# Heart and Soul

CW00496351

As pyschotherapies continue to proliferate, it has never been more important for the basic assumptions of psychotherapeutic practice to be clarified and reassessed. *Heart and Soul* shows psychotherapists, philosophers and general readers how an understanding of philosophical themes can transform the ways in which clinical issues are thought about and how psychotherapy is conducted.

Writers who have grappled with the practical implications of major philosophical interests – including ancient philosophy, positivism, existentialism, scepticism, Buddhism, hermeneutics, formal logic and linguistic philosophy – present resumés of relevant ideas and discuss their implications for the consulting room. Their discussions of the nature of psychotherapeutic theory, thinking, technique, relations and language raise issues of considerable philosophical interest.

By examining the interrelationship of philosophy and psychotherapy from many vantage points, *Heart and Soul* illustrates the importance of philosophical experience in the training of future psychotherapists and therapeutic potential of ideas underpinning many other areas of our culture.

**Chris Mace** is Senior Lecturer in Psychotherapy at Warwick University and Consultant Pyschotherapist to South Warwickshire Combined Care NHS Trust. His handbook *The Art and Science of Assessment for Psychotherapy* is also published by Routledge.

Contributors: Joady Brennan; Emmy van Deurzen; John M. Heaton; Jeremy Holmes; Joan Hurd; Paul Sepping Geraldine Shipton; Werdie van Staden; Paul Sturdee; Digby Tantam; Myra Thomas; John Wheway; Catherine Wieder.

# Heart and Soul

## The therapeutic face of philosophy

Edited by Chris Mace

London and New York

First published 1999 by Routledge
11 New Fetter Lane, London EC4P 4EE

Simultaneously published in the USA and Canada
by Routledge
29 West 35th Street, New York, NY 10001

Typeset in Goudy by The Florence Group, Stoodleigh, Devon
Printed and bound in Great Britain by
Creative Print and Design, Ebbw Vale, Gwent, Wales

*British Library Cataloguing in Publication Data*
A catalogue record for this book is available from the British Library

*Library of Congress Cataloging in Publication Data*
A catalog record for this book has been requested

ISBN 0–415–17000–1 (hbk)
ISBN 0–415–17001–X (pbk)

# Contents

# Contributors

**Joady Brennan** Dip.A.T., M.A. is a researcher at the Centre for Psychotherapeutic Studies, University of Sheffield. After using systemic and personal construct therapy with adults and children for over 20 years in community mental health teams, she is currently researching the moral construing of life prisoners. She has written on systemic and constructivist therapies, social understandings of abuse and perceptions of change in therapy.

**Emmy van Deurzen** Lic.Psy., Lic.Phil, M.Psy., M.Phil., A.F.B.Ps.S., C.Psychol. is Professor of Psychotherapy and Director of the New School of Psychotherapy and Counselling at Schiller International University, London. She has held senior posts in the United Kingdom Council for Psychotherapy, the European Association for Psychotherapy, the Society for Existential Analysis and the Universities Psychotherapy Association. Her most recent books are *Everyday Mysteries* (Routledge, 1997) and *Paradox and Passion in Psychotherapy* (John Wiley, 1998).

**K.W.M. (Bill) Fulford** D.Phil., FRCPsych. is Professor of Philosophy and Mental Health in the Department of Philosophy, University of Warwick, and honorary consultant psychiatrist in the Department of Psychiatry, University of Oxford. He is founder editor of *Philosophy, Psychiatry and Psychology* (PPP), the first international journal for philosophy and mental health, and founder chair and honorary secretary of the philosophy special interest group in the Royal College of Psychiatrists. He convenes the Masters and Ph.D. programme in the Philosophy and Ethics of Mental Health in the University of Warwick and has other visiting appointments. He has written widely on topics in philosophy, medicine, psychiatry and medical education. His books include *Moral Theory and Medical Practice* (Cambridge University Press, 1995).

**John M. Heaton** M.A., M.B., B.Chir., D.O. is a founder member of the Guild of Psychotherapists and sits on the training committee of the Philadelphia Association. He works in private practice in London. He has contributed many papers and chapters on medical, psychological and philosophical topics, including on ancient and existential philosophies. *Wittgenstein for Beginners* was published in 1996 (Icon Books).

**Jeremy Holmes** MD, MRCP, FRCPsych. is consultant psychotherapist in North Devon and an honorary consultant to the Tavistock Clinic, London. He is chair of the Psychotherapy Faculty of the Royal College of Psychiatrists and edits *Current Science* (psychotherapy). He has written extensively on psychotherapeutic ethics, attachment theory and personality disorder and his recent books include (with Anthony Bateman) *Introduction to Psychoanalysis* (Routledge, 1996) and *Attachment, Intimacy, Autonomy: Using attachment theory in adult psychiatry* (Jason Aronson, 1997).

**Joan Hurd** B.Sc., M.A. is an adult psychotherapist within the psychotherapy service of the South Warwickshire Combined Care NHS Trust. She has extensive experience in counselling as well as being an Associate Member of the Philadelphia Association. She uses ideas drawn from existential phenomenology in her work and undertakes private psychotherapy in Leicester.

**Chris Mace** MD, MRCPsych. is Senior Lecturer in Psychotherapy at Warwick University and consultant psychotherapist to South Warwickshire Combined Care NHS Trust. He teaches on many courses, including the Masters programme in the Philosophy and Ethics of Mental Health at Warwick University. Publications cover clinical research, the history of psychotherapy and a handbook, *The Art and Science of Assessment for Psychotherapy* (Routledge, 1995).

**Paul Sepping** FRCPsych., B.A.(Hons), B.Sc.(Hons) is consultant child and adolescent psychiatrist to Dorset Healthcare NHS Trust. A practising group analyst, his interest in narrative has led him to undertake postgraduate research at the University of Essex into the use of narrative in psychodynamic therapies.

**Geraldine Shipton** B.A. (Hons), Dip. Psychotherapy, Dip. COT is Lecturer in Psychotherapeutic Studies at the University of Sheffield and a psychoanalytic psychotherapist in private practice. She is course director for the M.A. in Psychoanalytic Psychotherapy and editor of *Psychoanalytic Studies* and of a handbook, *Supervision of Psychotherapy and Counselling* (Open University Press, 1997).

**C.W. (Werdie) van Staden** M.B., Ch.B., M.Med.(Psych.), F.T.C.L., U.P.L.M. is consultant psychiatrist to Weskoppies Hospital, Pretoria and Lecturer in Psychiatry at the University of Pretoria, South Africa. He has complemented his interest in the logic of relations with original research into pronomial usage in therapeutic conversation at the University of Warwick.

**Paul Sturdee** B.A.(Hons), M.A., SRN, RMN is Lecturer in the Philosophy and Ethics of Mental Health at the University of Warwick. He has extensive experience of teaching practioners and philosophers at postgraduate level, is reviews editor of *Philosophy, Psychiatry and Psychology*, and has contributed papers on irrationality and psychoanalysis.

**Digby Tantam** M.A., MPH, Ph.D., FRCPsych. is Clinical Professor of Psychotherapy in the Centre for Psychotherapeutic Studies and Associate Medical Director of the School of Health and Related Research at the University of Sheffield. A former chair of the United Kingdom Council for Psychotherapy and the Universities Psychotherapy Assocation, he has published widely in clinical psychiatry, psychotherapy and applied philosophy. He is editor of *Clinical Topics in Psychotherapy* (Gaskell, 1998).

**Myra Thomas** B.Sc. is an occupational psychologist working as a research consultant in private practice. She has undertaken postgraduate research into self-organised learning and its relationship to Zen psychology, and is chair of the trustees of the UK Zen Foundation.

**John Wheway** B.A., P.G.C.E., C.A.P.S., Dip. IDHP, Dip. HIP is a trainer at the Bath Centre for Psychotherapy and Counselling and has a private practice in Bristol. He has written on guilt, shame, gestalt psychotherapy and intersubjectivity.

**Catherine Wieder** D.Clin.Psych. is a practising psychoanalyst and Senior Lecturer and Maitre de Conference to the clinical psychology faculty at the University of Franche-Comté. She has published widely on the links between literature and psychoanalysis, including *Elements de Psychanalyse pour le texte littéraire* (Dunod, 1988) and *Lexique Trilingue de la Psychanalyse* (Masson, 1997).

# Foreword

*K.W.M. Fulford*

At a time when Freud-bashing has become a popular blood sport among the *literati*, it is a pleasure to welcome a book which so thoughtfully explores the links between philosophy and psychotherapy.

Neither subject is simply characterised: different generations, different cultures, have taken widely different views about what philosophy 'is': the search for foundations; an answer to the meaning of life; a spiritual praxis; the analysis of language. Psychotherapy, too, is heterogeneous, ranging from ten-year psychoanalyses, through a multitude of group therapies, counselling techniques and cognitive interventions, to the more austere forms of behavioural management.

Disciplines as diverse as these are easy targets. They offer no mainstream, no settled standards, no canon. But where there are no laws there are no outlaws. Any scandal – an overenthusiastic therapist inducing false memories of child abuse, a philosophical theory justifying infanticide – is a scandal for everyone. Such disciplines, moreover, are deeply divided internally. Psychoanalysis, notoriously, split into warring factions within a few years of its birth. There has been something of a truce recently, but as the psychoanalyst and writer Anthony Storr has remarked, it is an 'armed truce'. A recent *Farside* cartoon in the *London Evening Standard* showed Pavlov in his first experiment training his dog to attack Freud's cat! Philosophers, similarly, are fiercely tribal. There is little love lost, still less, meaningful communication, between existentialists and logicians; phenomenologists and ordinary language philosophers; metaphysicians and mystics.

Diversity, though, is also the mark of disciplines working at the creative edge. Such disciplines are necessarily undomesticated; they are wild strain, potential. The Oxford linguistic-analytical philosopher, J.L. Austin, used to describe philosophy as being concerned with all the questions we could not yet adequately frame. For Austin, philosophy was a central sun, in constant ferment, but occasionally spinning off planets – symbolic logic, mathematics, natural science, psychology – which then travelled on along relatively well ordered paths.

*Heart and Soul* owes something to this model. The therapeutic face of philosophy, with which it is concerned, is the philosophical influences – and they are rich indeed – on the varieties of modern psychotherapies. Therapists, preoccupied with the contingencies of their day-to-day practice, are often ignorant of the philosophical underpinnings of their work. Making these underpinnings explicit can help to improve mutual understanding. But besides the therapeutic face of philosophy, there is also a philosophical face of therapy. Austin anticipated this. Among practical disciplines, he identified those concerned with abnormal psychological phenomena as a particularly rich resource for philosophers concerned with questions of meaning. This is the point of contact, then, between philosophy and psychotherapy. Both are concerned with questions of meaning. Both are diverse disciplines because they work creatively at the edge of meaning.

K.W.M. Fulford
Universities of Oxford and Warwick
May 1998

# Acknowledgements

Many people have helped this book to become a reality. All the contributors have tolerated my demands with humour and forbearance. My colleagues at Warwick, Paul Sturdee and Bill Fulford, and students on the Masters programme in philosophy and mental health, have provided invaluable philosophical stimulation. The production has benefitted enormously from the faith and advice of Kate Hawes, Edwina Welham and their expert colleagues at Routledge. Thanks are due too to many people whose sterling support during its preparation has ensured that, despite potentially fatal threats, psychotherapy, training and opportunities to examine clinical relationships in depth remain available within the local mental health service. Lastly, I thank Graham Scambler. An undergraduate tutor in a thousand, he nurtured my early interest in therapeutic philosophy and showed me how it might be taught. The book is dedicated to him.

Every effort has been made to obtain permission to reproduce copyright material where appropriate. Special thanks are due to the estate of the late George Kelly for permission to reproduce the cited material in chapter 5, the estate of the late Jonathan Hey for permission to reproduce extracts from unpublished writings in chapter 12, and David Higham associates on behave of Jonathan Miller and Jean Renvoize. Permission is also gratefully acknowledged from the following publishers to quote copyright material under 'fair dealing' arrangements:

The kind permission of the following publishers to reproduce material under 'fair dealing' arrangements is gratefully acknowledged: Allen Lane; The Analytic Press; Jason Aronson; Blackwell Publishers; Caldar & Boyers; Cambridge University Press; Cornell University Press; Element Books; Free Association Books; Harper & Row; HarperCollins; Harvard University Press; Harvester Wheatsheaf; Hogarth Press; Johns Hopkins University Press; Kluwer Academic Publishers; Methuen & Co.; Modern Language Association; New York University Press; W.W.

Norton & Co.; Oxford University Press; Pan Books; Penguin Books; Princeton University Press; Random House, Inc.; Ross Erikson; Routledge; Sage Publications; Stenvalley Press; Tavistock Publications; Vantage Press; Vintage Books; Yale University Press.

# 1  Introduction
## Philosophy and psychotherapy

*Chris Mace*

How might philosophy enrich the practice of psychotherapy? This book will offer several suggestions. It is neither exhaustive nor systematic, trusting that illustrations of what can follow when a range of philosophical and therapeutic starting points are taken up will inspire other experiments of this kind. While the richness of psychotherapeutic ideas in general, and psychoanalytic theory in particular, have attracted a good deal of philosophical interest, this book is informed by practical values and concerns. Philosophical critiques of psychotherapy that fail to understand what its practitioners do, tend to take issue with models of psychotherapy which are incomplete or outdated. The present book takes several statements as granted: that psychotherapy is valued by many whose lives it has changed; that it must continue to evolve because of changing needs rather than prescriptive pronouncements; and that its practitioners will need new tools to enhance their ability to live and function in an ever shifting climate.

A given philosophical theme may find a place here because it represents a challenge to accepted models of the psyche or therapeutic change, or because of its potential impact on the way psychotherapy is practised. The specific implications of each theme for therapeutic strategy and technique will be discussed as it is introduced. Some cumulative lessons concerning the relationship of philosophy and practice, and how these bear on the future of philosophy and psychotherapy, will be considered at the close of the book. For the benefit of readers with little previous knowledge of either field, some notes follow on the broader contexts from which the detailed treatments are drawn.

## PHILOSOPHY

Anybody producing a course or book intended to orientate others to philosophy is beset by choices. Should it be presented through guiding questions (Who am I? How can anything be certain? What makes an action good?); or through key themes (the nature of universals, or of justice, or of love); or as the achievements of central figures or movements (Platonism, scepticism, the phenomenological movement); or is it reducible to the achievements of an array of discrete sub-disciplines (epistemology, philosophy of mind, aesthetics)? To some degree, all attempts to impose boundary and structure on philosophy are suspect. They somehow fail to contain a field whose own rules of procedure can never be beyond question, and whose achievements are sometimes as prey to the ravages of fashion as of reason. Among these different strategic approaches to philosophy, a clear preference is evident in the present collection. Philosophy is grasped either in the form of a key theme, figure or movement that can be related to therapeutic interests, or as a question arising within one of its sub-departments that can be re-addressed from inside a therapeutic tradition.

This selective and relatively focused attention to themes of common interest may leave some readers seeking to know more about the overall scope and limits of philosophy. One way is to read an historical overview. That of Tarnas (1996) is particularly approachable for psychotherapists, presenting a history of philosophical ideas in terms of their influence on collective perceptions, while showing the imprint of archetypal psychology in its own world view. Its sensitivity to the relevance of many developments to therapeutic thinking is offset by a lack of attention to the substance of philosophical argument, concentrating on how, rather than why, ideas succeeded one another. For this, and for sheer entertainment, Russell's *History of Western Philosophy* remains unmatched (Russell, 1961). An alternative is to approach the subject from the 'bottom up' via a freewheeling tour through one of the excellent dictionaries of philosophy now on the market (eg. Audi, 1995).

With the exception of a foray into the Buddhistic concept of self (chapter 12), this book deals with philosophy in Western Europe and the English speaking world. The philosophy of Ancient Greece and Rome is represented, as are major movements in modern thought from existentialism to linguistic philosophy, from formal logic to hermeneutics. Nevertheless, swathes of philsophical history, including medieval scholasticism, Cartesianism, and British and continental idealism, remain unexplored here. This selection may reflect some fashionable tastes, but it should not imply any judgment that other aspects of philosophy lack relevance for psychotherapy, nor that little could be gained from reexamining them.

## PSYCHOTHERAPY

While philosophers have been recognised within society for most of recorded history, psychotherapy remained an auxiliary activity, undertaken by sensitive physicians and priests in addition to their other work. It had already started to be professionalised through the activities of hypnotists, prior to the development of psychoanalysis. Psychoanalysis was, however, uniquely responsible for the theoreticisation of psychotherapy, allying developments in technique to new conceptions of psychopathology, and of normal psychological functioning. Most subsequent developments, both within psychoanalysis, and those that spawned alternative traditions such as humanistic, cognitive-behavioural and systemic therapies, can be characterised in terms of theoretical differences regarding the objectives of therapy, what their realisation requires, and differences in technique to complement these. Only a handful of people (for example, Jung, Rogers, Beck, Foulkes, Minuchin, Perls) have succeeded in effectively recasting psychotherapy so that profound modifications in all of these coincided and an original model was born. Even then, new paradigms have never remained static: they either disappear quickly or are progressively transformed as they become the shared tools of a community of psychotherapists. In this they are dependent to some extent on their amenability to revision in the light of clinical experience (itself often greatly influenced by the founder). In the course of such changes, innovations in theory and technique can straddle both theoretical schools and modalities of therapy (ie. whether the approach is used primarily with individual patients, groups, families etc.). This cross-fertilisation seems increasingly likely to happen, and at a faster rate than before, not only as a result of growing professional ecumenism (cf. Mace, 1995), but from consumer and governmental pressure. This consitutes a major pressure for continual revision in the face of 'evidence-based' practice, in which knowledge derived from mass observation of practice and its effects, rather than individual case study, is increasingly valued.

In the present book, explicit reference is made to many forms of psychotherapy: analytic, constructivist, humanistic and phenomenological. Sometimes discussion concerns models that are not yet fully realised, as well as others found almost everywhere. The interesting case of 'philosophical counselling' receives special consideration in the book's conclusion.

## PHILOSOPHY AND PSYCHOTHERAPY

If philosophy and psychotherapy are taken to be two independent traditions, how can their relationship be represented? Discussion of their
interface will reflect how this question is answered. I shall suggest that
different perspectives result when each tradition is taken as a vantage
point from which to view the other.

### Viewing psychotherapy from philosophy

Contributors to the book have tended to ignore the official image of
academic philosophy as a series of subdepartments. Indeed, these may
seem unpromising starting points from which to build bridges into
psychotherapy that will facilitate practice. However, a number of significant developments, dominating dialogue at the interdisciplinary
boundary until now, have been anchored in this way. For the sake of
completeness, two of these, of considerable interest in philosophical
and psychotherapeutic communities alike, will be briefly described here.

#### Psychotherapy and epistemology

In the first, psychotherapy is viewed as a system for acquiring knowledge, and assessed by the standards of epistemology. There have been
several such attempts, one of the best known being Karl Popper's negative verdict on Freudian psychoanalysis after evaluating it against his
falsificationist criterion of science (Popper, 1962). A more subtle exercise has followed from Adolf Grünbaum's (1984) attempt to identify
the nature of the knowledge claims of psychoanalysis rather than seeking
a wholesale judgement based on one set of inclusion criteria. The result
was a contention that psychoanalysis was neither scientific in the way
Freud conceived it to be, nor was it merely a hermeneutic exercise
whose claims held no truth beyond the extent to which they conferred
coherence on individual narratives. While Grünbaum maintained that
Freud was wrong to take evidence of the clinical impact of psychoanalysis as confirmation of his theories about the pathology of neurosis,
he argued the latter could and should be tested experimentally, outside
any clinical setting.

In his subtle arguments, Grünbaum avoids pitfalls that entrap less
sophisticated philosophical critics. Nevertheless, his recommendations
are revealing in the light of the present book's practical sympathies. It
remains possible, as some commentators did at the time (Strupp, 1986),
to take issue with Grünbaum's evaluation of the kind of 'knowledge'

that is actually central to Freudianism. Grünbaum had no doubt this was the idea of repression and the theory of neurosis arising as a consequence of conflict. Although concerns about 'repression' continue to be extremely topical (Brandon *et al.*, 1998), they are not necessarily central to a pragmatic view of Freud's legacy. His contributions to therapeutic technique have had a greater impact on practice than have his ideas on pathogenesis, and the former are based on other potentially testable ideas, especially the concept of transference. Attempts to explore the knowledge claims of a tradition like Freudian psychoanalysis can have a different starting point, and object of study, if they are guided by clinical values.

## Psychotherapy and ethics

A second traditional department of philosophy has a more complex relationship to psychotherapy. Within philosophy, ethics, especially in the form of aretaic morality, has placed great value on the improvement of character as an ethical end in itself. This means that psychotherapy has a peculiar position in respect of ethics. As a body of professional practice, it shares important ethical dilemmas, such as confidentiality, consent and the boundaries of the professional relationship, which, although they may raise special difficulties because of the unusually intimate nature of this relationship and its scope for exploitation, have much in common with other therapeutic professions. However, beyond these, there are peculiar ethical problems which arise because of the uniqueness of psychotherapy's aims and the entire way it goes about realising them.

It is not only the practices, but the theories of psychotherapy which have an ethical import, a point well illustrated by Hinshelwood's (1997) recent exploration of psychoanalytic ethics from a Kleinian perspective. Hinshelwood has demonstrated incompatibilities between the Kleinian view of the person and the assumptions of personal identity that underlie most traditional ethical thinking, including codes of professional ethics. However, when interactions with others are understood to involve processes of splitting, projection and introjection, with diffusion of personal identity a common consequence of these ordinary assumptions about personal autonomy cease to be valid. As a result, judgements of whether psychoanalysis is, in an ethical as well as a technical sense, achieving a 'good' result become fraught. Hinshelwood has attempted to resolve such questions by offering an ethical yardstick in the form of a 'principle of integration'. While this too is firmly rooted in one theoretical standpoint, and therefore not necessarily a complete answer to the concerns Hinshelwood has raised, his indication of the ethical complexities of analytic practice and of a residual need for more sophisticated ethical principles stands.

These concerns are not explicitly considered here, although many of the essays in this volume, in questioning underlying assumptions of the therapeutic process, will raise ethical questions too. Historically, when all learning was subsumed under 'logic', 'physics' or 'ethics', much of what is being discussed here would have been classed under 'ethics'. Now, developments in therapeutic practice will continue to pose a major stimulus to ethical thinking at all levels. It is a field ripe for theoretical and practical development.

Beyond epistemology and ethics, there are other areas of traditional philosophy – philosophy of mind, pragmatics, even aesthetics – which are more specialised, but whose questions could be brought to bear on psychotherapy with interest and value. However, just as the examples given of epistemological and ethical interest were far from comprehensive, gaining their strength from the specificity of the arguments they raised, so it may be at least as profitable to encourage connections between philosophy and psychotherapy to develop unplanned, leaving clarifications as to which components were involved on either side until afterwards. One of the intriguing points raised by Hinshelwood's discussion of psychoanalytic ethics is that a meaningful encounter cannot leave its participants untouched. Neither philosophy nor psychotherapy would necessarily remain unscathed if there were real exchange between them.

## Looking at philosophy from psychotherapy

If one looks at philosophy from psychotherapy, a view different from philosophy's usual self-image emerges. Individual contributors here, free to make their own connections, have been highly selective in their use of philosophy. None set out to provide a panoramic view, but it is clear that the philosophical landmarks thrown into relief by their selections are different from those that would arise if philosphy were viewed from, say, cosmology or economics. Had the interface between psychotherapy and philosophy been represented by a different collection of essays, other facets of philosophy might have been thrown into prominence too. Nevertheless, the contours apparent from what is here do suggest maps which encompass and bring some kind of order to them. Two distinct dimensions of philosophic concern run through the material here. One of these concerns the methods by which things become known. The other concerns what it is to be human.

## Method: positivism versus hermeneutics

Psychotherapeutic practice is based on knowledge from a number of channels, ranging across intuition, empathy, structured clinical observation, the humanities and experimental research. The refinement, scope and relative priority of these sources have been central concerns of philosophy. From the standpoint of the present discussion, a basic opposition, described by Windelband in the nineteenth century, between 'nomothetic' and 'idiographic' approaches, remains very relevant. This contrasted the effort of natural scientists to establish explicit, publicly verifiable, descriptions that were generally applicable despite differences between situations, with the work of humanists to capture and communicate whatever was unique to a given historical situation. It can be said to persist as a tension between positivist (nomothetic) and hermeneutic (idiographic) approaches to psychotherapy. Positivism, a term originating with the social philosopher Comte in the nineteenth century, seeks positive knowledge that can be justified through demonstration. It has generally valued empirical evidence, claimed at least neutrality with respect to questions of value, and resisted reference to causes or entities that cannot be demonstrated. It also values unity in method: although some fields of science may be less developed than others, there is no reason why their knowledge cannot be based on common, positivist principles (Kolakowski, 1972). In modern philosophy, the work of Descartes, Hume, Comte, Russell and Popper, as well as the so-called 'logical positivists' (whose work the early philosophy of Wittgenstein resembled) represent this trend.

Hermeneutics, originally a term that referred to biblical exegesis, was used in the seventeenth century to refer to the determination of what was meant, irrespective of whether it was true (Grondin, 1995). It has subsequently been seen as a route to knowledge in the idiographic tradition, and represents a current in philosophy that may be traced through Kant, Hegel, Schleiermacher, Dilthey and Gadamer. As a method, it emphasises the dependence of meaning on context and the primacy of interpretation in uncovering it. Unable to share positivism's aspiration to unity of method, it has nevertheless shared with it an aversion to metaphysical statements about underlying essences (as found in Platonism, for instance) because these remain impervious to both empirical demonstration and specific interpretation.

Tension between positivist and hermeneutic approaches continues to be felt in psychotherapy. Most major schools of psychotherapeutic thinking have been indebted to positivism at their inception, either because their originators were trying to develop universal models of the mind or, as in clinical behaviourism, because of an allegiance to experimental method. However, not only have gaps between theory and practice become evident when attempts are made to derive the rationale of specific treatments from first principles, but a tendency for new therapies to become more complex, relational and remote from direct observation with the passage of time have meant that even behavioural therapies become less positivist as they evolve. Instead, emphasis on the specificity of the case and the need to grapple with meaning and the interpersonal context in which treatment is occurring have continued to reassert themselves as newer psychotherapies come of age.

### Being human: naturalism versus transcendentalism

Beyond questions of how knowledge is constructed, psychotherapy cannot escape a concern with what is distinctively human. This has been an explicit concern of philosophy through the modern era (effectively, the last 400 years) during which a pre-eminent interest has been in our rationality as a defining characteristic. Alongside this, there has been intermittent interest in the irrational aspects of human nature. This had its clearest philosophical (and literary) expression in the Romantic movement of the late eighteenth century, from which existential and evolutionary philosophies have been important offshoots.

Romanticism is often portrayed as a rather undifferentiated urge to embrace many aspects of irrationality, from the instinctual, primitive and freely emoting, to those informed by a sense of higher purpose; urges to unify and exaltation of the imagination. Within the Romantic literature these have been conflated, often because of the ambiguous position of the natural world. Nature was often seen as an object of worship in itself, as well as something of which humanity was very much part. Nevertheless, it is possible to delineate retrospectively two opposing tendencies in Romantic philosophy. Both are richly present in those Romantic authors, notably Goethe, who were not merely idealists. Both challenge rationalistic images of humanity by emphasising continuities in different directions.

One tendency emphasises continuity between civilised humanity and the rest of the living world by reminders of the primitive, animalistic, blindly impassioned facets of life. This strand of Romanticism, which I shall refer to here as 'naturalism', was in some ways reinforced by biologism and evolutionism throughout the nineteenth century. It is overtly the school of Rousseau, Schelling, Nietzsche, Feuerbach, and even Sartre.

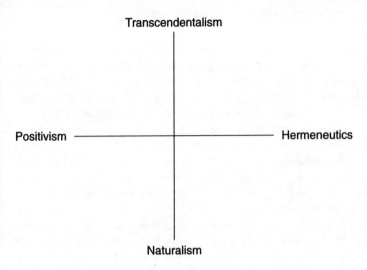

*Figure 1.1* A map of therapeutic philosophy

The other existed, sometimes uneasily, alongside it. It maintained a sense of mankind as being 'lower than the angels' even if official religion was rejected, and open to apprehensions of immanent purpose. I have termed this tendency 'transcendentalism', although the word has slighly different connotations in some philosophical contexts. Hegel, Schopenhauer, Kierkegaard and Heidegger are particularly prominent among its exponents.

While the two strands were not always easy to disentangle in individual Romantic authors, the tension between them was exposed once depth psychology identified the irrational with a substantive unconscious mind. Then, in the basic opposition between Freud's vision of a blind, anarchic, instinctually driven unconscious, and Jung's of the unconscious as an intrinsically wise repository for individual and collective ideals, irrationality emerged in, respectively, naturalistic and transcendental guises that took an unprecedentedly pure form. This tension has persisted in psychotherapeutic views of the person, not only in oppositions between established psychotherapeutic schools, or when orthodox psychotherapy is set against the 'transpersonal', but, perhaps inevitably, even between the reinterpretations that have been made of Freud's work. Bettelheim's (1982) reading appears transcendentalist alongside, say, Sulloway's (1979) naturalistic reading.

## A MAP OF THERAPEUTIC PHILOSOPHY

The two dimensions, of methodological and anthropological allegiances, help to frame a space within which individual philosophies, or philosophers whose work bears on psychotherapy, can be located. When both axes are used, it becomes possible to spread this philosophical field across four quadrants in an heuristically useful way (Figure 1.1).

To give just two examples, both of whom will appear in this book, Heidegger would be a hermeneutic transcendentalist, and Wittgenstein a positivist naturalist. This kind of exercise does involve looking back through lenses that are not only very modern but therapeutically attuned. It is understandably more difficult to locate figures who are more remote historically.

Nevertheless, the two-dimensional framework also allows psychotherapies to be more clearly located with respect to their underlying philosophies. Behavioural therapies remain very positivist, with a strong taint of naturalism; cognitive approaches are still strongly positivist but (by virtue of their rationalism) neither definitely naturalistic nor transcendalist. Humanistic approaches are usually clearly hermeneutic, often with a transcendalist leaning. Changes within schools can also be traced via this grid. For instance, although the historical shift in emphasis within psychoanalysis from appetitive drives to object-seeking ones did not involve much movement on the naturalism/transcendentalism axis, the loss of faith in psychic determinism and reframing of the role of the symbolic in analytic revisions has been consistent with a shift away from positivism towards a more hermeneutic stance. Some limits of the schema are indicated by at least one tradition that receives little attention here. Analytical psychology, already cited as the apotheosis of transcendentalism, defies easy location on the positivism/hermeneutic axis because its residual essentialism (seen in its archetypal psychology) is antithetical to both.

However, the main reason for proposing this structure is that it marks out the terrain of the remainder of this book. In the following chapters, positivism, hermeneutics, naturalism and transcendentalism are all represented in weak and strong forms and various combinations. All quadrants in Figure 1.1 will be found to be occupied, if not full. If this schema is heuristically useful, so much to the good. If it fails the reader in charting a course around the rest of the book, I hope they will draw up a better one rather than abandon the journey.

# REFERENCES

Audi, R. (1995) *The Cambridge Dictionary of Philosophy*. Cambridge: Cambridge University Press.

Bettelheim, B. (1982) *Freud and Man's Soul*. Harmondsworth: Penguin.

Brandon, S., Boakes, J., Glaser, D. et al (1998) Recovered memories of childhood sexual abuse: implications for clinical practice. *British Journal of Psychiatry* 172, 296–307.

Fisher, E. (1997) *Psychotherapy and Philosophy*. London: Sage.

Grondin, J. (1995) *Sources of Hermeneutics*. New York: State University of New York Press.

Grünbaum, A. (1984) *The Foundations of Psychoanalysis: A Philosophical Critique*. University of California Press.

Hinshelwood, D. (1997) *Therapy or Coercion?* London: Karnac.

Kolakowski, L. (1972) *Positivist Philosophy*. Harmondsworth: Penguin.

Mace, C.J. (1995) *The Art and Science of Assessment in Psychotherapy*. London: Routledge.

Popper, K. (1962) *Conjectures and Refutations*. London: Routledge.

Russell, B. (1961) *History of Western Philosophy*. London: George Allen and Unwin.

Solomon, R.C. (1988) *Continental Philosophy Since 1750: The Rise and Fall of the Self*. Oxford: Oxford University Press.

Strupp, H. (1986) 'Transference, one of Freud's basic discoveries'. *Brain and Behavioural Sciences* 9, 260–61.

Sulloway, F. (1979) *Freud, Biologist of the Mind*. London: Burnet

Tarnas, R. (1996) *The Passion of the Western Mind*. London: Pimlico.

# Introduction to chapter 2

Two thousand four hundred years after his death, Socrates remains one of the guiding spirits of our civilisation. He embodies a forceful individualism that has been an implicit ideal in Western cultures if not individual lives. Socrates urged contemporaries to look to their most basic aims, to take the attainment of happiness seriously, and insisted that the unexamined life was not worth living. Possessed of a personality formidable for its energy and one-pointedness, he would argue with all comers but left no writings. He died by drinking hemlock, his sentence at the most famous trial in history. His immortality is also tied to a number of phrases (Socratic irony, Socratic dialogue and Socratic questioning) and his unique status as Plato's teacher. A scholarly account of Socrates' life is given by Guthrie (1971).

Many later philosophers have claimed Socratic inspiration for their own work. Current developments, emphasising the relevance of philosophy for living, are also claiming Socratic ancestry (e.g. Sautet, 1995). Nevertheless, although Plato suggests that Socrates dispensed 'physic' to his fellow Athenians, the relevance of his life and work for psychotherapy has rarely been considered. This essay illustrates parallels and divergences between Socrates' technique and those of modern psychotherapy by focussing on the role of questioning in Socratic procedure. By reconsidering questioning in psychotherapy in this light, it is evident that, although it might inhibit personal change in some situations, some forms of questioning can also catalyse it in profound ways. The most potent questions, like those of Socrates, act from within to stimulate intense mental activity that becomes self-generating. The modern therapist attuned to the art of questioning might be more likely to emulate Socrates' ideal helper, the midwife assisting at birth.

# REFERENCES

Guthrie, W.K.C. (1971) *Socrates*. Cambridge: Cambridge University Press.
Sautet, M. (1995) *Un café pour Socrate*. Paris: Robert Laffont.

# 2  Therapeutic questioning and Socratic dialogue

*Chris Mace*

You may be sure none of you know Socrates' true nature; but I will reveal him to you.
Alcibiades in Plato's *Symposium* (Plato, 1973)

Ask a question and you'll get an answer. But it won't tell you much!
Michael Balint (quoted in Coltart, 1992)

Examining both myself and others is really the very best thing that a man can do . . . life without this sort of examination is not worth living.
Socrates in Plato's *Apology* (Plato, 1993)

## SOCRATES ANCIENT AND MODERN

Alcibiades' statement might be a warning to any of us who claim some special understanding of Socrates. It has rarely been heeded. The temptation to explain his enigmatic legacy is enormous, as if some spell was cast over Western philosophy that remains to be lifted. Greek and Hellenic schools of philosophy subsequently orientated themselves in relation to Socrates, and their differences might be reduced to how they individually exaggerate one or more elements of Socratic teaching at the expense of others. But modern philosophers too have continued to reinterpret Socrates as part of the process of shaping their own mature ideas. Hegel (1985), Nietzsche (1967) and Kierkegaard (1966) are key examples, to whom may be added Heidegger and Gadamer if their reluctance to disidentify Socrates and Plato is accepted (Zuckert, 1996). Socrates' influence is felt beyond particular arguments or doctrines. In the rare instances where a modern thinker manages to live so intensely that their life, personality and work seem indivisible, they are likely to be hailed as a modern Socrates. This applies to few more than to Wittgenstein.

Socrates is uniquely open to such treatment, not only because the facts of his own life and death were so remarkable, but because he wrote nothing. He is well known for engaging his contemporaries in sharp and often prolonged exchanges during which he would interrogate one or more willing Athenians on any topic bearing on how life should be lived. Professing not to know himself where this would lead, he would batter an interlocutor with questions until he reassessed his beliefs. Socrates' personal impact appears to have been enormous, and his style of questioning essential to it. Socrates never explained his method during these interactions, which is generally referred to as the Socratic elenchus.

Most of what we know about the content of these exchanges is based on a series of written dialogues by Plato in which Socrates is invariably a protagonist. It appears that the first such dialogues were intended to take the form of a historical record, setting out characteristic methods and teaching of Socrates. These conflict with the content of several of Plato's later writings in which Socrates remains a central character, and through which Plato appears to expound his own philosophy in the form of dialogue. (It might be said that Plato's reluctance to state his thoughts in the first person is equivalent to Socrates' reluctance to trust his thoughts to paper.) The dialogues provide an important taste of Socrates' style for any psychotherapist who is curious about how self-examination may be developed through persistent questioning.

In psychotherapy, questioning of patients by therapists has become suspect. It is the prerogative of the teacher or the lawyer but not someone who, instead of trying to convince or convict, is trying to help another person to find themselves. Although practices are changing, particularly through the need for therapists to be more active in the course of time-limited psychotherapies, there is little doubt that many practitioners find themselves in dilemmas over whether, when and how to question. Can Socrates help?

## APPROACHING SOCRATES

Commentators agree that four accounts of how Socrates lived and worked are pre-eminent. These come from the satirical playright, Aristophanes (Aristophanes, 1973); Xenophon, a military general and pupil of Socrates (Xenophon, 1990); Plato, his philosophical heir; and Aristotle, his most substantial philosophical critic (Aristotle, 1941). Socrates is most frequently depicted in the course of dialogue – exclusively in the case of Plato and Aristophanes; frequently in Xenophon but never in

Aristotle – with a broad range of contemporaries. The accounts differ considerably in form and content in ways that show consistent differences between the authors, suggesting that significant biases have been introduced that reflect their very different interests.

Socrates' interests appear to have been exclusively in human affairs – he helped to lead a sea change away from natural philosophy. One of Socrates' principal concerns was the nature of 'virtue' (*arete*). If striven for, virtue would bring happiness. Virtue itself was divisible into a small number of primary virtues prized especially by Socrates. Few translate precisely into modern language, but they can be termed bravery (*andreia*), moderation (*sophrosyne*), justice (*dikaiosyne*), wisdom (*sophia*) and piety (*hosiotes*) (Vlastos, 1991).

Virtue is a central theme in Plato's early dialogues where Socrates attempts to explore the nature of virtue with everyone he questions. Each dialogue usually concentrates on a single virtue (eg. *Laches* on bravery; *Euthyphro* on piety, *Charmides* on moderation, etc.). These give way to more metaphysical concerns in the later, Platonic, dialogues. Distinctions between Socratic and Platonic dialogues are not only about content, and cannot be ignored by an investigation of Socratic questioning. It is not necessary to adjudicate on whether individual dialogues are or are not truly 'Socratic' in order to sketch the characteristics that set the truly Socratic dialogues apart from the others.

There is a striking difference in conclusiveness between dialogues that portray a discussion as an end in itself, and those where it develops into greater things. In the vast sequences through the books of *The Republic*, Plato elaborates political arguments and develops a philosophy of ideal forms that do not appear in the earlier writing. Apart from the difference in focus, there is very little progression in the earliest dialogues. This lack of conclusiveness is associated in all of them with a particular mood or atmosphere. It engenders feelings of perplexity, confusion and, sometimes, irritation. This sensation of 'aporia' has been used to classify several of these early unresolved dialogues as 'aporetic' as well as 'elenctic'. Once Plato begins in later dialogues to allow Socrates to argue in favour of beliefs which he also owns, then his technique shades into 'dialectic'. As the emphasis on persuasion grows at the expense of deconstruction, aporia disperses and does not return.

## The Socratic elenchus

A very reasonable summary of elenchus has been offered by Terence Irwin:

The basic structure of a typical elenchus is simple. Socrates asks a question, either a request to be told what some virtue is (for instance, 'What is bravery'?), or some other question about a virtue. The interlocutor affirms some proposition p in answer to Socrates' initial question; under Socrates' questioning he agrees that he also believes q and r; and he discovers, under further questioning, that not-p can be derived from q and r; hence he finds that his beliefs commmit him to p and not-p. Finding himself in this situation, he is 'at a loss' (aporein) about what to believe.

It is not just the interlocutor who is at a loss. Socrates himself insists that he does not know the answers to the questions that he asks his interlocutors; and so he concludes that they are 'all alike at a loss'.

Irwin (1995, p.17)

All of this is true of interactions to be found in the typically 'elenctic' or 'aporetic' early dialogues (e.g. *Laches, Ion, Charmides, Hippias Minor, Euthyphro*). However, to obtain a full picture of Socratic questioning, it is necessary to distinguish elements that are conflated in Irwin's description – their content, structure and context. A painstaking analysis of all the questions Plato attributes to Socrates has been provided by Gerasimos Santas (1979). He distinguished their semantic, syntactic and pragmatic aspects. The semantic encompasses what a question is about, what it presupposes, and its validity in terms of its presuppositions. The syntactic refers to a question's form and the form of answers to it. Pragmatics include who the respondents were, the situation it was part of, and the presuppositions that made this questioning possible in the first place.

These distinctions will seem more real and useful if they illustrate an actual example. Among the uncontestably aporetic/elenctic dialogues, the *Laches* is a Socratic examination of the virtue of bravery (Plato, 1987). It is a good paradigm because this virtue seems closer to contemporary English usage than those of other elenctic dialogues. Its argument is relatively simple in structure and it also contains some helpful asides, as if Plato himself had intended it to be an introduction to Socrates' procedure and its impact.

The semantic account of the *Laches* would relate that a discussion of two boys' educational needs becomes a discussion of bravery. Socrates argues that bravery is really the good any training would bestow beyond what was already there. Three successive definitions of it are offered, as acts of not retreating, then as a quality of endurance, finally as knowledge of what is fearful and encouraging. None of these understandings is accepted as complete.

The syntactic account would emphasise how Socrates repeatedly invites definitions of bravery and then finds other statements that are seemingly true, but inconsistent with the definition that has been proffered. When Socrates subsequently invites opinion on the truth of the definition, it is rejected.

The pragmatic account would highlight how the two fathers seeking advice about their sons' education consulted two passing generals, Nicias and Laches, who then invite Socrates to help them. After listening patiently to lengthy expressions of opinion, Socrates suggests they need to clarify the subject at issue and that the parents should look to the generals, not himself, for expertise. In seeking their understanding of bravery, he responds to the simpler definitions of Laches alone, then involves Nicias in Laches' interrogation, before launching a more subtle examination of Nicias' beliefs. Accepting the need to start again, they disperse in an atmosphere of aporia.

I have introduced this analysis to try to pinpoint some of the ambiguity attaching to Socratic elenchus. The syntactic account of elenchus highlights the prominence of a search for definitions of the virtues. This does not necessarily mean that a wish to find and perfect such a definition was the reason why those questions were asked in the first place. (In Santas' terms, the point of the questioning as a whole, rather than individual questions, should be addressed within a pragmatic account.) However, it has sometimes been taken to be so. This search for definition became the basis of the metaphysical explorations of transcendent essences in Plato's later writings. In Aristotle, the definitions are identified with logical universals, as Socrates' achievement is hailed instead as an incomplete move in a different direction, towards a systematic and logically complete metaphysics:

> for two things may be fairly ascribed to Socrates – inductive arguments and universal definition, both of which are concerned with the starting point of science (*episteme*).
>
> Aristotle, *Metaphysics* (1941, p.894)

The latter claim in particular seems dubious on a number of counts, not only because of the apparent failure of Socrates' conclusions about any of the virtues to move beyond the negative, but also his lack of interest in building on previous arguments when he returns to a given topic again. Furthermore, he appears to adopt quite different tactics according to circumstance. Most disconcerting among these, from an Aristotelian standpoint, might be Socrates' willingness in dialogue with Protagoras to argue for the very definition of bravery that Nicias had proposed and then been persuaded by him to reject in the *Laches* (Santas, 1967). This is hardly how one moves inductively to a definition that is true in all circumstances. Whatever they are, Socrates' purpose seems more complex. The point is that a purely semantic and syntactic appreciation of elenctic method is incomplete. Its pragmatics, arguably the aspect most neglected by commentators, are essential too.

When the pragmatics of the elenctic dialogues are investigated further, it is clear that a good deal of filtering occurs before elenchus is brought into play. This means not only that, wherever it may have started, the argument is brought around to be a debate about the nature of virtue, but also that, however disinterested an interlocutor may have appeared to be at the outset, they are asked to examine and test personal beliefs.

> Whenever anyone comes face to face with Socrates . . . what invariably happens is . . . Socrates will keep heading him off until he has him trapped into giving an account of his present life-style and of the way he has spent his life in the past. . . . [H]e won't let him go until he has cross-examined him on every angle. . . . [Y]ou're bound to be more careful about your way of life in future if you don't shrink from this treatment.
>
> Nicias in Plato's *Laches* (1987, pp.95–96)

The way elenchus represents an examination of and challenge to essentially personal beliefs is concealed, in a purely syntactic account, and is a clue to its unique atmosphere and the generation of aporia. It complements a syntactic aspect that Vlastos draws attention to – the way these beliefs, once volunteered, are not challenged on the basis of their premises, but only on their compatibility with other simultaneously held beliefs (Vlastos, 1991). There is an element of stealth as well as deadly accuracy in this assault that is a clue to the generation of aporia. Socrates' stance during an elenctic examination is another important pragmatic feature. Although he may appear secure in knowing how to proceed in order to deliver an effective challenge, he is, in these early dialogues at least, seemingly unable or unwilling to provide any alternative definition of the concept in question when his companion's resources are exhausted. Socrates will deny this is guile on his part, simply insisting that, alongside his conviction that the quest is a proper one, he is ignorant of its outcome until it is achieved. At such times he can appear disingenuous, and his famous irony is experienced in the raw.

For a method that appears to be wholly negative in its workings, the impact of the elenchus can seem incomprehensibly powerful. Meno describes it:

> [a]t this moment I feel you are exercising magic and witchcraft upon me and positively laying me under your spell until I am just a mass of helplessness. If I may be flippant, I think that not only in outward appearance but in other respects as well you are exactly like the flat sting-ray that one meets in the sea. Whenever anyone comes into contact with it, it numbs him, and that is the sort of thing that you seem to be doing to me now. My mind and my lips are literally numb, and I have nothing to reply to you. Yet I have spoken about virtue hundreds of times ... now I can't even say what it is.
>
> Meno, in Plato's *Meno* (1956, p.127)

If the search for definition was not necessarily the purpose of this process, what was? And, although some of his discussants seemed to be simply irritated or repelled by it, why did others keep coming back for more despite a manifest lack of success?

## The virtue of answers

In simple terms, and despite appearances, the elenchus and its dynamo of doubt was not a wholly negative process. Certainly, Socrates appeared to inspire those he met with his confidence that it could yield results, and his suggestions that it could lead to lasting, highly beneficial change. Beyond this, Socrates admitted to a central belief that informed what he did, although it was one that aroused consternation then and at most times since. This is his equation between virtue and knowledge. Because virtue and knowledge are ultimately the same, no one who does wrong does so willingly. Wrongdoing can only be an expression of ignorance. (Socrates therefore had no need for the concept of *akrasia* that will be discussed in the following chapter.) At first glance the idea is so contrary to common sense that it seems preposterous, indeed sophistical. Socrates does spend a good deal of time in the course of elenctic questioning showing how x's definition of y is inadequate because it does not properly allow for, say, bravery, to be distinguished from the knowledge that the brave person has in order to be brave, or permit the concept to be taught to another person. However, any such knowledge is partial and unable to capture individual virtues because it does not connect with virtue in general. Were it to do so, all virtues would be known. Approached from many directions in the course of elenctic questioning, it becomes increasingly evident that the apparent unattainability of knowledge of virtue is a consequence of virtue being knowledge. An act of knowing can itself bring about virtue, but only an act of an extraordinary kind. This is not merely an understanding of what virtue comprises, but is inseparable from becoming disposed to always act virtuously. Realisation of virtue is indistinguishable from the certainty that brings it about. Knowing of this kind is only possible once, with the assistance of elenchus, false certainty has been removed.

This account of the underlying basis of elenchus is consistent with Navia's analysis of the role of virtue (Navia, 1985) and Hadot's identification of Socratic method with a form of spiritual exercise (Hadot, 1985). It contradicts both Plato's insistence that any intuitive identification of the nature of virtue depended on knowledge that corresponded to a parallel world of ideal forms, and Aristotle's efforts after a propositional understanding of the virtues. Had Socrates sought to be a proto-Aristotle, refining defintions as an end in itself, he would no doubt have bequeathed the world an Academy and a corpus of written works. If, instead, his principal aim was that of a teacher, concerned exclusively with the development of any individual who was consulting him, then what we know of his pattern of life, and his failure to write down a truth that was not transplantable, can seem inevitable.

The truth of this view of Socrates' project may be judged by any coherence it lends to these and other contradictions between the known facts of his life. It accords too with the few allusions he allowed himself about his stance. Socrates was fond of one simile for what he did before all others – it likens the service he offered others to his own mother's profession – midwifery. The midwife can facilitate birth of something which is already formed but unique. Although Socrates has been criticised for his apparent domination of others in the course of elenchus, Plato's dialogues are sufficiently vivid in their detail to suggest that, although Socrates would base many elenctic examinations around a given virtue, he never repeats the same arguments or counter-propositions in doing so.

While Plato has Socrates describing ethics and politics as 'sciences of the soul', psychotherapy was not a recognised activity in fifth-century Athens. Yet modern psychotherapists helping people, often painfully, towards a kind of rebirth might identify with his simile. What might be gained now from Socratic questioning?

## Socratic psychotherapy

There are parallels between Socratic and psychotherapeutic technique at semantic, syntactic and pragmatic levels. Semantically, Socrates' attention to belief rather than, say, feelings or behaviour, corresponds with cognitive therapists' insistence on the primacy of belief in psychological pathology and its remediation. The way in which dominant beliefs are personally constituted around central concepts is emphasised by the notion of 'personal constructs' in constructivist therapies (cf. chapter 5 this volume). The therapeutic potency of virtue concepts, that may only gradually yield their meaning, is the basis for contemplative techniques promoted in Assagioli's 'psychosynthesis' (Assagioli, 1975). Conversely the appeal to inherent knowledge, moral and otherwise, that informs a more Platonic understanding of the purpose of elenctic questions would correspond to the highly internalised conception of psychic reality that informs Jung's theory of archetypes (Jung, 1968).

Syntactically, the directed demonstration of inconsistency between simultaneously held beliefs in Socratic elenchus has technical parallels in cognitive psychotherapy and more analytic work, particularly that of the neo-Freudians and ego psychologists. Cognitive therapists often refer to a methodical process of 'Socratic questioning' (Padewsky, 1993) although in practice this often tries to expose the unfounded premises of automatic assumptions, rather than their mutual incompatibility. Overt demonstration of conflict between parts of the personality having mutually incompatible aims was part of neo-Freudian technique (Horney, 1951). Indeed, even in more traditional analytic work, recovery of 'repressed' or 'dissociated' beliefs can echo the surprise of Socrates' interlocutors at realising they must have believed things without having known they did so.

Pragmatically, the overall goal of insight ('know thyself') is claimed by many psychotherapies. In trying to achieve it, very different aspects of the context of Socratic questioning might be copied. Socrates' interventionism might be likened to the highly active and potentially paralysing argumentation of the rational-emotive therapist (Ellis and Dryden, 1987). The deliberate use of a distracting and frustrating tactic, such as demanding formal definitions, might be more in tune with modern day 'paradoxical' techniques that do not declare their methods, depending on surprise and an arrest of habitual operations (Selvini-Palazzoli et al., 1991). Socrates' refusal to prescribe any goal despite provocative requests to do so, and the inevitable generation of presumably facilitative discomfort has its analogues in a good deal of analytic technique. A classic instance is Wilfrid Bion's vivid description of a therapeutic group in which he effectively generates aporia through his dogged disavowal of expertise (Bion, 1961). The exploitation of small groups of interlocutors who stimulate one another in their analyses has much in common with other group therapy traditions. However, contemporaries' undoubted reliance on the sheer charisma of Socrates, and his own willingness to set about his task irrespective of audience, time or place, may have more parallels in revivalism than therapeutic practices.

With the parallels between Socratic technique and psychotherapy ranging as widely as this, it is not unreasonable to suppose that the fertility and genius that led to Platonism, Aristotelianism, scepticism, Epicureanism, and Stoicism all being indebted to Socrates might provide a basis for many modern psychotherapies to claim more kinship in spirit. However, apart from emphasising elements already evident within particular traditions in these ways, are there other senses in which psychotherapy might be more questioning and more Socratic?

A productive question at this point might be of the kind posed some years ago by R.H.S. Crossman – if one were building a new psychotherapy explicitly on Socratic principles, what form would it take? Here one is immediately thrust back on the enigma of Socrates' own character. His actions are informed by a project it might seem impossible to recapture – almost, but perhaps not wholly impossible. By an interesting quirk of history, there is a method that permits more retrospective access to the minds of the dead than can seem possible otherwise. Proposed by R.G. Collingwood (1944), it is disarmingly simple. To understand why an author wrote (or spoke) as he did, it is necessary to understand the questions that inspired him, and to which the material we have represents an answer. (A very similar method was adopted by the hermeneuticist Gadamer (Grondin, 1995).) Only in this way, Collingwood maintained, was it possible to appreciate all the parts of someone's work as a whole. However delicious the irony of putting questions to Socrates might be, any attempt at reconstruction must seem particularly forbidding when there are nearly two and a half milennia, a lack of direct writings, and a more impenetrable mound of scholarship intervening than for any almost any other historical figure.

However, Socrates does give an unusually coherent account of his own project and its central question. In his speech at the trial at which he was to be sentenced to death, reported by both Plato and Xenophon, he relates the impact of hearing the Delphic oracle's pronouncement that 'no one was wiser than Socrates'. Inspired by this to enquire what the nature of wisdom could be, he maintained that his attempts to understand this prompted all his interrogations, and that they univerally failed to teach him anything further about the nature of wisdom because wherever he looked he found none. There is perhaps one aspect to these that has been omitted from the account so far, one very relevant to his fate at that trial. Unlike the protagonists of the *Laches*, many of the people that Socrates engaged with, notably the sophists, did have claims of wisdom to uphold. (As recorded by Plato, Socrates' interactions with sophists such as Gorgias and Protagoras were liable to become particularly heated.) The sophists had already claimed an interest in similar themes, and were probably far more responsible than Socrates for a general renewal of interest in human affairs at the expense of the natural world. They taught sophisticated techniques of argument and persuasion, and at bottom maintained a relativistic stance that empowered them in this. If all arguments are potentially equally right, technique is all. Engagement with a sophist would often entail being invited to believe the world was very different from what you took it to be, just as engagement with Socrates would. The difference between them has to be expressed in terms of a difference in faith, and Socrates' unshakeable optimism that the kind of wisdom he spoke of was attainable.

One is therefore left with a figure looking two ways at once. On the one hand, we have a man able to question at such depth that the reverberations might propel a willing hearer to go on questioning themselves for the rest of their lives. It appears that Socrates lived as he did since this could only happen through direct contact. This impulse, of prompting internal questioning in a way that is self-sustaining and ultimately liberating, seems to represent a crucial element of what would make a therapy Socratic, independent of theoretical and technical affiliations.

On the other hand, Socrates could not fail to needle those professionally presuming to knowledge of things that he believed no one knew any better than himself, while failing to offer any new theories bar one. A philosophical autodidact, it is unlikely that he would complete training if reincarnated as a psychotherapist. If 'grandfathered' into professional practice by virtue of his great age, I suspect he would be aghast at the attempts made to deal with problems in the compartments that characterise modern practice, and that he would no longer attempt to use moral concepts as a vehicle when they were not universally shared. His first task, inspired by a radical perception of the roots of the malaise he found around him, would be to encourage others to share his vision. He would be most unlikely to endear himself to the custodians of established practice. But he would surely insist that the life that was not being constantly questioned was not worth living.

## REFERENCES

Assagioli, R. (1975) *Psychosynthesis: A Manual of Principles and Techniques*. Harmondsworth: Penguin.
Aristophanes (1973) *The Clouds*, tr. A.H. Sonnester. Harmondsworth: Penguin.
Aristotle (1941) *Metaphysics*. In *The Basic Works of Aristotle*, tr. R. McKeown. New York: Random House 689–934.
Bion, W. (1961) *Experiences in Groups*. London: Tavistock.
Collingwood, R.G. (1944) *An Autobiography*. Harmondsworth: Penguin.
Coltart, N. (1992) *Slouching Towards Bethlethem*. London: Free Association Books.
Ellis, A. and Dryden, W. (1987) *The Practice of Rational–Emotive Therapy*. New York: Springer.
Grondin, J. (1995) *Sources of Hermeneutics*. New York: State University of New York.
Guthrie (1971) *Socrates*. Cambridge: Cambridge University Press.
Hadot, P. (1985) *Philosophy as a Way of Life*, tr. M. Chase. Oxford: Blackwell.
Hegel, G.W.F. (1985) *Lectures on the History of Philosophy*, tr. T.M. Knox and A.V. Miller. Oxford: Oxford University Press.
Horney, K. (1951) *Neurosis and Human Growth*. New York: Norton.
Irwin, T. (1995) *Plato's Ethics*. Oxford: Oxford University Press.
Jung, C.G. (1968) *Archetypes and the Collective Unconscious*, Vol. 9 of Collected Works. Princeton: Princeton University Press.
Kierkegaard, S. (1966) *The Concept of Irony with Constant Reference to Socrates*, tr. L.M. Capel. London: Collins.
Navia, L.E. (1985) *Socrates: The Man and his Philosophy*. Lanham, MD: University Press of America.
Nietzsche, F. (1967) *The Birth of Tragedy*, tr. W. Kaufmann. New York: Random House.
Padewsky, C.A. (1993) Socratic questioning: changing minds or guiding discovery? Paper given to European Congress of Behavioural and Cognitive Therapies, September.
Plato (1951) *The Symposium*, tr. W. Hamilton. Harmondsworth: Penguin.
Plato (1956) *Protagoras and Meno*, tr. W.K.C. Guthrie. Harmondsworth: Penguin.
Plato (1987) *Laches*, tr. I. Lane. In *Early Socratic Dialogues*, ed. T.J. Saunders. Harmondsworth: Penguin 69–118.
Plato (1993) *The Apology*, tr. H. Tredennick. In *The Last Days of Socrates*, ed. H. Tarrant. Harmondsworth: Penguin 29–68.
Santas, G.X. (1971) Socrates at work on virtue and knowledge in Plato's *Laches*. In *The Philosophy of Socrates*, ed. G. Vlastos. New York: Anchor Books 177–208.

Santas, G.X. (1979) *Socrates: Philosophy in Plato's Early Dialogues*. London: Routledge Kegan Paul.

Selvini Palazzoli, M.S., Boscolo, L., Cecchin, G. and Prata, G. (1978) *Paradox and Counter-Paradox*. New York: Jason Aronson.

Vlastos, G. (1991) Happiness and virtue in Socrates' moral theory. In *Socrates: Ironist and Moral Philosopher*, ed. G. Vlastos. Cambridge: Cambridge University Press 200–232.

Vlastos, G. (1994) The Socratic elenchus: method is all. In *Socratic Studies*, ed. M Burnyeat. Cambridge: Cambridge University Press 1–37.

Walsh, J.J. (1971) The Socratic denial of akrasia. In *Socrates*, ed. G. Vlastos. New York: Anchor Books 235–263.

Xenophon (1990) *Conversations of Socrates*, tr. H. Tredennick and R. Waterfield. Harmondsworth: Penguin.

Zuckert, C.H. (1996) *Postmodern Platos*. Chicago, IL: Chicago University Press.

# Introduction to chapter 3

Socrates' equation of virtue and knowledge, and its corollary that no one could knowingly do harm, has been contentious since his own time. It seems to contradict the evidence of common sense that knowledge does not in itself guarantee virtuous behaviour, and that actions can be willed without them necessarily being carried out. The need to account for apparent failures of willing, or *akrasia*, stimulated philosophers to account for how the mind might be divided against itself. The most famous image of the soul in a state of conflict, that offered by Plato in the *Republic* and *Phaedrus*, is of a charioteer attempting to control two horses, one a model of obedience and restraint, the other driven by desire and resisting all attempts at control. This was a distant ancestor of models informing early psychoanalytic theories on psychological conflict (cf. Freud, 1923).

Among the theoretical traditions in modern psychotherapy, psychoanalysis has continued to provide models of the human mind of more than therapeutic interest. Some contemporary philosophers remain unaware of the extent to which these models have developed beyond those Freud was sketching almost a century ago. Nowadays, models based on the theory of internal object relations enjoy the greatest currency among analytic practitioners (cf. Greenberg and Mitchell, 1983). As Paul Sturdee illustrates here, the age-old issue of *akrasia* has not only failed to disappear, but remains of great relevance in therapeutic situations where issues of control and blame may be paramount. By asking how the theory of object relations copes with the phenomena of willing, he distinguishes between a model in which voluntarism makes the best sense of experience, and one where it depicts a sequence of cause and effect. He indicates how the benefits of internalising such an understanding might be realised in the expectations of therapists and patients alike.

# REFERENCES

Freud, S. 1923 *The Ego and the Id.* In *Complete Works of Sigmund Freud*, vol. XIX (ed. J. Strachey) London: Hogarth pp.3–67.

Greenberg, J.R. and Mitchell, S.A. (1983) *Object Relations in Psychoanalytic Theory* Cambridge, MA: Harvard.

# 3 The will in the light of object relations theory

*Paul Sturdee*

## INTRODUCTION

This chapter is concerned with the way in which the psychoanalytic idea of an object relations theory can help us understand an area of great philosophical difficulty, the notion of will. I will argue that 'will' is a semantic concept, that is, it is a concept which helps us to understand other concepts (like 'action' and 'intention') which are essential to our self-understanding. I will show how object relations theory can be used to explain a fundamental problem in the philosophy of action: the need to provide an account of how the representations we consciously and unconsciously entertain are related to the way we act.

I will begin with a case vignette (which is entirely fictional).

## THE CASE OF DICK

Dick is 18 years of age and has been referred for psychotherapy by his GP. He talks in a thin, strained voice which emphasizes his small physical stature. For some time he has been unable to work, remaining at home with his parents. The thought of resuming his occupation (as a panel-beater) causes him severe anxiety. His original reason for not going to work was because he felt his colleagues were laughing at him behind his back, but lately he has been having involuntary thoughts about harming himself, which he feels would be made worse if he attended work. In addition, his relationship with his parents has deteriorated to the extent where he will not speak to them. He experiences his father as menacing and overbearingly authoritarian. During one therapy session, he gets angry when talking about his father, and scratches out the face of a picture of a man in a magazine on the table in front of him. On yet another occasion, he says his mother is weak and 'spineless' because she will not take his side against his father. During therapy he experiences strong resentment towards his analyst. He says he feels bad about having such feelings, and that he has 'shredded' them. Dick is aware of there being conflicting motivations within him, and recognizes the rational conflict between different aspects of himself. For example, he feels desperately unhappy that he is unable to show love to his parents, whilst recognizing that they love him, despite his view of their behaviour as being unloving (because they seem unwilling to help him).

Now, although Dick's case might be straightforward psychotherapeutically, it raises a fundamental philosophical problem, one which philosophers, despite over two thousand five hundred years of inquiry, have so far failed to address, or even characterize, adequately.


## THE PROBLEM OF THE WILL

The problem is traditionally called the 'the problem of the will', although, since the philosophical focus has been mainly on the possibility of *failure* of will, it has also come to be called by the corresponding term from classical Greek, *akrasia*. In Dick's case we (apparently) have a paradigmatic case of failure of will. Dick acknowledges that he does not like, or indeed want, to have the mental experiences and behaviours which he finds troublesome, but nonetheless, he feels powerless to do anything about it. Perhaps we should say that his attempts to do anything about it seem more symbolic than effective.

Philosophers have long been troubled by an apparent paradox present in this sort of process. The standard analysis is to presuppose that an individual does what he wants to, and that what he wants is to do the thing he thinks best. He will thus do X rather than Y because he wants to do X *more* than he wants to do Y. So how can cases like that of Dick's happen?

There are two possible explanations which immediately present themselves: (i) in such cases there has been a disturbance of volition, that is, the normal mechanism by which the will expresses itself has been disrupted; and/or, (ii) there has been a failure of understanding, i.e., the individual's customary self-conception (and the methodology by which it is arrived at) has been found inadequate when faced with an occurrence which falls outside his usual self-understanding.

I will argue here that the primary explanation in Dick's case is (ii), with (i) being a consequence of this. Contrary to the commonsense view, in cases of this sort failure of will is secondary to failure of self-understanding.

## A PROBLEM OF SELF-UNDERSTANDING

With Dick, there appears to be an extreme case of dislocation of motivational forces, a dislocation so severe that he is perplexed and distressed by his failure to understand his mental experiences and actions.

We are normally accustomed to there being some parity between the representations which form an important part of our mental experiences, and the aims and focus of our actions. This is the case when we experience ourselves as being in control – i.e., the self is experienced as being the motivational origin of our acts. The mental representations we have, and the thoughts which accompany them, are congruent with the acts we perform. There is a compatibility between them, as when, for example, preparing a meal, I anticipate the experience of eating it, which in turn might stimulate me to add more seasoning.

Two kinds of disruption are possible here: first, I might be *over*-stimulated by my anticipation of enjoying the meal, and add too much seasoning, thus ruining the outcome. This is intelligible within the conventional model of belief–desire motivations, since it can be explained by an error of judgement. More troubling is the second possibility: I might respond to my anticipation of the enjoyment of eating the meal by adding too little seasoning. If this, too, can be explained by an error of judgement (I simply mistook too little seasoning for the right amount) then there is no problem. But if I added too little seasoning *despite* my intention (given my best, non-mistaken, judgement) to add the right amount, then there is indeed a serious explanatory problem.

What is happening in Dick's case is obviously more severe than this, but it has the same basic structure: a failure to recognize one's actions (and sometimes, as in Dick's case, one's wishes and representations) as one's own.

## A CONVENTIONAL VIEW OF THE WILL

The conventional view of the will portrays each individual as being possessed by a single source of conscious motivational control. This can exert itself to take control of almost the entire range of mental and physical processes, is used in the making of choices, and is the basis for any ascription of self-responsibility. The conventional notion of the will is therefore not purely descriptive, but also normative, in that it is motivated by evaluative concerns which seek expression in a particular conception of human nature.

Probably the most evocative term we use concerning the will, in the conventional sense, is 'will-power', as when one speaks of imposing, by force of will, one's intentions upon the failing executive powers of mind or body. This view lies behind the oft-heard exhortation 'Just pull yourself together!' – a common reaction to Dick's condition. But it does not, of course, do anything to explain how Dick's condition came about, still less his inability to overcome it.

However, if we reconstruct the concept of *weakness* of will in terms of a failure of self-understanding, it just might account for Dick's condition, as well as resolving the paradox identified above (of not doing what one most wants to do).

## AKRASIA AS A FAILURE OF SELF-UNDERSTANDING

This view of *akrasia* creates a difficulty in distinguishing *akrasic* acts having no moral dimension (for which the individual cannot be held responsible) from those which attract moral disapprobation (Austin 1979; Charles 1984; Charlton 1988). Fortunately, this difficulty can be avoided if we conceive *akrasia* as basically an issue in the philosophy of action, so that the moral dimension is secondary (Davidson 1980).

As an issue in the philosophy of action, the concept of *akrasia* is grounded on a fundamental requirement of rational action: that we should, if possessed of the appropriate self-understanding, be able to grasp the motives for our acts (this encompasses our thoughts, representations, and feelings). I am acting *akratically*, then, just when my behaviour, thoughts, phantasies, emotions, and so on, fail to be intelligible within the powers of rational judgement I possess. I simply do not understand myself, and hence find myself having experiences and being driven by motivational forces which I do not recognize to be under my conscious control. This does not preclude the existence of motivational forces which are actually beyond my conscious control but are nonetheless intelligible.

Now, under this conception of *akrasia*, the primary feature is a failure of self-understanding, with failure of the will to exert motivational control being only secondary. But the explanatory difficulty here is that, so long as the motivational processes at work in such cases remain inaccessible to (unaided) consciousness, the issue of a failure of self-understanding (as standing in some conceptual relationship to the *akrasic* outcome) does not seem to arise.

The explanatory difficulty arises, I suggest, because we are accustomed to treating the will as if it were causally linked to the phenomena we seek to explain, rather than as the source of our *seeking*, and, ultimately, of our motivation to understand, ourselves. In this alternative reading of 'will', the will is a *semantic engine* – it is what transforms the impact of the world upon us into intelligible information, and is also what lies behind our having a conception of self.

## THE WILL AS A SEMANTIC ENGINE AFFORDING SELF-UNDERSTANDING

We noted above that under the philosophy-of-action conception of *akrasia*, the explanation of Dick's case presents an explanatory problem in that, so long as the motivational processes at work in such cases remain inaccessible to (unaided) consciousness, the issue of a failure of self-understanding (as standing in some conceptual relationship to the *akrasic* outcome) does not seem to arise. Whilst it is still possible that a failure of self-understanding is involved in the psychical processes at work in Dick's case, for an explanation in these terms to be credible it must account for the development in Dick of an incapacity to arrive at an adequate self-understanding in the first place. This is just what conceiving of the will as a semantic engine would enable us to achieve.

Freud, in his formulation of classical psychoanalytic theory, antici-pated the need for such an account in his undermining of the conventional notion of the will. As mentioned above, the conventional view of the will takes mind and consciousness to be coterminous; it is an individual's strength of will which determines what he is and what he becomes. In his formulation of unconscious motivation Freud chal-lenged this conception with the claim that consciousness accesses only a tiny part of the mind (and its motivational structures), the greater proportion of it being unconscious and beyond the individual's powers of conscious control. The radical aspect of Freud's theoretical concept of the unconscious was a model of rational motivations interacting *irra-tionally*, as a result of being cathected with an affective component. In this way purely emotivist and purely rationalist accounts of human moti-vation can be replaced by one account which combines both kinds of experienced motive (see, e.g., Freud 1977, 1984).

The work of Melanie Klein goes even further, by offering a con-ception of the individual spontaneously creating his own symbolic relations in an inner world of phantasy, which may be out of harmony with his relations with 'objects' in the external world, and which may interfere with the individual's attempts to establish and maintain psychically healthy relations with 'objects' in the external world (see

Greenberg and Mitchell 1983, chapter 5; also Mitchell 1988, especially chapter 5).

The need for a semantic concept of the will comes down to this: whilst we have (or are perhaps indoctrinated with) commonsense conceptions of 'will' and 'person', these are revealed as inadequate in the light of our self-experience. Thus we are subject to complex and conflicting motivations which are, in part at least, beyond our common-sense understanding.

The Kleinian model of the individual affords a conception of the self in terms of the capacity for self-representation in the unconscious phantasy world, a representation which may owe nothing to conscious self-awareness (see, e.g., Klein 1932). In addition, this process of unconscious phantasy is conceived of as taking place in a biological system standing in dynamic relation to its surroundings. Here we have one possible account of the self which draws on the notion of the individual exercising a capacity to represent his surroundings symbolically, and himself as an 'object' in this symbolic world.

## THE PROBLEM OF THE REFLEXIVITY OF THE SELF

The self is one of the most complex conceptual problems facing contemporary philosophy, and it is one which is currently enjoying a high level of interest. It is a problem because it defies the traditional conceptual tools available to philosophy. The notion of something's being reflexive, that is, capable of maintaining an awareness of itself, presents a unique epistemological problem in terms of how the subject can know itself as an object – we are obliged (logically) to inquire how it is that the 'knowing' subject can be the same as the object of knowledge which is the self. So long as we take consciousness to be coterminous with mind, accounting for self-knowledge presents a seemingly intractable problem in that we must posit a knowing subject (the seat of conscious awareness) with the capacity to have knowledge of itself, which amounts to a contradiction in terms ('subject-as-object' on the one hand, and 'object-as-subject' on the other). However, if we treat these problems as being the result of a conceptual difficulty resulting from a disruption of our capacity for symbolization, rather than a purely philosophical issue, then we can address it in terms of the conceptual resources which are required to push against the boundaries of our existing conception of the self.

A very useful way of achieving this is to explore the conceptual roots of object relations theory. My proposal is that we do this by elaborating two fundamental constructs of object relations theory: 'boundary' and 'control'. These are implicit in Klein's work, and have since been rendered more explicit in the work of Donald Winnicott (e.g., 1971; see also Davis and Wallbridge 1990).

## BOUNDARY, CONTROL AND SELF

Perhaps the simplest way of understanding the conceptual roots of object relations theory is to see it as being built on two fundamental constructs: 'boundary' and 'control'. I will explain this by way of a reconstruction of the world of the Kleinian infant.

The Kleinian infant enters the world with minimal capacity to enter into relations with others in the external world, but with its mind working overtime constructing an inner world of phantastic objects. In making sense of the two worlds so that it can function adequately to meet its own needs, the infant must reconcile the demands of its relations with the objects in its inner world with the demands of the objects in the external world. In effect, what it is doing is to establish boundaries between objects (i.e., to distinguish one from the other in order to ensure reliable identification). But the only criteria it has, at least initially, is the extent to which these objects contribute to the meeting of its needs. Hence the distinction between 'good' and 'bad' objects.

In addition, the infant is biologically programmed to explore the external world in order to meet its needs – i.e., it can take the initiative in selecting objects with which to relate, which it will subsequently attempt to control as part of its needs-meeting system. This is a crucial activity, since it affords a functional[1] distinction between 'self' and 'other': in functional terms, the infant recognizes as 'self' anything which it can control as part of its needs-meeting system, whereas it recognizes as 'other' anything that it cannot control in this way. What we now have, in conceptual terms, is a theoretical relation between 'boundary' and 'control': boundaries are established on the basis of differential control.

What I suggest is that we conceive of the Kleinian infant as a functional system composed of a set of biological needs seeking fulfilment, together with a set of emotional and psychological needs seeking fulfilment. The emotional and psychological needs are a product of two factors: (i) the function of the central nervous system in process-ing inputs from the rest of the organism; and (ii) the innate need of the organism to enter into relations with others, a need which is expressed unconsciously through the exercise of a capacity for unconscious phantasy. In addition, we must recognize in the individual an innate capacity for functional representation and symbolization,[2] which enables it to model relations with its environment, as well as to ascribe symbolic roles to the objects it finds there or creates in its unconscious phantasy-world.[3]

To put in a little more detail: the Kleinian infant begins its life as a set of biological needs (which are genetically programmed) and an information-processing system (the central nervous system) which has, in evolutionary terms, developed its capacities as a survival-enhancing system far beyond that which is needed for mere survival, resulting in what we take to be the mind. In fact, so great are its information-processing capacities, and its need to process information, that the human mind spontaneously generates its own information in the form of unconscious phantasy. That is, it anticipates the external world of objects by entering into relations with the objects in its phantastic world.[4]

As the individual grows and develops, the infantile motivational and cognitive structures may be superseded by more sophisticated, adult, structures; but the old ones are not discarded entirely. Instead, the infantile structures are submerged below the level of the adult psyche, but they may remain functionally active in shaping motivations. When the adult psychic structures fail to maintain the individual's psychic integration, i.e., become dysfunctional, the dormant infantile psychic structures will re-assert themselves, overpowering the inadequate adult psychic structures so that infantile needs and needs-meeting become the dominant motivations.

There will be a crisis of self-understanding as the individual finds itself thinking, feeling, and behaving in a way which is incongruent or incompatible with its prevailing self-conception as an adult, rational being. On the one hand, it finds it difficult to disown the overwhelming feelings, needs and motivations which have erupted; but on the other hand, these feelings, needs and motivations undermine the capacity for rational action and responsible behaviour. The individual has been backed into a corner where the moral demand is that a choice must be made between being an adult or being a child, yet it is a choice which involves devastating loss either way: to disown one's adult psyche, and become an infantile psyche in the clothes of an adult body; or to disown the infantile psyche, thus rejecting one's entire developmental history together with the well-springs of one's emotions and intuitions. It is a choice we are not equipped to make.

## AN OBJECT RELATIONS ANALYSIS OF DICK'S CASE

The helplessness of all concerned in failing to gain a point of access to Dick's problem is consonant with the basic claim of Kleinian theory that we encounter the world from within the context of a primitive state of unconscious phantasy, which colours our experience of the world with symbolism, but which itself is far from transparent. An object relations analysis of Dick's case enables us to see how he is straining to recognize and control the boundary of his self, and protect it from intrusions, sometimes in a self-protective, sometimes in a self-destructive, way.

Dick believes his colleagues at work are laughing at him. This can be interpreted as Dick unconsciously experiencing his colleagues as belittling him – in his phantastic world, they are 'bad' objects, and not going to work is a way of annihilating them, of making them disappear. We can further interpret these features as being symbolic expressions of an unconscious wish to return to a child-like, dependent state, in which there is a removal of the demand to assume adult responsibility – a return, in effect, to the internal world of relating only to phantastic objects.

Dick's involuntary thoughts about self-harm are interesting, the more so because he is able to make a connection between returning to work and an increase in their intensity. His belief that he is being laughed at by his colleagues can be seen as an expression of a retreat to the paranoid position of isolation and helplessness, and may indicate a non-instrumental unconscious strategy, whereby Dick disowns the adult part of himself and projects it onto his colleagues. What Dick is doing is to separate out his own anger and hostility towards himself, and ascribe these characteristics to his work colleagues. However, he is not consciously doing this, and so is unaware of its significance or implications.

Unconsciously, Dick is projecting the adult, judgemental aspect of his psyche onto his work colleagues, and one might argue that there is some unconscious collusion on their part, in that they seem to be actively participating in this process.[5] In Dick's case the experience of his work colleagues laughing at him belittles him, and makes him feel small, more like a small child than an adult, and this can be interpreted as a further expression of an unconscious wish to return to the child-like state.

Dick's view of his father as being 'menacing and overbearingly authoritarian' and his mother as being 'weak and spineless' may simply be a continuation of the same kind of splitting, projection and introjection as happened with his work colleagues. Here Dick is projecting on to his father his own anger and hostility towards himself. On to his mother he is projecting his own child-like weakness and dependency. These two projections may indicate the existence of an unconscious nihilistic wish characteristic of depression, in that he is trying to project all of his psyche onto others, trying to become nothing, to annihilate himself psychically.

Dick has unconsciously assigned a strong, masculine role to his father; male sexuality is here being associated with physical violence, or the threat of it, whilst his mother is unable to support Dick against his father's (perhaps only phantasised) hostility. It is possible, using this sort of interpretation, to analyse this situation as being part of a classical Freudian Oedipal complex, which would (normally) have been resolved years earlier, but which is now expressing itself pathologically.

Dick's ambivalence towards the therapist is another indication of splitting. Dick's use of the term 'shredding' for his way of dealing with his unhappiness at having such feelings is ambiguous, in that by scratching out the face in a magazine photograph he is symbolically 'shredding' his anger towards his father. This ambiguity is an important feature of Dick's mental state, in that it combines two important characteristics of his coping mechanisms.

The first characteristic is the tendency for Dick to unconsciously split off parts of his psyche and project them onto others. This can be seen either as a discrete defence mechanism or as an indication of a more fundamental pathological defensive move (in Kleinian terms, a retreat from the 'depressive position' to the 'paranoid-schizoid' position). The second characteristic Dick displays is a tendency to annihilate symbolically aspects of his world which he has identified as 'bad' objects (e.g., by 'shredding' the face in the magazine photograph as he talks about his father). There is a possibility that the symbolic annihilation will come to be expressed by actual attempts to harm or destroy his father. The process may be turned inwards onto Dick himself (he is already experiencing involuntary thoughts about self-harm), and seems more likely than violence to his father.

Dick's feeling unhappy about his resentment towards his therapist, and his 'shredding' of such feelings, may indicate a resolution of unconscious conflicts, but on the other hand may simply express a transference – i.e., he has transferred on the therapist positive feelings which originate in another relationship, and thus he may be trying to please the therapist by giving her what he thinks she wants to hear.

An overall assessment of Dick's situation might be that he is undergoing a regression to the paranoid-schizoid position (the splitting and projection, together with the symbolic annihilation of 'bad' objects, supports this assessment), and that there is a risk that he might come to see himself as a 'bad' object and attempt to annihilate himself. We can say that, whatever the root cause of Dick's problems, he has been unable to achieve or maintain a satisfactory reconciliation between the demands of his infantile phantasy world and the external world. He is losing the battle to influence the setting of the boundary between himself and others.

## THE WILL IN THE LIGHT OF OBJECT RELATIONS THEORY

We are now in a position to reflect on how the concept of an object relations theory sheds light on the problem of the will, and in particular on the problem of *akrasia*. The most significant concession forced upon us by object relations theory is the acceptance that we are far less in control of our lives than we might believe, given the over-optimistic stance represented by the conventional view of the will.

Both classical psychoanalysis and object relations theory view the source of motivations as being differentiated, that is, motivation expresses itself in a complex way which can involve separating into different strands which may then work in opposition to one another, and, in the limiting case, they may cancel each other out.

This view of how the mind is motivated is strikingly different from the standard philosophical view, which takes there to be one (logically simple) will motivating one single stream of thought which produces identifiably straightforward results (if the process works correctly). A similar process is held to operate in terms of the will controlling the actions of the body.

We can now see that this conventional philosophical view of the will and its operations on the mind and body is, in conceptual terms, so at odds with aspects of our ordinary experience accounted for by object relations theory, that wholesale overhaul is required. Object relations theory prompts us to think of the will as being involved primarily with the *making sense* of our motivations and experience rather than with the problem of control over empirical forces. In other words, the concept of will is invoked when we wish to refer to our ability to function as a semantic engine, which enables us, conceptually, to set boundaries between ourselves and other selves. Contemporary philosophy emphasizes the role of language in this 'making sense', and the distinction between conscious and unconscious states in self-understanding has recently been drawn in terms of propositional awareness and pre-propositional awareness in the context of a neo-Kleinian reconstruction of irrationality (Gardner 1993, pp.104, 122, 131, 155–6, 187–91).

It is the capacity to redraw our mental experience in the semantics of natural language which enables us to render explicit meanings which previously were available only as implicit knowledge. This redrawing of experience affords us conscious awareness of our surroundings and of ourselves, but it does not of itself constitute that awareness. Awareness and experience are always *of* something. It is the essential relatedness of different factors of experience which provides us with the 'objects' of our world, and it is the relatedness of awareness which enables us to make these 'objects' available to reflection in a communicable form.

The rendering of experience intelligible by redrawing it in the semantics of natural language affords a conception of the will as a semantic engine – the will is what drives the transformation of information generated by the capacity for functional symbolization into communicable form.

Conceived in these terms, the notion of the will is a purely *semantic* concept, i.e., its function is to render intelligible our experience as agentive beings. We would still want to say that it is the having of a will which enables an individual to qualify as an agent and as a person, but now we can add that the having of a will is not something we experience directly – all we can do is infer we have a will from the possession of the ability to apply the semantics of natural language to the things we find in the world, and this is as much to do with understanding language as with the capacity for linguistic expressiveness.

This inferential capacity relies on the meanings provided by the semantics of natural language, plus rules of inference, rather than direct observation. This means that the products of this inferential capacity are open to challenge in just the way the interpretations of psychoanalysis have been challenged: that they are not observations in the same sense as the observations of natural science, and therefore do not qualify as 'data'.

Whilst there is some substance in this, it does not follow that the semantic concept of the will is empty of content (still less the concepts afforded by psychoanalysis). What it does mean is that we must be very careful to ensure that the postulates in question are conceptually licensed as being preconditions to our rendering our mental experiences intelligible. On this basis, the semantic concept of the will does have content, but it does not have to be interpreted as empirical content. It is a necessary precondition for our having intelligible mental experiences, and it is arrived at by a rational reconstruction of the reason relations we find in the spontaneous expressions of mental life. There need be no necessary connection (systematic or otherwise) with empirical causes – it may be that no systematic psychology of the will is possible.

Conceiving of the will as a semantic concept enables us to make a clear distinction between it and notions of biological drives and instincts, which may or may not have anything to do with the semantic concept of will – this can remain a moot issue without affecting the intelligibility and usefulness of the semantic concept of will. The semantic concept of will can stand quite independently of other concepts of motivation – it is what helps us to understand our selves in terms of the having of motivations, and it may contribute to the redirecting or restructuring of our motivations, but of itself it requires no theoretical account to bolster its credibility. It is conceptually licensed by our demonstrable capacity to render our mental experiences intelligible in the terms provided by our grasp of semantics and our powers of rational thought.

We can now recast the concept of *akrasia* in terms of the individual's failure to engage successfully with the semantics of natural language concerned with achieving sufficient self-understanding to render the problematic motivations transparent. Once the problematic motivations are rendered transparent, the individual can make informed decisions about restructuring his life (reconditioning himself, if necessary) so that he can affirm those aspects of himself which he considers the most important and desirable aspects of his being. This is consistent with the basic psychoanalytic claim that awareness of an individual's motivations is sufficient to empower that individual to make autonomous decisions on the basis of this new understanding. In terms of the object relations school of psychoanalysis, this depends upon awareness of the operation of his defence mechanisms, such as splitting, projection, and introjection.

## THE WILL AND THE PRACTICE OF PSYCHOTHERAPY

How does understanding the notion of the will as a semantic engine engage with the theory and practice of psychotherapy? Psychotherapy is essentially a practical skill, and the concerns of psychotherapists are essentially pragmatic – to enable their clients to achieve a better accommodation between their mental experiences and the demands of the external world. Clearly, there must be some conception of human nature motivating the therapeutic approach being used, but this does not have to be presented in terms of a causal account of the will.

The semantic conception of the will is consistent with the aims and concerns of psychotherapy. To talk of the will as a semantic engine is no longer to be making a claim about the will as a metaphysical entity or as a cause of events in the physical world, still less to be implying any moral obligations to exercise the will in a particular way.

Even more important, we can acknowledge that the impact of the will is felt in rational and affective terms rather than as a 'power' effecting empirical causation. This means that the impact of the will upon our lives as empirical beings will always be problematic: the notion of full autonomy is an illusory ideal. Taking this view of the will may help us better understand the problematic relationship between the concepts of 'willing' and 'wishing'. For example, the experience of anxiety may have a phenomenological connection with wishing what cannot be willed, i.e., what is beyond our capacity to influence.

Perhaps the best we can hope for is to arrive at an understanding of ourselves which enables us to recognize, accept, and (perhaps) ameliorate the constraints within which we are condemned to live.

## NOTES

1   I am using 'functional' as a means of indicating a limitation of language and consequently of our explicit understanding. A 'functional distinction' is therefore a distinction which we must infer on the basis of our grasp of the preconditions for the system to operate globally. We may not know *how* the infant makes such a distinction, but we can infer that it must do so, since without this capacity it would not be able to develop sophisticated behaviours (i.e., in addition to its genetically programmed behavioural repertoire) as a means of exploiting its environment in order to meet its needs better.

2   Functional symbolization, being a capacity which is inferred from its effects, can be understood as a capacity to operate with symbols which do not have signs.

3   In the terms in which I am reconstructing Kleinian theory, the unconscious is merely a theoretical convenience for referring to a functional system – for all we know, the unconscious exists merely in terms of a functional system. At this level of theory, all is speculation, and what gives it cogency is its capacity to help us understand better our conscious mental life.

4   It is thus possible to grasp the basic, unresolvable ambiguity in the use of 'object' in object relations theory. This ambiguity is between 'object' as the

aim or goal of an instinct or drive, and 'object' as a characterizable focus of the individual's needs-meeting behaviour (usually this focus is another person). For the infant, an 'object' in the second sense exists only insofar as it impacts upon the infant as a potential source of needs-meeting, i.e., the infant is attracted to it or repulsed from it on the basis of a genetically programmed motivation for needs-meeting. Such an 'object' will be experienced (in the widest sense, i.e., functionally) not as an object (in the literal sense) but as a dynamic focus of processes which the infant struggles to control. To what extent the 'genetically programmed motivation for needs-meeting' is susceptible to modification by the individual is a moot point.

5    If this is the case, then they may have introjected the part of Dick's psyche that Dick has projected onto them. Splitting, projection, and introjection are difficult concepts, but they reward careful study with insight into psychic processes which are otherwise undetectable (see, for example, Hinshelwood 1997).

# REFERENCES

Austin, J.L., 1979 'A plea for excuses' in *Philosophical Papers*. Oxford: Oxford University Press (3rd edn)

Charles, D., 1984 *Aristotle's Philosophy of Action*. London: Duckworth

Charlton, W., 1988 *Weakness of Will*. Oxford: Blackwell

Davidson, D., 1980 'How is Weakness of the Will Possible?' in *Essays on Actions and Events*. Oxford: Oxford University Press

Davis, M., and Wallbridge, D., 1990 *Boundary and Space: An Introduction to the Work of D.W. Winnicott*. New York: Brunner/Mazel; London: H. Karnac

Freud, S., 1977 (1900) *The Interpretation of Dreams*. Freud Pelican Library, Vol. 4. London: Penguin

—— 1984 (1915) 'The Unconscious' Freud Pelican Library, Vol.11, pp.159–222. London: Penguin

Gardner, S., 1993 *Irrationality and the Philosophy of Psychoanalysis*. Cambridge: Cambridge University Press

Greenberg, J.R., and Mitchell, S.A., 1983 *Object Relations in Psychoanalytic Theory*. Cambridge, MA: Harvard University Press

Hinshelwood, R.D., 1997 'Primitive mental processes: psychoanalysis and the ethics of integration' in *Philosophy, Psychiatry, Psychology* 4:4, pp.121–143

Klein, M., 1932 *The Psycho-Analysis of Children*. London: Hogarth Press

Mitchell, J.R., 1988 *Relational Concepts in Psychoanalysis*. Cambridge, MA: Harvard University Press

Winnicott, D., 1971 *Playing and Reality*. London: Routledge

# Introduction to chapter 4

The scepticism associated with Pyrrho (4th century BC) is the basis of one of the central movements within Hellenistic philosophy. Like its other principal schools (notably Stoicism and Epicurianism, both very influential in Roman and Renaissance literature) these share a fundamental humanism and a concern to apply philosophical method to establish principles for good living. Sharples (1996) provides a very clear introduction to the methods and doctrines of all three. Like Socrates, Pyrrho wrote nothing, most 'Pyrrhonic' writings being authored by Sextus Empiricus in the 3rd century AD.

Within philosophy, scepticism has undergone several subsequent metamorphoses, Wittgenstein promoting an important modern variant, informed by linguistic philosophy. It proposes that, doubt should bear not on propositions taken on their own terms, but on the dubious use of language they perpetuate. Wittgenstein appears to imply that the central questions of philosophy might all be remedied through consistent adoption of such an attitude. As Heaton notes, both here and in his own introduction to Wittgenstein (Heaton and Groves, 1994) Wittgenstein reserved particular scorn for the antics of psychological theorists. Accordingly, strict hygiene should be practised in the way mental entities are spoken about, and therefore thought about. Heaton argues for the value of doing so before framing any clinical problems. In the spirit of the Pyrrhonians, he examines some implications for the lives of therapists and their clients. He points out that some consumers of psychotherapy may be particularly vulnerable to linguistic misuse, accruing a repertoire of unhelpful linguistic devices during therapy in the absence of deeper change. In such cases, Heaton proposes how sceptically oriented consultations may be of particular benefit.

## REFERENCES

Sharples, R.W. (1996) *Stoics, Epicureans and Sceptics.* London: Routledge.
Heaton, J. and Groves, J. (1994) *Wittgenstein for Beginners.* London: Icon Books.

# 4 Scepticism and psychotherapy: A Wittgensteinian approach

*John M. Heaton*

A true story: Peter, aged 5, who was due to start school the next day, was running around excitedly telling his mother about how much he was going to learn at school, suddenly stopped and said: 'Mummy, what if when I go to school all my blood goes to my head and I don't have enough blood in my heart to love you?' His brother, two years older, then said: 'Don't talk like that Peter, nobody talks like that at my school and it's not even in the books'.

I will juxtapose this with a remark from Wittgenstein:

> One of the most dangerous of ideas for a philosopher is, oddly enough, that we think with our heads or in our heads. The idea of thinking as a process in the head, in a completely enclosed space, gives him something occult.
>
> (Wittgenstein 1967: §§605–6)

I want to understand Peter's remark and show the relevance of it. I will argue that Wittgenstein's thought and Pyrrhonian scepticism make far more sense of it than any psychoanalytic explanation. Sceptical therapy is concerned to refind the heart – in Peter's sense – whereas psychological explanations send 'blood to the head' and are deeply implicated in thinking with the head.

## SCEPTICAL THERAPY

I will first make a few general remarks on sceptical therapy, a large subject which has been recently discussed (Hankinson 1995, Heaton 1993:106 and 1997:80). It is a way of life and thought that leads to human well being. It is informal and discontinuous because its practitioners question dogma and have never depended on institutional trappings for their status. Its effectiveness is shown more on the example of their lives and through conversation and debate. So it is not a school with well defined boundaries and it is not doctrinaire. Sceptical insights can be found in the work of many different therapists.

There is a long tradition in philosophy and medicine which argues that practice is more fundamental to therapy than knowledge or theory. The roots of this tradition lie in Pyrrhonian scepticism which is named after Pyrrho, a Greek, who died in 270 BC. He wrote nothing but taught through discussion and example. His teaching eventually took over Plato's Academy and became one of the main schools of philosophy in the Hellenistic and Roman periods. It was particularly popular with physicians because of its emphasis on practice. The tradition has waxed and waned in Europe; Erasmus, Montaigne and Gassendi are amongst the famous teachers of it. In this century Wittgenstein can be understood as being in this tradition (Fogelin 1987:226). He gave a linguistic turn to scepticism emphasizing the lack of sense or meaning in perplexity arising from mental conflict.

The word 'sceptic' derives from the Greek *skeptikos* meaning 'thoughtful', 'paying attention to'. So one learns sceptical therapy by thinking on one's feet – attentiveness in acting, speaking, listening and reading – rather than sitting in one's study learning theories and how to apply them.

There is a paradox about my attempt to understand Peter. Here am I, writing an article which, if it is read at all, will be read by people who are academics or learned therapy in a training institute, well schooled, almost certainly with lots of 'blood in their head'. Furthermore I will be using academic language which would certainly not be understood by Peter when he was 5.

Sextus Empiricus, the main source of our knowledge of the Pyrrhonian sceptics, wrote books with titles which are translated as *Against the Logicians*, *Against the Physicists*, *Against the Ethicists*, and *Against the Professors* yet few others than professors, logicians and academic philosophers read or are even aware of him! Wittgenstein, our other source was, for a time, a professor of philosophy but he considered it an 'absurd job' and 'a kind of living death' (Monk 1990:483) and resigned long before he had to; he was notoriously rude about professional philosophers and said he found more philosophy in Street and Smith's *Detective Story Magazine* than in *Mind*!

So what is going on here? When we go to school we go to learn. At elementary school we learn how to behave socially and elementary skills like reading, writing and arithmetic. As we become more advanced we learn more and more difficult skills like how to write an essay, how to solve a differential equation and so on. At the same time we increase our knowledge; in the modern world the rate of increase of knowledge is rapidly expanding year by year so that it is impossible to keep up with it except in one's own special field which gets narrower as knowledge increases.

But philosophy, according to the thinkers I am concerned with, is very different from all this. It is not concerned with increasing knowledge; of course this does not mean a philosopher is an ignoramus. If he/she wants to clarify the confusions of quantum theory then obviously he/she must be familiar with it, but the learning of quantum theory is not a philosophical activity as such. So philosophy is not one of the sciences, it does not increase our knowledge of the world or of the mind or of ultimate reality – whatever that is; it does not seek to explain anything or to construct theories or to make hypotheses; in philosophy there is nothing hypothetical. Philosophy is not progressive, it is not concerned to increase anything or to prove anything. There are not even any philosophical propositions for if there were theses in philosophy they would be trivial as everyone would agree with them (Wittgenstein 1958:§128).

As many philosophers have noted, the source of philosophy is wonder, as Wittgenstein put it 'It is not *how* things are in the world that is mystical but *that* it exists' (Wittgenstein 1961:6.44). And by 'mystical' he is not referring to any sort of religious or emotional experience but to wonder at the commonplace and familiar. Philosophy is an activity which involves inquiry but also a suspension of feeling (Sextus Empiricus 1994: Bk 1 §7) or as Wittgenstein wrote: 'a resignation, but one of feeling and not of intellect' and he continues: 'that is what makes it so difficult for many' (Wittgenstein 1993:161). It is enormously difficult to stand back and suspend judgement as we are all conditioned to pursue questions and give answers, to take hold of and increase our knowledge and to make immediate judgements. Learned beliefs, inward compulsions and urges drive us on.

The Pyrrhonian sceptics describe their philosophy as a way of life leading to *ataraxia*, freedom from mental conflict. It was a therapy involving suspension of judgement over conflicting accounts of affairs and was particularly attractive to physicians, Sextus Empiricus was himself a practising physician. Their aim was tranquillity, but they realised that if it is seen as an aim then it becomes a good, an object of desire, and so something to be striven for and compulsively thought about; this of course leads to conflict. I try to reach what my conditioning makes me think is the goal but fail, so I am thrown into conflict. They used this story to illustrate the sceptical way:

The painter Apelles was painting a horse and wanted to represent in his picture the lather on the horse's mouth; but he was so unsuccessful that he gave up, took the sponge on which he had been wiping off the colours from his brush, and flung it at the picture. And when it hit the picture, it produced a representation of the horse's lather.

(Sextus Empiricus 1994: Bk 1 §27)

Tranquillity follows suspension of judgement as it were fortuitously, it is not the result of ambition. In other words, it is in the very activity of thinking clearly, reasoning critically and sanely that one discovers for oneself the limits of thought and language.

Wittgenstein too thought that his philosophical activity was a therapy whose aim was peace of mind. 'The philosopher's treatment of a question is like the treatment of an illness' (Wittgenstein 1958: §133). He recognised the similarity between his philosophy and psychoanalysis but with the huge difference that psychoanalysis rests on theories about mental mechanisms which rest on assumptions about the nature of the mind. Wittgenstein thought this is a sign that the psychoanalyst is in the grip of a false picture created by illusions leading to the misuse of language. So structures are imposed on mental concepts without the necessary grounding in the ordinary use of these concepts.

Psychotherapists are known by the theory they adhere to; there are some three hundred theories of psychotherapy at present and no doubt by the time this essay is published there will be some more as psychotherapy 'advances'. To the sceptic these three hundred theories are the names of three hundred pairs of blinkers hiding certain differences and complexities of human life that the therapist has been persuaded to ignore. 'Our investigation, however, is directed not towards phenomena, but, as one might say, towards the "*possibilities*" of phenomena' (Wittgenstein 1958: §90). Every theory hides certain possibilities.

Wittgenstein thought that the job of therapeutic philosophy is simply to put everything before us and not try to explain anything, for the real foundations of the enquiry are the aspects of things that are hidden because of their simplicity and familiarity. We need to be '*reminded*' of what we have overlooked in our anxiety to find answers to our troubles. We are so busy looking for answers and explanations that we stare into the distance and create theories instead of seeing what is under our noses. We fail to be *struck* by what, once seen, is most striking and powerful (Wittgenstein 1958: §126–9).

He depicts his general strategy thus:

You want to straighten out a knot by pulling at the ends of the string. And as long as you pull, the knot can't come undone. You feel there is still a knot, so you pull. And the knot becomes smaller and harder. One way of solving a philosophical problem is to tell yourself: *it is insoluble*. It isn't answerable or it would have been answered, you would have answered long ago. It's not a kink, it's a knot. Don't look for an answer, look for a cure. Don't try to pull it straight, try to unravel it.

(Baker and Hacker 1980: 486)

To unravel a knot we do not need new knowledge or clever theories but patience and attention, two prime qualities in the practice of therapy.

The philosophy I am discussing is particularly concerned with language as that is the medium in which it acts. The philosopher strives to find the liberating word that allows us to grasp what intangibly weighs down our consciousness. He/she seeks to express all false thoughts so characteristically that we can acknowledge that this really is the correct expression of the thought or feeling. He/she seeks to make a tracing of the physiognomy of every error and this is an interminable task as nearly every advance or cultural change contains the potentiality for confusion and every person has his/her unique way of expressing it (Wittgenstein 1993:165).

There is no particular method in philosophy for it seeks to convert error into truth. This involves finding the source of error, as merely hearing the truth is no good. For truth cannot force its way in when falsehood is occupying its place. To see the truth it is not enough to state it, but rather one must find the *path* from error to truth (Wittgenstein 1993:119). Of course this adds to the enormous difficulty of philosophy, as it is not easy to find the path, for it is not only the confusion that needs clarifying but the person in the sway of the confusion. So the therapeutic philosopher must not be ignorant of the current psychological theories. He/she must be so familiar with them that he/she is able to uncover what the theory hides. Sextus Empiricus is a good example as his writing is the chief source of our knowledge of the Stoic and other theories around in his time but he viewed them critically and eschewed all theory himself.

## UNDERSTANDING

Our task is '"to *understand*" something that is already in plain view. For *this* is what we seem in some sense not to understand' (Wittgenstein

1958:§89). The temptation is to seek to penetrate phenomena, to seek explanations and causes which lie below or above phenomena. Instead we need to be reminded of the kinds of statement that we make about phenomena as misunderstandings about the use of words caused by the analogies and pictures embedded in language confuse us.

For example we are told that 'analysis of direct inner perception' is the source of psychological knowledge (Ferenczi 1926:18). This goes along with Freud's belief that

> consciousness makes each of us aware only of his own states of mind; that other people, too, possess a consciousness is an infer- ence which we draw by analogy from their observable utterances and actions, in order to make this behaviour of theirs intelligible to us.
>
> (Freud 1984: 170)

The individual mind is taken as basic, other people and society are sec- ondary. Fulfilment is sought on an individual level, society is necessary but tends to get in the way of fulfilment. This cluster of beliefs are amongst the fundamental assumptions of psychoanalysis. It characterises the dualism of the mental and physical which is taken for granted by most people in our culture. The physical world is public, whereas the human mind is a private world hidden behind our behaviour. Each indi- vidual has a privileged access to his own mind, while only inference or identification gives us access to other minds. Fulfilment and happiness are essentially private affairs and other people merely means to this end.

Now this hypnotic picture of the nature of the mind has been crit- icised by Wittgenstein (1958: §§243–397) and his critique has been commented on and simplified by numerous commentators (Bouveresse 1995, McGinn 1997). Briefly, he shows that we have a picture of the inner world of mental processes and the outer world of public things. This division is empty in practice because it is grounded in the gram- matical distinctions between concepts which describe our world. A friendly smile, a depressed look are neither inner nor outer events but expressions whose meaning lies in the context in which they occur. 'What determines our judgement, our concepts and reactions, is not what *one* man is doing *now*, an individual action, but the whole hurly- burly of human actions, the background against which we see any action' (Wittgenstein 1981: §567). 'What goes on inwardly, too, only has meaning in the river of life' (Wittgenstein 1992:30).

The interesting point is that these criticisms have had little or no effect on psychoanalysis although they have been generally known for some fifty years. This is not because any psychoanalyst or anyone else has given a reasoned rebuttal of Wittgenstein. The same popular beliefs soldier on. Why is this? Part of the answer lies in the narrow intellectual horizon of psychoanalysis and that most specialists will only read within their own speciality. But a more interesting answer lies in the very different approach of Wittgenstein to self-knowledge from that of most people in our culture.

## SELF-KNOWLEDGE

One of the most prevalent beliefs in our culture is that the way to wisdom, mental health, relief of mental conflict and mental pain is through self-knowledge. This belief goes back at least as far as Socrates. Thus in a famous passage in the *Phaedrus* Socrates criticises those who try to explain myths and legends (Freud and Jung would be modern examples), suggesting that their explanations are laborious and over-clever and, in any case, never more than probable. Then he adds:

> In no way do I have leisure for these things. The reason, my friend, is this. I am not yet able to 'know myself' in accordance with the Delphic inscription. It seems to me to be absurd to study alien things so long as that ignorance remains.
>
> (Plato, *Phaedrus*: §229e, author's translation)

Plato only wrote dialogues because he was more interested in the way of inquiry than of demonstration. His method was not to derive consequences from postulates and so build up theories but to ask fertile questions which can lead to the formulation of the real issues which can lead to self-confirming answers. All answers are discounted except those given by the person being questioned so that he genuinely consents to the evidence; this makes sure that the question belongs to him and no one else. It is a method in which a person is thrust into being both inquisitor and witness and so can learn to know himself.

Freud too thought that self-knowledge was the way to the cure of neurosis but he had a very different notion of what that meant. He thought of himself as a scientist and so had a scientist's notion of knowledge. Thus he starts his *Introductory Lectures on Psychoanalysis* (Freud 1973:39) with these words: 'I cannot tell how much knowledge about psychoanalysis each one of you has already acquired from what you have read or from hearsay'. He continues to tell us about his observations and discoveries regarding the contents and mechanisms of the mind in much the same way as a neurophysiologist would lecture us about the brain. Our troubles, he claims, arise because we do not know our minds in the way a psychoanalyst does. Our instinctual impulses have been repressed so that their representatives lie in the unconscious where they are governed by mechanisms such as condensation and displacement. The mechanism of cure is to free the libido from its attachments which are withdrawn from the ego and so making it once more serviceable to the ego. Freud claimed to have discovered these mechanisms and the unconscious itself and psychoanalysts have been working out the details ever since. The assumptions about the nature of the mind, of consciousness, of language, which undergird this theory are never mentioned, let alone questioned. Inquisitor and witness have been torn apart so now it is the analyst alone who is the inquisitor.

Wittgenstein's notion of self-knowledge is very different. He wrote: 'I ought to be no more than a mirror, in which my reader can see his own thinking with all its deformities so that, helped in this way, he can put it right' (Wittgenstein 1980:18).

So self-knowledge is obtained, not by telling someone what is in their minds or what their minds are like, but by enabling them to see what is confusing them and see their own temptations and so recognise them as temptations to be avoided. The problem of the self and our knowledge of it is not resolved by advancing theories but like the problem of life, it finds its solution in the dissolving of the problem. That is when we no longer concern ourselves with ourselves but live in the world appropriately.

Wittgenstein reflected on the notion of the self, the I, the soul and the subject throughout his philosophical life. In his 1914–16 notebooks he was writing: '[t]he I, the I is what is deeply mysterious'; '[a]s the subject is not a part of the world but a presupposition of its existence, so good and evil which are predicates of the subject, are not properties in the world'; '[t]he I is not an object'; and so on (Wittgenstein 1979:80).

In the *Tractatus* he developed very sophisticated notions about the confusions surrounding the notion of the self. He made a crucial distinction between the philosophical and the psychological meaning of the self (Wittgenstein 1961: §5.641). The philosophical meaning of the self is that it is the limit of the world and not a part of it and happiness depends on the understanding of this. Thus 'the world of the happy man is a different one from that of the unhappy man' (Wittgenstein 1961: §6.43).

In vulgar psychological thinking we tend to think of the self as some sort of a mental substance, a ghost in the machine. The first person

pronoun, I, is thought to name a self which is assumed to be something essential inside one's mind or in the inner world, so it forms a
nucleus for the formation of images and so phantasy. Suppose I believe
I am a failure. Now objectively I may have failed in many things; I
failed my school exams so I am only a road sweeper, I have had several
'failed' marriages and I drink too much and so on. But if I am confused
about the meaning of 'I' I will believe that *I*, this named 'substance'
inside me is a failure and will feel and act accordingly; this will manifest perhaps in chronic depression and my always placing myself in a
situation so that I fail, confirming to me that I am a failure.

When we come to see that all this is a nonsense and that the pronoun
I does not name any object then we can be a 'failure' but be happy.
Our failures are real enough, they are facts and can be stated as such,
but sentences state facts and do not name mythical substances. But
Wittgenstein goes much further than this. In the penultimate words of
the *Tractatus* he states:

> [m]y propositions serve as elucidations in the following way: anyone
> who understands me eventually recognizes them as nonsensical,
> when he has used them – as steps – to climb up beyond them. (He
> must, so to speak, throw away the ladder after he has climbed up
> it.) He must transcend these propositions, and then he will see the
> world aright.
>
> (Wittgenstein 1961: §6.54)

The point is that if we argue that the self is not an object we are
putting forward a philosophical proposition and so people may be led
to believe that with no self there is an emptiness inside them which
they feel compelled to fill. So Wittgenstein and the sceptics insist that
they are not putting forward philosophical doctrines or theses, for they
are therapists (Diamond 1991: 179–204). If they put forward any thesis
about the self it would simply leads to arguments as to whether 'I' is a
referring expression or not and would not be returning words home to
the ordinary from the non-places to which they had been dragged by
people hypnotised by crude notions of language. Clinically, it would
lead to the nonsense of telling a depressed person a thesis about the
self and expecting this would be helpful!

This applies to putting forward any thesis about a neurosis. It simply
leads to a hysteric hysterically trying to cure his hysteria; an obsessional
obsessionally trying to cure his obsessions and so on. The ancient sceptics put it thus: 'People who hold beliefs posit as real the things they
hold beliefs about, while Sceptics utter their own phrases in such a way

that they are implicitly cancelled by themselves, then they cannot be said to hold beliefs in uttering them' (Sextus Empiricus: Bk 1 §15). The field of psychotherapy is full of beliefs about the nature and causes of neurosis, whereas neuroses are due to people holding false beliefs positing as real what is not a fact. Theories of neurosis therefore simply reproduce on a meta-level the very disease they seek to cure.

A person deeply embroiled in confusions about the self may take many years or a lifetime to get a clear view of his confusions; stating philosophical propositions will be of little help as eventually he must recognise them as nonsensical as they try to say of reality what cannot be said. The Pyrrhonian sceptics suspended judgement about all dogmatic assertions about reality and so they could listen without the intervening screen of theories and conclusions at the same time being aware that speakers do not say what they seem to say. As Sextus (1994: Bk 1 §14) put it, therapists: 'say what is apparent to themselves and report their own feelings without holding opinions, affirming nothing about external objects'. Or we must say as clearly as we can what can be said and 'it will mean the unspeakable (*das Unsagbare*) by clearly displaying (*darstellt*) the speakable' (Wittgenstein 1961: §4.115).

Self-knowledge implies that we need to know ourselves; but knowledge here is easily taken to mean that we know our own psychological states by observing ourselves in much the same way as we know what we perceive by observing it. Thus it makes sense to say that we know someone is in pain if we observe particular behaviour – he looks ill, he is holding himself tensely, he groans from time to time and so on. But of course it is possible to speak of doubt here, he may be a very good actor. But do we know our own experience in the same way? Can we doubt it? Do we report or describe on our own experience by observing our inner experience as an analysand is supposed to do in psychoanalysis?

Supposing someone has just heard that a person he dearly loves is gravely ill and will probably die. He may feel sad. Does he observe himself and then report the presence of sadness? Of course if someone else were sad one may observe them and report that they are sad but does one observe one's own sadness? Does it make sense that he can doubt whether he is sad or not? Does it make sense for him to say: 'I know I am sad' as if that is a report of some observed mental process? He may say: 'I am sad' but this is an expression of sadness, not a report of a process. Of course he may keep his sadness to himself, perhaps with a stiff upper lip, but that does not mean that he does not feel sad, although it may mean that others do not know he is sad. In short it makes no sense to say that we know our own experiences or that we do not know them. Rather sadness is better understood as an instinc-tive expression, a natural response to a particular situation.

We may deceive ourselves and pretend that we are sad when we are not or pretend that we do not care and perhaps become manic, but self-deception only makes sense if at root there are natural responses. Self-deception does not depend on reporting an inner event falsely, but is a capacity to mislead for some purpose or other.

Let me give some examples of self-deception in therapy. A lot of psychotherapeutic talk concerns motives. But these are very tricky to handle and easily lead to self-deception. Thus a patient who is English and a Christian, and whom I had seen for two years or so, sends me a Christmas card at Christmas. What should I do? What is her motive? Perhaps it is an expression of an infantile wish and so I should respond in the classical manner and refuse the gift and interpret her act. But perhaps this would be mean on my part and be a manifestation of my anal-retentive wish for control of the patient. But on the other hand if I 'gave in' and accepted the card perhaps I would be acting out of a maternal countertransference and surrendering to the patient's control-ling projective identification.

There is no end to the motives one can impute to the therapist and patient. But perhaps sending a card is a natural response to the partic-ular situation for this patient and we do not seek motives for these. It would be absurd to ask what my motive is for putting on my trousers when I get up in the morning, but it might be worth enquiring why I took them off at a public meeting. Here again there is endless room for dispute. I say I took them off as a protest against bourgeois respectability; someone else might say it was because I am very narcis-sistic. How do we assess these claims? If I said I took them off because the man in the moon told me to then this would be unintelligible.

People who have seen several therapists have told me how each one takes exception to different aspects of the person's life and so will inter-pret accordingly. Some do not like signs of aggression, others have a fine eye for obsessional features, others concentrate on sexual devia-tions, others on breaks in therapy and so on. Thus one woman was married to a sexually inhibited man and during analysis started an affair. The analyst took exception to this and interpreted it as an acting out of transference fantasies. Her second analyst on the other hand thought analysis had strengthened her ego's capacity for decision which had accompanied the liberation of her sexuality and so did not interpret her motives as acting out.

The sceptical question is, why does this patient go from one thera-pist to another to have her actions interpreted in terms of one theoretical system or another? These systems hide an implicit moral stance under the guise of objective science. Self-knowledge is to be discovered in the action of relationship, not by cutting oneself off from the flow of life and then seeking an answer to one's problems which is conditioned by a theoretical system. That is one type of self-deception.

One particular move in sceptical therapy which causes bemusement and anger is questioning 'the good'. Therapists are full of what is good for people; to them 'obviously' therapy is good; but it is also good to be Kleinian, or person-centered, or lesbian, or heterosexual, etc. All this may be questioned at appropriate times by the sceptic. Sextus Empiricus produces many arguments on this (1994: Bk 3 §§21–3). This stance towards 'the good', in my experience, produces apoplexy in many therapists and one is labelled homophobic, anti-psychoanalysis, etc. Sceptics, on the whole, have to bear the burden of being seen as particularly wicked by most people. My impression is that patients who have seen a number of therapists do best with a sceptical approach to therapy.

So self-knowledge is not at all what it seems to be; for there is no self to know and the concept of knowledge cannot be applied in a straightforward way to one's own experience. So what was Peter expressing when he said that he feared going to school might threaten his love for his mother?

## PRIMITIVE REACTIONS

A Freudian explanation comes to mind. Peter is in the throes of the Oedipus Complex. His head symbolises his penis and blood going to it is an erection so Peter is fearful of his mother's sexual envy. But this is an argument from analogy; we have to see the analogy between the head and penis and between blood going to the head and an erection for it to make sense. An analogy is a way of looking at things, but it does not give us any proof that that is the actual way that Peter understood what he was saying, let alone that it is the final truth of the matter, as analogies are endless. How do we know that is the true reason for his statement and not an explanation imposed by people who see certain phenomena through the spectacles of sexual analogies?

I want to show that Peter's response to the situation of starting school can best be understood as expressing a fear that he would lose touch with the primitive language game of expressing his love for his mother which requires no justification or evidence. At school he would learn to reason, argue, doubt, and absorb and justify knowledge. These are secondary activities which are built on primitive language games but can

easily take over so that we forget the primitive on which the rest depends
to make sense.

How does one learn one's mother tongue?

> When a child learns language it learns at the same time what is
> to be investigated and what not. When it learns that there is a
> cupboard in the room, it isn't taught to doubt whether what it sees
> later on is still a cupboard or only a kind of stage set.
>
> (Wittgenstein 1969: §172)

Learning one's native language is a kind of training depending on man's
primitive, that is, prelinguistic, innate ability to recognise regularities
in the world and in the actions of human beings. Infants are surrounded
by speakers much of the time and they respond to the rhythm of language
and attune themselves to its harmony. Their behaviour is responded to
by the people around them in appropriate ways, so they are brought to
act as other competent members of their family. 'The origin and the
primitive form of the language game is a reaction; only from this can
more complicated forms develop. Language – I want to say – is a refinement. "In the beginning was the deed"' (Wittgenstein 1993:395).
Children do not learn first that books exist, rather, they learn to fetch
and look at books, sit in chairs, sit on the potty etc. (Wittgenstein
1969: §476). So children gradually get the point and follow the rules
of the respective practices just as others do. 'Does a child believe that
milk exists? Or does it know that milk exists? Does a cat know that a
mouse exists?' (Wittgenstein 1969: §478). Knowledge, belief, justification come much later than the natural associations and significations
that are primitive; children simply have to trust the adults first of all,
otherwise they could not learn to speak. 'The primitive form of the
language game is certainty, not uncertainty. For uncertainty could never
lead to action' (Wittgenstein 1993:397). 'A child learns there are reliable and unreliable informants much later than it learns facts which
are told it' (Wittgenstein 1969: §143). 'What is essential for us is, after
all, spontaneous agreement, spontaneous sympathy' (Wittgenstein
1980(a): §699). '"Knowledge" and "certainty" belong to different *categories*. They are not two "mental states" like, say "surmising" and "being
sure"' (Wittgenstein 1969: §308).

So the certainties of primitive language games like: 'this is a hand'
or 'this is red' or 'Mummy loves me' cannot be justified, for they are
basic to our human form of life. The more elaborate language games
that one learns at school need more than the simple training and spontaneous agreement on which primitive language games depend. Facts

like 'the earth is round', 'William the Conqueror came in 1066', 'mammals are warm-blooded' require reflection to make sense and the more sophisticated the game, the more it depends on reflection, quietening doubts and questioning. Such facts require a rational foundation, in contrast to primitive language games which have no rational foundation (which does not mean they are irrational).

Primitive language games, such as the expression of a child's love for its mother, are independent in the sense that the language and the ways of acting with which it is connected are independent of the ways we speak about and act in relation to physical objects and processes. So there cannot be a single principle which accounts for both. Also, the meaningfulness of the form of language cannot be separated from an understanding of the activities connected with it – playing with the mother, kissing her and so on; an insight made use of in play therapy.

Primitive language games are independent as they are not grounded in beliefs and cannot be justified (Hertzberg 1992:24–39). Thus in adult love we may love a person because they are pretty, or wealthy, or dependable, or because the parents approve etc. and of course we may doubt our love or the other person's love for us. So instead of encountering another's love and allowing it to be sustaining we may seek evidence for it; this is deeply destructive as when basic trust is destroyed it will not be restored by a sufficiency of evidence. We may then be led to worry about something hidden – in the unconscious perhaps. None of this applies to the primitive language game of a child's love for its mother which is open and this is why it used to be called innocent. But this innocence has a double edge. For if the mother actually hates the child – tries to smother it etc. – then the child will understand this as love. People brought up in this way, in which hate masquerades as love, tend to have deep confusions which take a long time to clarify.

When we see the rich variety of primitive reactions in human life we are less inclined to impose theoretical models on them and this enables us to escape from the impoverished view of human existence that ensues when the variety of human relations are forced into a single mould. The innocence of a child's love for its mother is perverted when it is explained through theory which can never be more than possibly true.

So Peter understood himself and his situation quite well. Going to school would mean he would learn to doubt, he would learn information that would be far removed from his heart – the seat of spontaneous response – and could go to his head – the seat of reflection. He could easily lose touch with the forms of life fundamental to being human that escape our notice because they are so ordinary and are right in front of our eyes. They are a requirement for our understanding anything at all and so are exempt from explanation. Our hopes and fears, science and mathematics, religions and therapies, in the end focus on what is distinctively human, our form of life; when this is forgotten we will create therapeutic theories and so lose ourselves in one or other of the three hundred or so current intellectual castles in the air.

## REFERENCES

Baker, G.P. and Hacker, P.M.S. (1980) *Wittgenstein: Understanding and Meaning*, Oxford: Blackwell.

Bouveresse, J. (1995) *Wittgenstein Reads Freud*, trans. C. Cosman, Princeton, NJ: Princeton University Press.

Diamond, C. (1991) 'Throwing Away the Ladder: How to Read the *Tractatus*', in *The Realistic Spirit*, Cambridge, MA: MIT Press.

Ferenczi, S. (1926) *Further Contributions to the Theory and Technique of Psychoanalysis*, London: Hogarth Press.

Fogelin, R.J. (1987) *Wittgenstein*, 2nd edn, London: Routledge.

Freud, S. (1973) *Introductory Lectures on Psychoanalysis*, Harmondsworth: Penguin Books.

Freud, S. (1984) *On Metapsychology: The Theory of Psychoanalysis*, Harmondsworth: Penguin Books.

Hankinson, R.J. (1995) *The Sceptics*, London: Routledge.

Heaton, J.M. (1993) 'The Sceptical Tradition in Psychotherapy', in *From the Words of my Mouth: Tradition in Psychotherapy*, ed. L. Spurling, London: Routledge.

Heaton, J.M. (1997) 'Pyrrhonian Scepticism: A Therapeutic Phenomenology', *Journal of the British Society for Phenomenology* 28.

Hertzberg, L. (1992) 'Primitive Reactions – Logic or Anthropology?', in *Midwest Studies in Philosophy*, Volume 16, Notre Dame, IN: University of Notre Dame Press.

McGinn, M. (1997) *Wittgenstein and the Philosophical Investigations*, London: Routledge.

Monk, R. (1990) *Ludwig Wittgenstein*, London: Jonathan Cape.

Sextus Empiricus (1994) *Outlines of Scepticism*, trans. J. Annas and J. Barnes, Cambridge: Cambridge University Press.

Wittgenstein, L. (1958) *Philosophical Investigations*, trans. G.E.M. Anscombe, 2nd edn, Oxford: Blackwell.

Wittgenstein, L. (1961) *Tractatus Logico-Philosophicus*, trans. D.F. Pears and B.F. McGuiness, London: Routledge and Kegan Paul.

Wittgenstein, L. (1967) *Zettel*, trans. G.E.M. Anscombe, Oxford: Blackwell.

Wittgenstein, L. (1969) *On Certainty*, trans. D. Paul and G.E.M. Anscombe, Oxford: Blackwell.

Wittgenstein, L. (1979) *Notebooks 1914–1916*, trans. G.E.M. Anscombe, 2nd edn, Oxford: Blackwell.

Wittgenstein, L. (1980) *Culture and Value*, trans. P. Winch, Oxford: Blackwell.

Wittgenstein, L. (1980a) *Remarks on the Philosophy of Psychology*, Volume 2, trans. C.G. Luckhardt and M.A.E. Aue, Oxford: Blackwell.

Wittgenstein, L. (1992) *Last Writings on the Philosophy of Psychology*, trans. C.G. Luckhardt and M.A.E. Aue, Oxford: Blackwell.

Wittgenstein, L. (1993) *Philosophical Occasions 1912–1951*, ed. J.C. Klagge and A. Nordmann, Indianopolis, IN: Hackett Publishing Company.

# Introduction to chapter 5

Throughout his life, Ludwig Wittgenstein was one of the most influential philosophers of the present century. He twice presented a novel yet unusually complete way of doing philosophy, demonstrating its power to view thorny problems in a blindingly different light. His own originality can inspire commentators to try to overhaul rather than simply summarise his work, but a reliable and readable introduction is provided by Kenny (1973). Despite apparent differences, Wittgenstein's early and late philosophies were both concerned with fundamental questions of the nature of meaning, and informed by a profound ethical sensitivity. As well as the potentially distorting impact of psychological language that Heaton has highlighted, Wittgenstein's work also demonstrates paradoxes about the relation of understanding to action that cannot be ignored in psychotherapeutic work.

Joady Brennan selects aspects of Wittgenstein's later philosophy, in which meaning was identified with communal understandings inseparable from linguistic habits, and a strand of psychology that has informed significant therapeutic innovations within 'constructivist' psychotherapy (a helpful reading list will be found at the end of the chapter). While many traditional therapies from psychoanalysis to behaviourism have been redescribed to accommodate the active creation and maintenance of meaning through social interactions, the theory of personal constructs places such processes centre stage. At the same time, the relationships between linguistic habit and other human activities it presupposes are reminiscent of Wittgenstein's inferences about the interdependence of 'language games' and 'forms of life'.

Brennan uses these comparisons to draw conclusions about the importance of language in therapy, its potential for misuse, and the cultural limitations of psychotherapy which demand attention from practitioners of non-constructivist therapies and personal construct therapy alike.

## REFERENCES

Kenny, A. (1973) *Wittgenstein*. Harmondsworth: Penguin.

# 5 Picture this
## Wittgenstein and personal construct theory

*Joady Brennan*

Scholars customarily distinguish sharply between the forms of thought and the actual thinking behaviour of people. The study of the former is classified under philosophy – or, more particularly, logic – while the latter is considered to be psychology. But we have taken the basic view that whatever is characteristic of thought is descriptive of the thinker; that the essentials of scientific curiosity must underlie human curiosity in general. If we examine a person's philosophy closely, we find ourselves staring at the person himself. If we reach an understanding of how a person behaves, we discover it in the manner in which he represents his circumstances to himself.

(Kelly 1955:15)

I am sitting with a philosopher in the garden; he says again and again 'I know that that's a tree.' pointing to a tree that is near us. Someone else arrives and hears this, and I tell him 'This fellow isn't insane. We are only doing philosophy.'

(Wittgenstein 1969: #467)

*One of the most interesting aspects of writing this chapter has been my uneasy awareness that neither Wittgenstein nor Kelly would particularly approve the undertaking. Although themselves voluminous writers and generous, serious teachers, who actively sought criticism and response to their ideas, the prospect of yet more words on paper might seem equally redundant to them both. The bond between them that I hope to illustrate here is their specific interest in words in action, in use, as our form of life. Kelly created a psychological model of an inventive, inquiring human being whose perceptions and use of language are uniquely personal. Wittgenstein offers a philosophical approach to language as our form of life, where use, not dictionary definition, gives meaning. Our language defines and modulates us, how we describe our situation may imprison or free us; Kelly and Wittgenstein are concerned with the everyday human enterprise, what we do with words, rather than solemn academic reformulations of their theories.*

## TWO KINDS OF CONSTRUCTIVIST

Ludwig Wittgenstein (1889–1951) and George Kelly (1905–1966) are both known for the density and difficulty of their written works, which have spawned schools of specialist commentators, many of whom in the course of time have come to refer to each other, rather than back to the originals. Although profoundly disparate in background and culture, these two men can be seen to have similar ways of looking at things, and to have embarked on a similar quest, though from two very different starting-points, and in two very different modes. Interestingly, the huge disparity between each undertaking demonstrates the point each was trying to illustrate, from the angle of therapy and that of philosophy. As far as the *Psychology of Personal Constructs* and the *Philosophical Investigations* go, it might help to think of them as trying to lead you to the same awareness, one by detailed explication, one by posing questions; the Old Testament versus Zen koans. Different people learn from whichever method suits them best – do you prefer to have someone patiently lead you through the material until it makes sense, or to have someone set up little scenarios and inquiries until suddenly something clicks? Does it depend on what the subject is, on whether you're studying to learn practical skills or to write a paper?

Wittgenstein grew up in a cultured family in pre-war Vienna, giving his inheritance away on principle; Kelly's family struggled in severe rural poverty in Depression America. Originally, both studied engineering, and although Kelly became a clinical psychologist, and Wittgenstein a philosopher, both were natural mathematicians and pragmatists, builders of houses and abstract systems. Wittgenstein was uncertain about the usefulness of being a philosopher, and exhorted his students instead to become shop assistants, doctors or mechanics. Kelly frequently stresses that psychology is supposed to *do* something in real-life terms, and as an academic clinician, did not have Wittgenstein's need to find alternative practical work. As well as teaching philosophy on and off at Cambridge, Wittgenstein was variously a gardener, a hospital porter, and a schoolteacher. A concern with, and respect for, the mundane, the workaday, is what distinguishes their thinking, and underpins the self-reflexive nature of their speculations.

With the encouragement of his early mentor, Bertrand Russell, Wittgenstein published the pamphlet *Tractatus Logico-Philisophicus* in 1921, having written it while a foot-soldier in the trenches, and as a prisoner of war. He at first believed he had completely dealt with the issue of language by clearly elaborating it as a signatory system, a word in the head corresponding with the object out there, but he soon began to work on rebutting his early modernist conclusions. 'In the Tractatus, Wittgenstein made a philosophy consistent with the modern view of nature, but in so doing what was incompatible with that view was ignored, namely, human experience' (Bolton 1979:107).

Although he devoted the greater part of his life thereafter to this task, the only other philosophy text he actually prepared for publication, and our main focus here, was *Philosophical Investigations* (henceforth PI), which came out after his death. The rest of his body of work has since been devotedly assembled for print from notes, reports of his lectures and scraps of paper in box-files.

The intellectual context for these two books was a time of great change. The main model of scientific thinking current in the last century and the beginning of this one was the cause-and-effect chains of Newtonian mechanics, which assumed one 'true' observable reality available to an objective observer; this was the medium in which the medical, psychological, philosophical, and sociological theories of the nineteenth and twentieth centuries had been cultured.

From our present vantage-point, Kelly and Wittgenstein are situated towards the end of modernist thinking, both in the hard and the human sciences, in that a confident assumption of linear certainties was giving way to the more complex visions of quantum physics, which recognized levels of connectedness, the myth of the independent observer and the multiplicity of possible explanations and descriptions. 'Construct theory, or better, personal construct theory – a term which implies that a construct is as much a personal undertaking as it is a disembodied scheme for putting nature in its place – suggests that human behaviour is to be understood in a context of relevance' (Kelly 1969:11). 'Why should there not be a psychological regularity to which *no* physiological regularity corresponds? If this upsets our concept of causality then it is high time it was upset' (Wittgenstein 1967: #610).

*Philosophical Investigations* and *Psychology of Personal Constructs* are both situated in and contributive to this paradigm shift in our thinking about language, reality, change, and description, with Wittgenstein and Kelly examining, in their different ways, the questions raised by the disappearance of the modernist world view.

Science is often understood by students as a way of avoiding subjective judgements and getting down to the hard facts of reality. But
I am suggesting that the avoidance of subjectivity is not the way
to get down to hard realities. Subjective thinking is, rather, an
essential step in the process the scientist must follow in grasping
the nature of the universe. . . . When we know something, or think
we do, we make up sentences about it, using verbs cast in the
indicative mood. We talk about it in a way that appears to be
objective.

(Kelly 1969:150)

Perception of reality – how we know what we know – has always been
a thread of concern running through the classical modernist weave, and
although in some ways wild cards, our two subjects, philosophy and
psychology, are cornerstones in the elaboration of the notion of the
constructivist world. Watzlawick in his introduction to *The Invented
Reality* speaks of 'the development of constructivism from the days of
antiquity to Giambattista Vico, Immanuel Kant, David Hume, Eduard
Zeller, Wilhelm Dilthey, Edmund Husserl, Ludwig Wittgenstein and
the Vienna Circle, Jean Piaget, Erwin Schrodinger, Werner Heisenberg,
George Kelly, Nelson Goodman, and many competent thinkers'
(Watzlawick 1984:10). It is here that Wittgenstein and Kelly most fully
overlap, illuminating the shift from observation of the world to active,
personal construction – from description to process. Both demonstrate
the constructivist viewpoint by asking us to imagine what it might be
like if it were so – to think about constructivism propositionally, and
see how it fits. 'Cybernetics, for me, is the point where you can overcome Russell's theory of types by taking a proper approach to the notions
of paradox, self-reference, etc., something that transfers the whole
notion of ontology – how things are – to an ontogenesis – how things
become' (Von Foerster 1995:9).

Wittgenstein speaks about 'language games' (PI #7 and on), where
people share common assumptions, angles of perception, and use words
in similar ways and thus create and negotiate their 'form of life' (PI ##
19, 23, 241). This equates with Kelly's 'Commonality Corollary', where
construing experience in similar ways implies that one's 'psychological
processes are similar to those of the other person'. The questions raised
lead us to think about the ways words bring us to certain conclusions
about the world; Wittgenstein uses the example of describing something as though it were a machine, and how this abstract figure of
speech has pragmatic consequences. We see machine-like qualities;
limitations, essences, and other aspects are no longer on the cards. The

tunnel vision inherent in language forms is particularly familiar in the field of mental health, where a mechanistic or internal-drive model may limit our options, lead us to certain conclusions, attributions or reductions. Wittgenstein points out that this is 'not reasonable (or unreasonable). It is there – like our life' (Wittgenstein 1969: #559).

Wittgenstein offers a philosophical reading on language as our form of life, where use and action, not dictionary definition nor an unmediated external reality, impart meaning. Whether or not there is 'really' a reality out there is not just a philosophy exam-paper question, and the relativity of 'truth' has personal significance in more contexts than the case-conference, care proceedings, or the court-room; ethical questions attach to how we think the world works. Kelly is moved not to debate reality but to respond to it: 'As in phenomenology, personal construct theory sees man looking out on his environment, but, unlike phenomenology, does not portray that environment as a figment of his imagination. It's a real world that he lives in. The trick is for him to make something out of it' (Kelly 1969:219).

While a professor in Kansas, Kelly set out initially to write a practice handbook for the travelling clinic staffed by himself and a variety of students. Twenty years later, in 1955, he published the two weighty volumes of *The Psychology of Personal Constructs*, saying '[p]resumably it was the sort of thing more likely to be purchased than read' (Kelly 1963:xi). Here, Kelly sets out a psychological model (henceforth PCT) based on the proposition that language-meanings, like points of perception, are unique to each person, and that these meanings are the basis for active elaboration in the real world. His framework of therapeutic practice rests on assumptions not of pathology, but difficulties in transition.

Although Kelly began teaching psychology as soon as he qualified, while progressing up the academic ladder he also continuously carried a clinical caseload. He describes how alternate sessions with clients for therapy, and graduate students for supervision gradually brought home to him that these two undertakings involved similar problems and responses, and could be viewed as very similar human enterprises. Most of his clients lived in disadvantaged rural areas, in a time of recession, and Kelly found that the current mainstream psychological approaches, behaviourism and psychoanalysis, seemed too circumscribed, too procrustean in practice, so he began to formulate a more comprehensive model. He tells how he was educated by his clients into seeing their 'symptoms' as questions they were posing their world. Kelly speaks as a researcher, who formulated theories to explain his observations, testing his hypotheses, both clinically and academically. The psychological model he created is of an inventive inquiring human being whose perceptions and use of language are uniquely personal.

Kelly's bulky volumes constitute a basic philosophical exposition, abstract theoretical statements, and a descriptive elaboration of the theory, followed by a scientifically laid out methodology with: 'its mathematical construction of psychological space, its more humanistic approaches to man as a person, and its multifaceted ways of coping with human distress' (Kelly 1963:xi).

Wittgenstein presents the reader with numbered paragraphs, some of which can be read sequentially, some of which are free-standing. Many of these are epigrammatic, terse, and puzzling: none of them spells out any answers: 'the difficulty is to see the point of Wittgenstein's plain remarks and observations' (Bolton 1979:xii).

People sigh over Wittgenstein because he offers terse epiphanies, brief illuminations – he rarely states or advises, but merely keeps on querying things and giving alternate readings in a way that may, or may not, lead you to his stated goal: a 'perspicuous representation' which consists in 'seeing connexions' (PI #122). Kelly, on the other hand, is greeted with a sigh because his is an extraordinarily painstaking, dense attempt to spell *everything* out – a philosophy, how a psychotherapeutic stance follows on, and how to do that sort of therapy – down to the meticulous discussion of the therapist's breathing patterns and the layout of consulting rooms. People get fed up with Kelly 'because he goes on and on', and with Wittgenstein because 'he never explains anything'; both are extremely hard work. However, these can be seen as two deeply serious attempts to look at the same questions – if objective knowledge is not an option, then how are we subjective creatures to live, how are we to change, how are we to help each other?

PCT, then, is a psychological and philosophical model of humanity that strives to account for the person as a situated active being:

> A personal construct system is not a collection of treasured and guarded hallucinations, it is the person's guide to living. It is the repository of what people have learned, a statement of their intents, the values whereby they live, the banner under which they fight. A personal construct system is a theory being put to a perpetual test.
>
> (Bannister and Fransella 1986:14)

One of the most engaging features of PCT for practitioners is that this is a comprehensively self-reflexive theory, which adequately explains the therapist, or the theorist, in with all the rest of humanity, while, as Kelly reflects:

> curiously enough, psychologists rarely credit the human subjects in their experiments with having similar aspirations. It is as though the psychologist were saying to himself, 'I, being a psychologist, and therefore a scientist, am performing this experiment in order to improve the prediction and control of certain human phenomena; but my subject, being merely a human organism, is obviously propelled by inexorable drives welling up within him, or else he is in gluttonous pursuit of food and shelter.'
>
> (Kelly 1955:4)

PCT methodology includes elicitation of personal constructs, fixed-role and enactment exercises, and repertory grids, mathematical formats which map the person's understanding of themselves and others within their personal dimensions of meaning. The repertory grid has been by far the most commonly used aspect of Kelly's work, and he did voice regrets at having opened that particular Pandora's box, which with its appealing trappings of scientism and replicability can be – and have been – taken up as a technique without reference to PCT. Within construct theory, grids have been used in creative, respectful work with individuals, families, and groups, in both therapy and research. Given the sizeable literature on repertory grids I shall only clarify here that Kelly originally designed them to provide therapist and client with a clearer picture of the personal construct system, and possible areas of movement and change.

Kelly tries to give us a different aspect on how we get along in the world by using the analogy of a scientist; active, experimenting, moving forward on the basis of personal hypotheses about likely outcomes. He describes our perceptual net as made up of our unique bipolar constructs or discriminations, such as wealthy/struggling, European/American, cryptic/detailed; comparison lines on which we locate ourselves, our experiences, and the relationships between different aspects of our particular world. He offers a model of humanity as moving through time in an inquiry, an investigation into life. Behaviour is seen as an experiment, and each person as construing outcomes in their own unique way, making sense of their lives in their own terms, revising their constructs in the light of their experiences. Kelly's stance is that of a humanist, with an emphasis on the self-creating capacity of the person.

In talking about constructs, Kelly does not mean formal lists of generalized opposites, or Cartesian dualistic dichotomies, but personal discriminations, contrasts, ways we differentiate or put together occur-rences, people, ideas; 'distinctions which our ordinary forms of language easily make us overlook' (PI: #132). The personal construct system is how we distinguish, give meaning, and make sense of the world, it is what makes each of us a person, an individual; or rather, it is *how* we are a person. This is the 'form of life' Wittgenstein speaks of – our language is our way of being our particular selves.

The construct system envisaged by Kelly is hierarchical, in that there are 'superordinate' or 'core' constructs which may subsume others which are less personally crucial or less well elaborated. Constructs are seen as inter-related, although not necessarily consistent with each other. Someone whose core constructs are to do with fair play and universal justice, for instance, may manage to behave in a way you might see as unjust by applying these constructs only to 'all humanity', but not includ-ing women, or blacks, in the universal human picture. We have all too many vivid examples of this: the words Jew, Palestinian, Serb, Croat or Muslim are, as I write and as you read, used as descriptions which over-ride our usual constructs about right conduct. Writing on white racist use of stock black characters in American literature, Ralph Ellison illustrates such conflicting points of view, and the often ludicrously baroque lengths people go to to make the contradiction fit in a coherent way:

> whatever else the Negro stereotype might be as a social instru-mentality, it is also a key figure in a magic rite by which the white American seeks to resolve the dilemma arising between his demo-cratic beliefs and certain antidemocratic practices, between his acceptance that all men are created equal and his treatment of every tenth man as though he were not.
>
> (Ellison 1994:28)

Think of this in terms of mental health, clarifying how we as professionals may find our clinical labels allow us to deviate from our generally caring humanistic stance, without dislodging us from our core role structures. Think of this allowing us to comprehend the complexity of any particu-lar human system without having to search for some ideal internal con-sistency or logical coherence: 'predicaments into which we have been cast by the language of objectivity' (Kelly 1969:158).

Both Wittgenstein and Kelly remind us that at some point 'talk', that is, abstract discussion, explanation, theorizing, have to come to an end, and we have to get down to the real conversation of daily living, the stories of our lives. This is a scary business, and Kelly provides us with some different ways of thinking about how and why we may find things so difficult, by taking key psychological concepts and putting them in terms of the one 'doing' them rather than the one perceiving (and often labelling) the process. In this way stress is laid on actively elaborating the understanding of other people.

Writing at a time when psychoanalysis and behaviourism were equally popular 'explanations', Kelly used aspects of both, placing them in a more complex picture. He neutralises pejorative terms by describing them from the inside, as personal and unique processes. In particular, he changes the aspect of words more usually viewed in a psychodynamic light – hostility, aggression, threat, anxiety, and so on, and reconstructs them according to their internal significance, rather than as labels to be applied to behaviour by an onlooker.

Try seeing threat as 'the awareness of an imminent comprehensive change in one's core structures', and hostility as 'the continued effort to extort validational evidence in favour of a type of social prediction which has already been recognised as a failure' (Kelly 1955:565). What Kelly does for us here is let us see not just hostile, threatened behaviour, but the fears of change and personal invalidation which inform such behaviour. How can you recognize blacks as equal if that might shatter your whole personal template for life? Will pointing out the error of racist thinking *work* here?

Studs Terkel interviewed a former racist and Klu Klux Klan member, C.P. Ellis, who unwillingly found his version of the world changed when he began to look at people in terms of a rich–poor discrimination, rather than a black–white one; he could shift the aspect he saw, and become a different person, not just in how he spoke, but in what he did (Terkel 1992). Wittgenstein uses an exercise with Jastrow's duck/rabbit image, where the same shape can look like two things, now duck, now rabbit, to get us thinking about this sort of process (PI: #194). We may have exactly the same input, the same physical evidence, the same information, but we make different sense of it, not only from each other, but from ourselves, at different moments.

## MEANING, USE AND THERAPY

> We have to remember that what we observe is not nature in itself, but nature exposed to our method of questioning.
>
> (Heisenberg 1958:58)

Now, how is this of any importance; why should this matter at all to a clinician? Because this question of how we know what we know is not merely of academic interest; for philosophers to mull over how they know something is an apple tree does matter, if you think of it in terms of how someone *knows* it is best to kill themselves, or that they are grossly fat, or that it is all right to beat their child or to hospitalize someone. These are the questions of personal knowledge we run up against all the time.

What Kelly's model offers is some ways of describing how we can formulate human talking and acting in ways which mean that the possibility of change is available. Where Wittgenstein struggles to free us from the traps of language, its deceptively linear mode, its convincing reifications, by clearing away the rubble of modernist philosophies, and leaving space clear for social context and personal meaning, Kelly offers us propositional tasks and methods to explore and elaborate the space available.

> Probably there is nothing more exciting in the whole field of clinical psychology than the notion that persons in distress can couch their problems in the language of hypothesis, and that one can think with verbs in the invitational mood, even though our language has no structural form for designating such verbs.
>
> (Kelly 1969:153)

The therapeutic techniques Kelly described are based foremost on achieving an understanding of what the client's words mean to them, rather than the therapist assuming that language is shared because the words are common. This is an area of equal concern to Wittgenstein and Kelly – it is very easy to think that words are equivalent to their dictionary definitions, when in practice they are idiosyncratic tools. And just like the person who uses the screwdriver to open cans of paint, and tightens screws with the blunt end of a nail-file, no one can be tied down to a 'proper' usage in real life. That only happens in grammar tests, psychiatric assessments, philosophical debates. If the nail-file got the brackets attached, it was the right tool. Someone may use the word 'behaviourist' to mean superficial, mechanistic; that's not the dictionary definition, but it is what it means in their personal language-game. 'Let the use of words teach you their meaning' (Wittgenstein PI:220e).

In one PCT exercise you ask someone to describe the people who make up their social repertory by asking 'How would you see two of these three people as alike and therefore different from the third?' A person I once worked with described everyone initially in terms of 'man' as compared to 'woman'. On elaboration, 'man' meant, to him, 'tough, strong, reliable, white', and 'a proper fighter'. People who were 'women' he described as weak, 'always yakking', corrupt, 'stab you in the back', invasive, and of all colours. Can you see how by seeing someone as 'man' he is building a world-picture that does not necessarily fall into a gender division, but has a definite racist component? Talkative, foreign or black, you could be either male or female, all would be equally threatening to this person, and part of the same collection put together in the despicable 'not like me', women's group. Of course, this meant that women he admired, like his mum and sisters, had to be distinguished as 'female', because he couldn't lump them in with what the word 'woman' denoted to him. Kelly's theoretical position is based on personal meaning, personal significance, and the human being as a unique, languaged, form of movement, with all the opportunities and pitfalls that involves.

Kelly designed ways of eliciting personal meaning and constructs, and describes how these can be used to help the client along the road they want to travel, as well as clarifying that there is always more than just one road. Structured role-play and a variety of 'as if' exercises allow the client to try out other versions of the world in a comparatively safe environment. The switching of roles, so that people get the chance to look through others' glasses, try on others' constructs, is seen by Kelly as a crucial experience. This is a tack frequently taken by Wittgenstein, who poses propositional questions, asking us to imagine ourselves in a different tribe, with different rules, or preferring a different style of painting, and many sections of *Philosophical Investigations* (for instance, ## 21, 32, 172, 207 and 258) can be seen as fixed-role exercises. What if we were in a strange country where we didn't know the language, or if we wanted to enslave people, or if we weren't sure what 'pain' really meant, what would follow on?

The PCT client–therapist relationship is described as being ideally egalitarian, like that of a research student and supervisor undertaking to work together, with the onus on the therapist to guide, question, and check while the client follows up possible leads. The therapist is also expected to take an active role in ensuring these experiments are useful, by practically helping reformulation and revision of situations or people: 'Okay. Now, if you *had* spoken your mind then, what might have happened next? And if that hadn't upset her? How else might it have gone? Let's go through that again and this time I'll be you and you be her'.

[A] lot of the most prestigious preparation today seems to me to unfit the therapist for joining his client in a truly sensitive and humble exploration of the world. Too often the training substitutes doctrine for inquiry; it makes the therapist feel respectable rather than responsible – and there is a lot of difference between the two.
(Kelly 1969:53)

It often sounds, and perhaps sounds here, as though PCT is primarily a verbal therapy, but Kelly studied Moreno and psychodrama, and in the main, discussion is a basis for action, practice at living differently, either in role-play in the therapeutic setting, or outside, at home and at work, back in the real world. This stress on language is a stress on communication, on understanding. Fixed-role exercises involve the therapist writing a description of a person who is not the opposite of the client, but *different* – whose constructs would be as it were at right angles, not contrary to, the client's present constructs. ('Slot-rattling', shifting from one end of a construct to another, say 'helpless alcoholic' to 'absolute teetotaler', is not a shift in construing; it doesn't reflect a change in points of reference, merely in where you situate yourself in the same picture.) Checking and rewriting the role into one which seems internally coherent, the therapist and client discuss and elaborate this different character, until the client has a clear enough picture to be able to *be* that person, for a day or two at a time. Kelly is very specific that this is to be a detailed and thorough undertaking, eating what they would eat, saying what they would say, dreaming what they would dream, but that it is not an attempt to permanently change, merely a bit of research into being different, checking this out in real life, with real people, but without laying your own personal core constructs on the line. To do this is not an answer to your problems, but an experiment in asking different sorts of questions, as Wittgenstein does in his philosophical approach. As you can imagine, this is also a useful training exercise; trainees can try on different clinical hats without the massive personal investment or invalidation which looking at things from another point of view may at times seem to involve.

> Any word, whether an oath or a benediction, has a meaning in the context of its usage, and within the construct system of the speaker that no dictionary can make clear. This is because dictionaries cannot provide the framework of relevance that makes language come alive.
>
> (Kelly 1969:35)

So why does a therapist think there is any point in mulling over the abstruse, elliptical words of a philosopher famous mainly for being obscure? Or the wordy, 1950s theory of some American academic/clinician who failed to set the world on fire? Just how many people go round saying 'I'm a Kellyian' or 'I'm a Wittgensteinian' on the wards, in mental health centres, probation offices, child guidance, or GP surgeries? Not many. But good practice, which I am here defining as the sort of practice you yourself would prefer to receive, whatever the details might be – good practice is demonstrably what Kelly and Wittgensteins' ideas look like when put into action. There may be no objective truths or values, but there are unique personal realities to be elaborated and respected. In particular, Kelly and Wittgenstein share an awareness of language as power – not just in the matter of who speaks, who gets to be voiced, but in the very structure of language, its phrasing, its grammar, as control. 'In our language there is an entire methodology embodied. The primitive forms of our language: noun, adjective and verb, show the simple picture into whose form language tries to force everything' (Wittgenstein 1993:199).

Freud and scientism have between them, some think, created a lamb-like willingness to accept expert opinions on private experiences. But if you pursue the consequences of that belief (and this is what Wittgenstein's concept of language-games makes clear; language lives in human context, and hence has/is social consequences) you come very soon to ethical questions about who the experts are.

> When he agrees with me I tell him he has 'insight' and when he doesn't I tell him he is 'resisting' – both of these being terms that grow out of objective speech and the prestigeful use of the indicative mood in talking about psychological matters.
>
> (Kelly 1969:153)

As Wittgenstein says, explanations have to stop somewhere, and if they stop in the hands of an expert, rather than on your own doorstep, the consequences are that decisions about how to live, what is true, right or wrong, all the questions that are the backbone of ethical private life, become the domain of the person who 'knows best'. For instance, he asks us to imagine we meet people where:

> [i]nstead of the physicist, they consult an oracle. (And for that we consider them primitive.) Is it wrong for them to consult an oracle and be guided by it? – If we call this 'wrong' aren't we using our language-game as a base from which to *combat* theirs?
>
> (Wittgenstein 1969: #609)

So Kelly and Wittgenstein are not merely involved in tilting at the language of scientism and its superficiality, but focusing on the deep consequences of scientism, about how philosophical stances are used, when those descriptive practices become common usage, part of how we talk together.

If we say that inappropriateness or unpredictability is an essential feature of the behaviour that helps define schizophrenia we are saying, in effect, that schizophrenia is anything which we do not understand. If we really understood why a client laughed, his laughter would not be unexpected. If we understood his point of view, the behaviour could not appear to be emotionally inappropriate. Thus, when we say that a person's behaviour is emotionally inappropriate, we are likely to be saying simply that we do not understand him. We certainly do not make him any more understandable when we reify our own confusion and call it a symptom of the client's.

(Kelly 1955:781)

If someone wanted to test out some of these concepts, what might they do in their daily practice? Perhaps they would ask more propositional questions, be more uncertain, check more carefully, ask what the opposites and contrasts to any statement or description might be? Perhaps they would think, 'What does this *mean* here, in practical terms – What would change involve, in practical terms?' Perhaps they would try to listen more credulously, as if there was always some sense to be found. 'From a phenomenological point of view, the client – like the proverbial customer – is always right. This is to say that his words and his symbolic behaviour possess an intrinsic truth which the clinician should not ignore' (Kelly 1955:241). Look at the words this 17-year-old battered child/wife, and child-batterer, uses:

[b]ut I only hit him once, once at a time I mean. I never keep battering him. I usually kick him, push me foot against his back, and then he falls over and starts crying and that's it. I'm sorry then. . . . [Shocked] No! Oh no! I'd never ever punch his face or anything like that, or hit his ears. I'd never punch him. I'll push him over or slap his face or his hands or his legs, but oh no! I couldn't, I just couldn't do it.'

(Renvoize 1978:12)

How do you think she came to see 'a punch' as something specific, reprehensible, while 'a slap, a kick, a push' describe things people *can* do to children – or wives? What language-game did she grow up in, what practices do these words entail, how does someone live when they talk like this? 'If someone sees a smile and does not know it for a smile, does not understand it as such, does he see it differently from someone who understands it?' (PI:198).

Wittgenstein makes it clear that someone just pointing out that this isn't dictionary-defined as proper usage won't help change things: 'it is not a kind of *seeing* on our part, it is our *acting*, which lies at the bottom of the language-game' (Wittgenstein 1969: #204).

How would Kelly suggest we might offer some change of aspect? Maybe elaborating 'people who punch', 'people who hit', 'people who get hit', might clarify the construing. Perhaps some propositional experiments, trying out different angles of perception and description – her son's, her husband's, her father's, her mother's – on various interactions might be useful. There could be a shift of construing to enable a different form of life. A new language – or new meanings for the old language.

> [W]hat matters is not so much the conclusions arrived at as the terms within which arguments are conducted. For to talk in new ways, is to 'construct' new forms of social relation, and to construct new forms of social relation (of self–other relationships) is to construct new ways of being (of person–world relations) for ourselves.
>
> (Shotter 1993: 9)

Neither Kelly nor Wittgenstein can be adequately represented in a brief chapter. It seems to me that for them the important thing about philosophy and psychology is not whether they give us some scientific or academic rationales, make us sound respectable or impressive, but whether they help us to live better, to struggle more carefully, and in better heart, with the details of our everyday contacts with others, and to respect and value others' points of view. Neither of these men would be interested only in words on paper, but in what follows, how they are used. Rather than further expounding, let us ask ourselves some questions:

- What if it were possible to treat everyone as if they made sense, if you paid enough attention to their language, in terms of what their words mean to them, and what that would then tell you about the world they see themselves living in?
- What stops us doing that? Practise, next time you really cannot comprehend someone, next time someone makes no sense at all to you – your partner, your child, your boss, your client or your Prime Minister or President. What stops us?
- What if there are serious ethical dimensions to our philosophical stance, our use of language, the way that it controls, empowers, represents, disempowers, negates . . . as therapists, who presumably want to help people, how do we best go about using language as if it didn't

represent 'reality', but represented people, who are, like us, so tenuous, changeable, complex?

> Even the questioning act of man is a disturbance of nature, as well as a provocation to it. The more interrogations he presses upon his world, and the more vigorously he plies his resources, the more altered his world of resources becomes. His act of questioning even changes himself, to the consternation of psychologists who want to understand him as the stabilized product of antecedent events – evolutionary, biographical, and official. Thus a man comes to understand for himself what is happening – within and without – not as an academic dilettante whose ethereal propositions impinge on nothing, but as the impact of his own actions demonstrates what is possible.
>
> (Kelly 1969:26)

## FURTHER READING

### On Kelly

Bannister, D. and Fransella, F. (1995) *Inquiring Man; The Psychology of Personal Constructs* (3rd edition), London: Penguin Books. [The best basic introduction]
Dunnett, G. (ed.) (1988) *Working with People*, London: Routledge.
Fransella, F. and Bannister, D. (1977) *A Manual for Repertory Grid Technique*, London: Academic Press.
Fransella, F. (1995) *George Kelly*, London: Sage Publications.
Kelly, G. (1963) *The Theory of Personality: The Psychology of Personal Constructs*, New York: Norton. [A short introductory version]
Shaw, M. (1980) *On Becoming a Personal Scientist*, London: Academic Press.

### On Wittgenstein

Bloor, D. (1983) *Wittgenstein: A Social Theory of Knowledge*, London: Macmillan. [Lucid and helpful, even for non-philosophers]
Fenichel Pitkin, H. (1972) *Wittgenstein and Justice*, Berkeley: University of California Press.
Rees, R. (1981) *Recollections of Ludwig Wittgenstein*, Oxford: Oxford University Press.
Shotter, J. (1993) *Conversational Realities: Constructing Life Through Language*, London: Sage Publications. [Extremely clear and helpful]

## On Language and Therapy

Fisch, R., Weakland, J.H. and Segal, L. (1982) *The Tactics of Change: Doing Therapy Briefly*, San Francisco: Jossey-Bass.

Maturana, H. and Varela, F. (1992) *The Tree of Knowledge: The Biological Roots of Human Understanding*, Boston and London: Shambala Books.

Sarbin, T. and Mancuso, J. (1980) *Schizophrenia: Medical Diagnosis or Moral Verdict?*, New York: Pergamon Press.

Watzlawick, P. (1978) *The Language of Change*, New York: Basic Books

White, M. and Epston, D. (1990) *Narrative Means to Therapeutic Ends*, New York: Norton.

## REFERENCES

Bannister, D. and Fransella, F. (1986) *Inquiring Man; The Psychology of Personal Constructs*, (2nd edition) London: Penguin Books.

Bolton, D. (1979) *An Approach to Wittgenstein's Philosophy*, London: Macmillan.

Ellison, R. (1994) *Shadow and Act*, New York: Random House.

Heisenberg, W. (1958) *Physics and Philosophy; The Revolution in Modern Science*, New York: Harper and Row.

Kelly, G.A. (1955) *The Psychology of Personal Constructs*, Vols I and II, New York: Norton. (Reissued 1991 by Routledge, London, in association with the Centre for Personal Construct Psychology)

Kelly, G.A. (1963) *The Theory of Personality: The Psychology of Personal Constructs*, New York: Norton.

Kelly, G.A. (1969) *Clinical Psychology and Personality: The Selected Papers of George Kelly*, ed. B. Maher, New York: John Wiley and Sons, Inc.

Renvoize, J. (1978) *Web of Violence*, London: Routledge Kegan Paul.

Shotter, J. (1993) *Conversational Realities*, London: Sage.

Terkel, S. (1992) *Race*, New York: New Press.

Von Foerster, H. (1995) 'Constructions of The Mind', Interview in *Stanford Humanities Review* vol. 4, issue 2.

Watzlawick, P. (ed.) (1984) *The Invented Reality: How Do We Know What We Believe We Know?* New York: Norton.

Wittgenstein, L. (1953) *Philosophical Investigations*, Oxford: Blackwell.

—— (1967) *Zettel*, Oxford: Blackwell.

—— (1969) *On Certainty*, Oxford: Blackwell.

—— (1993) *Philosophical Occasions 1912 – 1951*, Indianapolis: Hackett Publishing Company, Inc.

# Introduction to chapter 6

Wittgenstein owed much to a seminal figure of twentieth-century philosophy, to whom philosophers in the English-speaking tradition of analytic philosophy (which he joined) and continental positivism have been equally indebted. Gottlob Frege was responsible for making the most substantial contributions to formal logic since Aristotle, and then applying this new understanding of inference in attempts to refound mathematics within the discipline of logic. If ultimately unsuccessful, his methods and programmes remained highly influential beyond his own field. Originally one of the three principal divisions of philosophy (alongside physics, which incorporated the whole of natural philosophy, and ethics), logic has been returned to a pre-eminent place in our century through the efforts of neo-Fregeans. Although thinking in other areas has benefitted from attempts to apply insights from logic, psychotherapy has been untouched, with the exception of one prominent example. It will be mentioned because, in contrasting sharply with van Staden's tack here, it illustrates its significance.

Freud had proposed that the unconscious mind operated in fundamentally different ways from the conscious mind, designating these primary process and secondary process respectively. Ignacio Matte Blanco (1975) used formal logic to reinterpret Freud's concept of primary process in terms of the logic of symmetry. Levels of unconscious processing could be discriminated according to the degree of symmetry apparent. Distortions of ordinary reality would occur as asymmetries in relations and were overlooked in favour of symmetries, with one relation becoming conflated with or substituting for another. Accordingly, linking would occur on the basis of sound or image rather than meaning, by metaphor rather than analysis as Freud had described. Van Staden's essay here complements Matte Blanco in its focus and method. In what is in effect a radical philosophy of the ego, van Staden uses Fregean logic to look outwards in order to recognise asymmetries overlooked even in conscious thinking.

Van Staden introduces some of the basic tools of Fregean analysis, in particular the apparatus it provides for the formal description of relationship. (Anthony Kenny provides helpful notes on Frege in his book on Wittgenstein, and a fuller account in Kenny (1995)). This highlights many ambiguities that arise in any attempt to discriminate one relationship from another. He draws attention back from the transactions that are the logician's principal concern, to the characterisation of the objects being related, and the relationship between the way relations are expressed in formal terminology and in everyday language. Our relations are revealed as being broader in extent, and open to far more accurate specification, than ordinary language implies. Only by paying attention to the full field of relations can it become clear how far these relations are germane to health, or to therapeutic change. Examples are provided to suggest how logical analysis may have a particular contribution to make in unravelling the convolutions of non-relationship characterised as clinical narcissism.

## REFERENCES

Matte Blanco, I. (1975) *The Unconscious as Infinite Sets*. London: Duckworth.
Kenny, A. (1995) *Frege*. Harmondsworth: Penguin.

# 6  'I' or 'me'
## The logic of human relations

*Werdie van Staden*

The philosophy of 'I' and 'me' may contribute to the therapeutic understanding of a patient's relations and complement the practice of several kinds of therapy. This claim presupposes that a patient in psychotherapy occupies positions in various relations. A patient occupies positions in relations with people, and these are the relations with which psychotherapy is conventionally concerned. However, it is often erroneously assumed that either these are the only relations, or what applies for these relations also applies for relations more generally. I shall argue here that a patient occupies positions in relations that extend beyond the scope of relations between people. Moreover, a patient expresses these relations, and the positions s/he occupies in these relations, in his/her account or narrative during the psychotherapeutic encounter.

If we set aside, at least temporarily, preconceived ideas about relations as ordinarily approached in psychotherapy, we may discover a rich source in philosophy to inform discussion of relations and the positions a patient occupies in his/her relations. I shall first draw from this source to describe philosophy's approach to relations. In the second section, a patient's positions in relations will be traced according to the way they are ordinarily marked with the use of 'I' and 'me'. Thereafter, I shall consider psychotherapeutic applications by which an understanding of the use of 'I' and 'me' in relational expressions may be utilised in psychotherapeutic practice.

## RELATIONS

According to the century-old semantic theory of Gottlob Frege (1952) and contemporary philosophical logic, a relation allows for the occupancy of at least two relata. Relata are those items between which a relation holds or fails to hold. For example, in the sentence 'Brutus

killed Caesar', 'Brutus' and 'Caesar' are the relata and '. . . killed . . .'
expresses a certain relation. This is close to the ordinary conception of
a 'relation', which is something that pertains *between* entities. Of course
there are many kinds of relations, and in a language these are expressed
with the use of a great variety of sentences in which verbs are crucial.

It is well recognised in logic that the *positions* of relata are of significance in some relations, but not all relations (Lemmon, 1965/1996).
For example, in the relation 'Brutus killed Caesar' the positions of the
relata 'Brutus' and 'Caesar' matter, because it is true that 'Brutus killed
Caesar' but not true that 'Caesar killed Brutus'. Thus, in '$x$ killed $y$'
the position of $x$ is different from the position of $y$. In some relations
the relata are interchangeable and an interchange does not result in
different meanings. For these relations, we may say the positions of the
relata are identical insofar as they do not imply different meanings. For
example, the positions of $x$ and $y$ do not matter to the meaning of the
expression '$x$ is the neighbour of $y$' because '$x$ is the neighbour of $y$'
means the same as '$y$ is the neighbour of $x$'.

Whether the positions of the relata matter, is determined by the *kind*
of relation. A 'symmetric' relation is defined as a relation in which the
positions of the relata are identical. More precisely in terms of logic, a
relation $R$ is said to be symmetric if, for any $x$ and $y$, if $R$ holds between
$x$ and $y$ then $R$ holds between $y$ and $x$. Conversely, for a relation that
is not symmetric the positions of $x$ and $y$ are different. That is, the
meaning expressed depends on the respective positions of $x$ and $y$. This
is evidenced in 'asymmetric' relations and 'non-symmetric' relations. A
relation $R$ is 'asymmetric' if, for any $x$ or $y$, if $R$ holds between $x$ and
$y$ then $R$ does not hold between $y$ and $x$. '. . . Being a parent of . . .' is
an example of an asymmetric relation. If a relation is neither symmetric
nor asymmetric, then it is non-symmetric. A relation is 'non-symmetric'
if a relation holds between $x$ and $y$ it could also hold between $y$ and
$x$ but a relation between $y$ and $x$ is no necessity. An example of this
kind of relation is 'loving'. If $x$ loves $y$, it is possibly true that $y$ loves
$x$ but this is not necessarily the case. Whether a relation is asymmetric
or non-symmetric, the positions of the relata are different insofar as
interchanging the relata would result in a different meaning.

Consider the distinct positions of relata in the relation of 'hurting'.
Say, 'Jack hurts the dog' and 'The dog hurts Jack'. The position of Jack
when he hurts the dog is the same as the position of the dog when it
hurts Jack. Also, the position of the dog when Jack hurts it is the same
as the position of Jack when the dog hurts him. Besides these similarities, there are also differences between the two positions of either Jack
or the dog. *Jack is in a different position when he hurts the dog compared with*

*his position when the dog hurts him.* Also, the dog is in a different position when it hurts Jack compared with its position when Jack hurts it.

The positions that occur first in each of these sentences are similar and the positions that occur second are similar. The difference between the positions, for both *these* sentences, appears as a difference in the *order* of the positions. Also, in some other languages like Latin or German, the positions would be 'declined' differently. The first position in each of these sentences is the nominative and the second is the accusative.

For many relational expressions like these, the order of the relata seems to exemplify the distinction between the positions of relata. Subsequently, the 'order' of relata has received much attention. For example, Strawson (1974, pp. 84–92) identifies the relatum in the first position as the 'primary term' and the second relatum as the 'secondary term'. Russell (1913/1984, Ch. VII) addresses this distinction in terms of the 'sense' of a relation and the 'sequence' of the terms. In set theory (Suppes, 1960; Quine, 1940/1962), the first position of an 'ordered pair' of relata is considered the 'domain' of the relation and the second position is considered the 'range' or 'converse domain'. If the order of an ordered pair changes, say from (*a;b*) to (*b;a*), then another relation results which is called the converse relation. This converse relation is taken as another relation, of which the first position is again considered the 'domain' and the second position is considered the 'range'. The first and the second positions in relations are treated similarly in linguistics, where the first position (or nominative) is occupied by the 'subject' and the second position (dative/accusative) is occupied by the 'object' in the grammatical *surface* structure (Brown, 1984).

If the order of relata is taken as the starting-point, then the distinction between the positions of the relata seems little more than a distinction between the 'first' position and the 'second' position of relata. However, the *meaning* of the positions of relata could alternatively be the starting-point. Consider the next two sentences: 'Jack hurts the dog' and 'The dog is hurt by Jack'. The *meaning* of both sentences is essentially the same, and the positions of the relata in terms of their expressed meaning are as follows: 'Jack' is in the same position in relation to 'the dog', and 'the dog' is in the same position in relation to 'Jack' for both these sentences. For *both* sentences, Jack is in the position of hurting whereas the dog is in the position of being hurt. The order of the positions of the first sentence is different from the order of the second sentence. Also, 'Jack' is the nominative and 'the dog' is the accusative in the first sentence but in the second sentence, 'Jack' is the accusative and 'the dog' is the nominative.

Therefore, notwithstanding a case for distinguishing between the positions of relata as the 'first' and the 'second', or according to their inflection, a distinction between the positions of the relata may be made in terms of *meaning*. In linguistics, positions distinguished in terms of meaning are called the 'subject' and 'object' positions in the grammatical *deep* structure of the sentence. Accordingly, 'Jack' would be the 'subject' and 'the dog' the 'object' for *both* the sentences: 'Jack hurts the dog' and 'The dog is hurt by Jack'. Chomsky (1965) distinguishes between the grammatical 'surface' and the grammatical 'deep' structure by saying the distinction is between the phonology and the semantics of a sentence. He does not clarify, though, what is the semantic difference between the 'subject' and 'object' in the grammatical *deep* structure of sentences.

For the sake of clarity, I shall refrain from using the concepts 'subject' and 'object' because of their different meanings in the grammatical *surface* structure (the more commonly meant use) and the grammatical *deep* structure, also because of their divergent meanings when comparing their use in philosophy, linguistics, scientific research on 'subjects', ordinary usage, and in psychotherapy (especially object relations theory). Moreover, there is sometimes also confusion between the concepts 'subject' and 'subjective', and between 'object' and 'objective'. By refraining from using these concepts, I attempt to circumvent preconceived notions here, and allow, perhaps more importantly, for the positions of relata to be identical, as it is the case for symmetric relations.

If we follow the meaning, rather than the order or grammatical inflection, of the positions of relata, we have two distinct positions without a presupposed order to them, although an interchange of the positions results in different meanings. Say we call these positions '$\alpha$' and '$\omega$'. That is, for a relation that is not symmetric, the one position of the relatum would be the $\alpha$ position and the other position would be the $\omega$ position. However, it is not clear yet how we shall assign either $\alpha$ or $\omega$ to the positions of the relata in relations that are not symmetric. For this, we shall need a criterion to identify a position as the $\alpha$ position or the $\omega$ position.

Although Frege (p.155, 1952/1966) does not provide a way by which the distinct positions of relata could be identified, he does *suggest* a way, insofar as he clearly makes the distinction in virtue of *differences* and *similarities* when the positions of relata are compared. Frege calls the positions of the relata 'argument-places' and he designates the argument-places with '$\xi$' and '$\zeta$' He recognises a difference between $\xi$ argument-places and $\zeta$-argument-places insofar, he says, they are not akin ('*verwandt*') whereas $\zeta$-argument-places are akin to one another and $\zeta$-argument-places are akin to one another. The questions he does not address, though, are: (i) what do $\zeta$-argument-places have in common to be akin to one another; and (ii) what do $\zeta$-argument-places have in common to be akin to one another? Answers would provide criteria by which the argument-places could be identified as $\xi$ or $\zeta$, or in present terms, criteria by which the positions of relata could be identified as $\alpha$ or $\omega$.

Thus, a similarity of position amongst various relations that are not symmetric is called for according to which one position can be marked as, say, the $\alpha$ position. Likewise, a similarity of position amongst various relations is called for that can mark the 'distinct from the $\alpha$ position' position as, say, the $\omega$ position. Moreover, each position should not have the other's similarity in common. And the positions should be distinguished in terms of the meaning rather than them being 'first' or 'second'.

Finding similarities that stretch across all kinds of relations that are not symmetric, is no lightweight undertaking. Nevertheless, I propose two similarities, suspecting that they might have their shortfalls, but they might prove adequate to take us quite some way. I shall phrase the two similarities in terms of criteria:

The first criterion is:

> The relatum in the $\alpha$ position is **owner** of a particular relation rather than the one in the $\omega$ position.

The 'particular' here emphasises the narrow context, and necessary condition to the criterion. This condition attempts to preclude an *a priori* ownership. This means the condition requires that the owner to a relation is so deemed only in virtue of the position this one occupies in a particular relation, and not in virtue of ownership derived in some other way. Furthermore, the 'rather than' in the criterion leaves it open to debate whether the $\omega$ position is a position of ownership at all. It should also be noted that the ownership here refers to the ownership of the *relation* and not necessarily of the other relatum.

The answer to the question 'whose relation is expressed?' would pick out the one in the $\alpha$ position.

The second criterion is:

> The one in the $\omega$ position is **accidental** to a particular relation rather than the one in the $\alpha$ position.

Conditions similar to those for the first criterion apply for the second criterion. The answer to the question 'who is accidental to the relation?' would pick out the one in the $\omega$ position.

For *action* relations, the criteria clearly demarcate α and ω positions. The *owner of an action is the one in the α position*. In 'Jack acts upon Mary', Jack is owner of the action rather than Mary. And in 'Mary acts upon Jack', Mary is the owner of the action rather than Jack. Moreover, whether the relation is expressed in the active or the passive voice, the owner of the action is still the one in the α position. Jack is the owner of the action rather than Mary, whether 'Jack acts upon Mary' or 'Mary is acted upon by Jack'. *The accidental to an action is the one in the ω position*. In 'Jack acts upon Mary', Mary is accidental to the action rather than Jack. And in 'Mary acts upon Jack', Jack is accidental to the action rather than Mary. Moreover, whether the relation is expressed in the active or the passive voice, the accidental of the action is still the one in the ω position. Another example follows: whose action was it in 'Brutus killed Caesar' or in 'Caesar was killed by Brutus'? It was the action of Brutus. 'Brutus' is in the α position. Who was accidental to the action? Caesar was accidental to the killing. 'Caesar' is in the ω position.

For action relations, there are other similarities and differences. The similarity of the α positions amongst action relations may be described as the position from which one performs an action. The similarity of the ω positions amongst action relations may be described as the position upon which actions are performed. The difference between the α position and the ω position in action relations may be regarded as a difference in *agency*. The directedness of the α position and α position in action relations differs in that the one in the α position is directed at the one in the ω position, and the one in the α position is directed towards. Other differences between the positions of relata in action relations are: the α position is the *powerful* position in a particular action relation, whereas the ω position is less powerful, if powerful at all; the α position is the *active* position whereas the ω position is the *passive* position; the α position is the *executive* position whereas the ω position is the *non-executive* position.

However, the distinction between the positions of the relata extends beyond action relations. For the non-action relations, the above criteria demarcate α and ω positions, whereas the other similarities mentioned in the previous paragraph fail to capture the distinction fully. Consider the following examples where, according to the two proposed criteria, x is in the α position and y is in the ω position: In 'x needs y', x is the owner of the need and y is accidental to the need. In 'x wants y', x is the owner of wanting, and y is accidental to the wanting. In 'x knows y', x is the owner of the knowledge, and y is accidental to the knowledge; and so forth for 'x omitted y', 'x doubts y', 'x discovers y', and 'x despises y'. Even when these relations are expressed in the passive voice, the criteria clearly demarcate α and ω positions.

Consider the following example of a relation expressed with 'having': 'Jack has Mary as teacher'. The criterion suggests that Jack is the owner of the relation rather than Mary. But 'have' already implies ownership. Thus, we have a case of 'owner of ownership' which may be tautology or it may even be objected against as too abstract. Yet, it is intelligible, because a claim such as 'The ownership is Mary's' or 'Mary has the ownership' is intelligible despite a comparable level of abstraction.

However, too much should not be made of the distinct positions of relata in relations expressed with 'having', because a *specifier* to these relations is significant to the difference in meaning. First, a specifier may render a relation symmetric, in which case there is no difference in the positions of relata. For example, the specifier 'as neighbour' renders symmetric the relation 'x has y as neighbour'. Second, consider 'x has y as *employer*' which is different from 'y has x as employer'. Yet the meaning of 'x has y as employer' is hardly, if at all, different from 'y has x as employee' (thus *different* specifiers), although x occupies the α position in the former relational expression whereas y occupies the ω position in the latter relational expression. Thus, a distinction between the positions of relata in a relation expressed with 'having' is constrained by a specifier of such a relation. Nonetheless, within such constraints, the positions are discernible as α and ω.

For relations expressed with 'being', we should not overstate the case for distinct positions of relata either. Certain specifiers render the relation symmetric, for example 'being next to', 'being the same age as', and 'being either brother or sister of'. Specifiers also constrain the distinct positions of relata in the way as seen in the example 'x is the husband of y'. x is the owner of this relation *as specified* (being the husband) rather than y, yet the similarity between 'x is the husband of y' and 'y is the wife of x' (thus *different* specifiers) should not be overlooked. The *meaning* of a relation expressed with 'being' is also a constraint. For example, the positions of the relata in 'Jack is against the government' are distinct in that this sentence's meaning is different from 'the government is against Jack'. But 'Jack is against the wall' is hardly, if at all, different from 'the wall is against Jack'.

It is important to notice that the one in the α position is owner of the *relation* and not necessarily of the other relatum. Consider an example that makes this distinction clear. In 'Jack belongs to Mary', Jack is the owner of this *relation*, whereas Mary is the 'owner' of *Jack* and not of the relation as it is expressed here. A more familiar phrase would be to say that the 'sense of belonging' is Jack's even though Jack is the belonging of Mary's. If the example were 'Mary owns Jack', Mary is not only owner of *Jack* but also owner of the owning *relation*. Moreover, Mary is accidental to the belonging in the former example, and Jack is accidental to the owning in the latter example.

An objection might be raised that the first criterion presupposes ownership to a relation. And a presupposition of this kind, it might be claimed, would be contrary to the notion of a relation as *between* entities and not belonging to anyone/anything. In order to consider this objection, a distinction should be acknowledged. This distinction is between what Frege calls a 'saturated' relation and an 'unsaturated' relation. The latter is something with at least two empty places ('argument-places') whereas a 'saturated' relation has 'arguments' that occupy these places. It would thus be correct to claim an 'unsaturated' relation (that is, with at least two empty argument-places) belongs to no one or nothing. However, once a relation is 'saturated', there is a necessary connection between the relata and the relation. The above criteria, then, describe the nature of the connections between the relata and the relation in the case of an asymmetric or non-symmetric relation.

The ownership of relations is not too far-fetched a notion. Russell (1913/1984, p. 88, Ch. VII), for example, makes a brief reference suggestive of ownership of relations as a way to distinguish the positions of relata from each other. Unfortunately, he does not explore this possibility.

Nevertheless, the objection against ownership of relations highlights a further point. For some relational expressions, neither of the relata is the owner of the relation. That is, neither of the relata is in the $\alpha$ position. Consider for example, '$x$ is given to $y$'. Clearly, the owner of this action, that is, the one who executed the action 'giving', does not present in this relational expression. If it did, as in '$x$ is given to $y$ by $z$', it would have been a triadic relation with one relatum ('$z$') in the $\alpha$ position and the other relata ($x$ and $y$) in $\omega$ positions. But since an owner of the relation is absent in this expression, we have here a relation expressed between relata ($x$ and $y$) *both* in $\omega$ positions. However, in this example $x$ and $y$ are in different positions, since an interchange of the relata would result in a different meaning. This suggests that the $\omega$ position is in need of a further distinction, but for present purposes, the distinction between the $\alpha$ and the $\omega$ positions will suffice.

In the light of this philosophical description of the positions of relata, we shall now turn to the most important relations in psychotherapy – those relations in which a patient is (at least) one of the relata.

# THE DIFFERENTIAL USE OF 'I' AND 'ME'

A patient may use various ways to indicate him/her rather than someone else or something else as a relatum. Ordinarily, though, patients use the linguistic signs 'I' or 'me'. The ordinary use of 'I' and 'me' in the expression of relations corresponds to the positions that 'I' and 'me' occupy in relations. *'I' is used in the α position unless the relation is expressed in the passive voice in which case 'me' is used in the α position. 'Me' is used in the ω position unless the relation is expressed in the passive voice in which case 'I' is used in the ω position.* Schematically we may present this as follows:

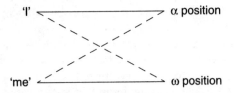

The crossing connections (dotted lines) represent the expressions in the passive voice, and these are the ordinary exceptions. The non-crossing connections (solid lines) represent the ordinary pattern of use for all expressions other than those in the passive voice. For those relations that do not allow for their expression in the passive voice, there are no crossing connections. For example, a relation 'having someone as father' (as in 'I have Jack as father' and 'Jack has me as father') does not allow for passive transformations, and 'I' is used in only the α position and 'me' only in the ω position. Passive transformations are not confined to action relations. Just consider the examples I have given above of non-action relations. It follows that the cross-connections are not confined to action relations either. For example, in a relation of need, 'I need Jack' may be expressed as 'Jack is needed by me' but 'I' and 'me' in these sentences are both in the α position, that is, 'I' is owner of the need as well as 'me'.

Insofar as this pattern of the use of 'I' and 'me' is adhered to, 'I' and 'me' may be used as markers of the positions the user of 'I' and 'me' occupies in the relations that s/he expresses. So far, I have qualified this pattern of the use of 'I' and 'me' as 'ordinary' since we have to acknowledge the possibilities of colloquial variations, and instances of wrong or mistaken use. For example, a common colloquialism is to say, 'it is me who hurt the dog' instead of 'it is I who hurt the dog'. This certainly bears on the extent to which 'I' and 'me' could be used as markers of the positions expressed.

Relational expressions are subject to temporal specification. Consider a relation of 'hurting' between 'the dog' and 'I'/'me'. (Henceforth, I shall use 'self' to designate the user of 'I' and 'me'.) This relation of 'hurting' between the dog and self necessarily has a temporal specification. This specification, though, is contingent on the distinction between the positions 'I' and 'me' may occupy in relations. According to tense indicators, of course, 'I hurt (past tense) the dog', 'I hurt (present tense) the dog' and 'I shall hurt the dog' are temporal variants depicting the relation of 'I' (in the α position) with the dog. 'The dog hurt (present or past tense) me' and 'The dog will hurt me' depict the temporal variation in the relation of 'me' (in the ω position) with the dog. The self, either in the α position or the ω position, is in relation with the dog where any temporal possibility is conceivable for a relation.

This diverges from the 'trialogical' model of the 'semiotic self' as put forward by Wiley (1994), drawing from the works of the pragmatists Mead and Peirce, in which the present self is designated as 'I', the past self is designated as 'me', and the future self is designated as 'you'. Mead (1934), for example, like Hume, treats 'I' as something to be found or caught and the failure to succeed in this makes Mead say, '"I" of this moment is present in the "me" of the next moment'. The temporality of their account of 'I' and 'me' is the moment of this relation between them and their use of these signs. Over and against this, in this essay the temporality associated with 'I' and 'me' is not found in the moment of the use of these signs, but the temporality associated with 'I' and 'me' is the temporality of the expression of which 'I' or 'me' is part. It is thus an account of 'I' and 'me' as they *present* in time-specified relational expressions.

If 'I' or 'me' is one of the relata, who or what could the other relatum conceivably be? This is perhaps too broad a question for easy answers, but we may say the *kind* of relation constrains the conceivable relata. For example, in a relation of hurting it is not conceivable that 'I hurt an *insult* (or *measles*)', nor is it conceivable that 'A *table* swears at me'. It is conceivable that the other relatum is someone or something in particular. It is conceivable that the other relatum is some people or something in general. It could conceivably be singular or plural, it could be spatiotemporal entities or an abstract notion. In philosophical terms, the other relatum could conceivably be universals or particulars. Surely, the scope of conceivable relata extends way beyond 'significant others' and the 'generalised other' with which we are more familiar in psychotherapy.

If 'I' is one of the relata, it is also conceivable that this very person, who uses 'I', is the other relatum as well. 'I hurt myself', 'I despise myself', 'I know myself' are examples. The 'other' relatum may also be an *ascription*(s) of this very one who uses 'I' or 'me'. 'I touch my arm', 'I consider my thoughts' and 'My emotions overwhelm me' are examples where 'I' or 'me' is one of the relata and an ascription(s) is the other relatum.

Relations between 'I' and 'myself', and between 'I' or 'me' and ascriptions of the user of 'I' and 'me', allow for alienation between 'I' and 'myself', or between 'I' or 'me' and ascriptions. A few familiar examples in psychotherapy are 'I am not myself', 'I am not my body', 'I hate my thoughts', 'My feelings persecute me' and 'My thoughts control me'. Needless to say, these relations are often paramount in psychotherapy.

Not all expressions where 'I' or 'me' is used, are relational as they present in sentences. These expressions are those that have only one position (or 'argument-place') to them. Consider the example 'I eat'. This could be taken as a relation of eating, where 'I' is one relatum and the other relatum is implied contextually, say 'the food'. Then, the position of 'I' is the $\alpha$ position. Similarly, imperatives such as 'Tell me' would imply 'you' as the other relatum and then 'me' would be in the $\omega$ position. However, in some non-relational expressions it is difficult, if not impossible, to say whether 'I' or 'me' is in the $\alpha$ or the $\omega$ position. For example, consider the position of 'I' in 'I am exhausted'. If there is an implied 'by someone/something', then 'I' is in the $\omega$ position and this someone/something is owner of the exhausting. But if this example is to express a way of being, then 'I' is the owner of this way of being. Clearly, there is ambiguity to the position of 'I' in this example. Nevertheless, the positions of 'I' and 'me' in non-relational expressions could still be discerned in many instances, despite this ambiguity in some instances.

## PSYCHOTHERAPEUTIC APPLICATIONS

The philosophy I portrayed above enhances understanding and may complement psychotherapeutic practice. The way 'I' and 'me' are used allows for an understanding of a patient's relations. Moreover, *by looking at the markers 'I' and 'me', we can trace a patient's positions in relations*. We can trace a patient's positions in certain *kinds* of relations. And we can trace a patient's positions in relations with specific people (for example, the therapist or significant others), a generalised other, a patient's relations with him/herself and his/her ascriptions, and a patient's relations with other items in the universe and the universe itself. This understanding of the scope of a patient's relations is not too narrow, but extends as far as the scope of the relations that the patient expresses.

Tracing a patient's positions in relations may be taken even further. That is, *an assessment* of a patient's positions may be done, not only for the understanding of that patient but also to understand patients more generally in the course of empirical research. Such assessments would be potentially very informative, since the difference between the $\alpha$ position and the $\omega$ position is meaningful. This is, the meaningful difference will correlate with differences in experiences, emotions, cognition and behaviour associated with the $\alpha$ and the $\omega$ position respectively. Furthermore, such *assessments may reveal change* in the positions of a patient in the course of the therapeutic process.

It may be asked what changes are expected in a patient's positions in relations. In particular, an answer to this question would amount to an open-ended list of changes according to the kinds of relations and the 'other' relatum in each relation. Holmes and Lindley (1989) describe the change in most kinds of psychotherapy as a procurement of *autonomy*. Insofar as this is correct, it suggests *that a patient procures more frequent occupancy of the $\alpha$ position and less frequent occupancy of the $\omega$ position in relations*, since the $\alpha$ positions encompass the positions of a patient as agent, and the $\omega$ positions encompass the positions of a patient when s/he is influenced, controlled or restricted by (for example) someone, something, thoughts, or emotions.

However, this is not to say the $\alpha$ position is the all-healthy position and the $\omega$ position should be relinquished altogether, because it may be a therapeutic aim for a patient to be able to occupy the $\omega$ position. An example is a patient who cannot bear being in the $\omega$ position of a loving relation with his/her partner, but is restricted to the $\alpha$ position in this relation with his/her partner. Rather, Anthony Ryle's (1990; 1994) notion of expanding a patient's repertoire of reciprocal roles has a parallel here, in that the changes to a patient's positions in relations may entail *an expansion of a patient's repertoire of positions in various relations*.

The above philosophy may complement the practice of various kinds of therapy. Consider the following of a patient suffering from a social phobia, and note her positions in her relations with 'group situations', people ('they'), her father, her 'thoughts of failure' and her 'incompetence':

> Group situations make me ($\omega$ position) nervous. They ask me ($\omega$ position) things or expect me ($\omega$ position) to do something, and then I can't say (failure of $\alpha$ position) or do anything. Actually, I

don't even know (failure of α position) what they asked me (ω position) most of the time. Then I am so embarrassed (ω position) by it all. What do they think of me (ω position)? And when I try (α position) to say something, they all stare at me (ω position). I don't know ... (failure of α position). I am overwhelmed (ω position) by my incompetence. Thoughts of failure really get me (ω position) down. My father used to mock me (ω position) about this, as if he got some satisfaction from seeing me (ω position) cringe. Sometimes he shouted at me (ω position) or when his friends were about, he ridiculed me (ω position) in front of them. I still hate (α position) him for that.

Analytically and dynamically oriented therapies could use the relational positions in their *understanding* of a patient's difficulties as and when a patient expresses them. This may not only enhance empathy, but could also be reflected to a patient more explicitly. To employ a patient's use of personal pronouns in a similar way, is not unfamiliar to analytic practice. Spence (1995), for example, examined the use of first and second person pronouns in analytic therapy. He used the relation between the first and the second person pronouns as reference for the analyst–analysand relationship. A high degree of co-occurrence of the first and second person pronouns correlated with more comprehensive and probing interpretations, and these interpretations had greater effect on a patient's associations. He even depicts 'you' and 'me' as 'transference' pronouns. Another of his studies (1994) suggested that the clustering of 'you' and 'me' represents an important aspect used by the analyst to determine when to intervene, marking whether the patient considered the therapeutic space to be safe and whether she was sharing the space with the analyst. The analyst's sensitivity to these patterns increased over the course of treatment and concurred with his responsiveness.

Cognitive-behaviourally oriented therapies (Hawton *et al.*, 1989/1996) could build the understanding of a patient's positions in relations, into the *restructuring* of thoughts and modification of behaviour. Sentences a patient uses to express difficult situations could be rephrased in order for a patient to learn to occupy a preferred position in these situations. The preferable position could be determined according to the agreed goals of the therapy. Occupancy of the preferable position in relations could be practised during and after therapy sessions. Reconsider the relations expressed by the above phobic patient. In each of the relations, and for each of the relata, the patient might contemplate and practise being in the preferable position (say the α position). Again, restructuring of a similar kind is not unfamiliar. For example, rational emotive therapy (Ellis, 1984) changes prescriptively modal specifiers such as 'ought to', 'have to', 'must', and 'should', into 'prefer to' and 'would like to'.

The various theories that inform the many kinds of therapies might benefit from self-scrutiny in the light of the above philosophical presentation in order to ensure that any particular theory does not omit or neglect some of the positions in which patients experience themselves. For example, the predominant account of the 'self' in object relations theory is an account of the 'self' in the α position. This lacks justification to date. But not only object relations theory uses the concept 'self'. Others might also benefit from scrutiny of their understanding of 'self'. Another example is those therapies that put 'control' central to their enterprise (such as reality therapy (Glasser, 1984)). They should not only account for a patient's position of control (the α position) that s/he lacks initially and aims to gain in therapy, but also for a patient's position of being controlled (ω position) and his/her renunciation of this position. Therapies that focus exclusively on what a patient does or fails to do, or on how a patient behaves or fails to behave or on what a patient thinks or fails to think (the α position), would not account therapeutically for a patient's experiences of having things done to them, and being exposed to (traumatic) events and causes of distress (the ω position). Such an exclusive focus would be in need of amendment. For example, some therapists call upon Buber's (1970) ideas (as elsewhere in this book), but their potential therapeutic value notwithstanding, his consideration of 'I' seems unfortunately limited to an 'I' in the α position.

Furthermore, the psychotherapy literature on first person pronouns should acknowledge the distinctive uses of 'I' and 'me', which are not as simple as is often assumed. I shall mention a couple of examples. The excellent papers by De Waele (1995; 1996) address 'I' but not a word is written about 'me'. Rizzuto (1993) addresses 'me' as well as 'I', but clarity on the uses of 'I' and 'me' is elusive. Moreover, she does not view 'I' or 'me' as a (first) person in relational positions, but takes 'I' and 'me' as constituents of the 'psyche' and likened them to the Freudian 'ego' and 'id'.

The so-called 'ego' is often assumed to be reflected in the use of 'I', yet it is unclear whether this 'I' would be related to the α position or the ω position or both of these positions. Moreover, clarity is needed on the link between 'ego' and 'me'. Furthermore, egoism, egocentricity and narcissism are sometimes supposed to relate to excessive use of 'I' and 'me', and this would suggest that 'I' and 'me' should be used less.

Less use of 'I' and 'me' contrasts with the procurement of agency and autonomy in that such procurement might suggest an increased frequency of use of 'I' and 'me'. A resolution is called for here, and I suspect such a resolution could be found by examining the positions that 'I' and 'me' occupy in cases of egoism, egocentricity or narcissism. For example, if the problems associated with egoism, egocentricity or narcissism arise due to the ways 'people and the world treat and consider *me*, or ought to treat and consider *me*' (that is, the patient is in the ω position), then egoism, egocentricity or narcissism is not associated with the use of 'I' and 'me' indiscriminate of a patient's positions (α and ω) but it is associated with the use of 'I' and 'me' in the ω position. Thus, 'excessive "I" and "me" use' is an insufficient account for egoism, egocentricity or narcissism if the *pattern* is not specified in which 'excessive' use occurs. Conversely, the *pattern* of 'I' and 'me' use needs to be specified in which it would be true that the procurement of agency or autonomy would concur with a higher frequency of 'I' and 'me' use. Accordingly then, the procurement of agency and autonomy concur with a higher frequency of 'I' and 'me' use only for those instances (the specification) where 'I' and 'me' occupy the α position. Thus, specification of the use of 'I' and 'me' from which higher or lower frequencies would be brought about by psychotherapy, is necessary. Neither egoism, egocentricity or narcissism is expressed with *all* instances of 'I' and 'me', nor is autonomy or agency expressed by *all* instances of 'I' and 'me'.

## CONCLUSIONS

I described distinct positions in relations and called them α and ω positions. Moreover, the one in the α position is identified as *owner* of a particular relation. The ordinary pattern of 'I' and 'me' use is such that 'I' is used in the α position unless the relation is expressed in the passive voice in which case 'me' is used in the ω position. 'Me' is used in the ω position unless the relation is expressed in the passive voice in which case 'I' is used in the ω position. This pattern allows patients' positions in relations to be traced and assessed by looking at their use of 'I' and 'me'. Insofar as autonomy (or agency) is procured in therapy, this would entail a patient's more frequent occupancy of the α position and less frequent occupancy of the ω position in relations. Furthermore, a patient occupies positions in various relations with people, but also with themselves, their ascriptions, and with particular and universal entities.

A rich source for understanding our patients' positions in relations lies in the ways they use 'I' and 'me'. Certainly, the ways patients use

'I' and 'me' follow meaningful patterns. These patterns may not only reflect healing change, but may be used in therapeutic practice to procure that change.

## REFERENCES

Brown, K. (1984) *Linguistics Today*, Suffolk: Fontana.
Buber, M. (1970) *I and Thou*, trans. W. Kaufman, Edinburgh: T. and T. Clark.
Chomsky (1965) *Aspects of the Theory of Syntax*, Cambridge, MA: MIT Press.
De Waele, M. (1995) 'A clinical concept of self: The experiential being', *British Journal of Medical Psychology*, 68: 223–242.
—— (1996) 'A process view of the self', *British Journal of Medical Psychology*, 69: 299–311.
Ellis, A. (1984) 'Rational-Emotive Therapy', in R.J. Corsini (ed.) *Current Psychotherapies* (third edn.), Itasca, Illinois: F.E. Peacock Publishers Inc.
Frege, G. (1952/1966) *Translations from the Philosophical Writings of Gottlob Frege*, trans. P. Geach and M. Black, Oxford: Basil Blackwell.
Glasser, W. (1984) 'Reality Therapy', in R.J. Corsini (ed.) *Current Psychotherapies* (third edn.), Itasca, IL: F.E. Peacock Publishers Inc.
Hawton, K., Salkovskis, P.M., Kirk, J. and Clark, D.M. (eds.) (1989/1996) *Cognitive Behavioural Therapy for Psychiatric Problems*, Oxford: Oxford University Press.
Holmes, J. and Lindley, R. (1989) *The Values of Psychotherapy*, Oxford: Oxford University Press.
Lemmon, E.J. (1965/1996) *Beginning Logic* (second edn.), London: Chapman and Hall Medical.
Mead, G.H. (1934) *Mind, Self, and Society*, London: University of Chicago Press.
Quine, W. van O. (1940/1962) *Mathematical Logic*, New York: Harper and Row.
Rizzuto, A.M. (1993) 'First person personal pronouns and their psychic referents', *International Journal of Psycho-Analysis*, 74, 3: 535–546 .
Russell, B. (1913/1984) *Theory of Knowledge: The 1913 Manuscript*, ed. E.R. Eames and K. Blackwell, London: George Allen and Unwin.
Ryle, A. (1990) *Cognitive Analytic Therapy: Active Participation in Change*, Chichester: Wiley.
—— (1994) 'Consciousness and psychotherapy', *British Journal of Medical Psychology*, 67: 115–123.
Spence, D.P. (1995) 'When do interpretations make a difference? A partial answer to Fliess's Achensee question', *Journal of the American Psychoanalytic Association*, 43, 3: 689–712.
Spence, D.P., Mayes, L.C. and Dahl, H. (1994) 'Monitoring the analytic surface', *Journal of the American Psychoanalytic Association*, 42, 1: 43–64.
Strawson, P.F. (1974) *Subject and Predicate in Logic and Grammar*, London: Methuen and Co. Ltd.

Suppes, P. (1960) *Axiomatic Set Theory*, Princeton, New Jersey: D. Van Nostrand
    Company, Inc.
Wiley, N. (1994) *The Semiotic Self*, Cambridge: Polity Press.

# Introduction to chapter 7

The logical construction of relationship in the previous chapter contrasts sharply with the phenomenological approach of this one. Emphasis shifts to the experientially, rather than the formally, unique and from formal agreement as the criterion of truth to certainty based on immediate perceptions. The phenomenological movement, most closely identified within philosophy with Husserl's attempts to establish a method of objective perception, has influenced many methodological initiatives in the humanities and social sciences. From among these, Wheway introduces two approaches to relationship that have already been championed by people with a keen interest in their philosophical application. They have been termed the intersubjective and the dialogical. Descriptions of their separate application within psychotherapy will be found in Atwood and Stolorow (1984) and Friedman (1992) respectively.

In a careful consideration, Wheway suggests that the practical and explanatory merits and defects of these schools are complementary. He indicates how a synthesis can facilitate a more flexible and sensitive approach not only to psychotherapy, but also to other disciplines where understanding of the particular is paramount.

## REFERENCES

Atwood, G.E. and Stolorow, R.D. (1984) *Structures of Subjectivity: Explorations in Psychoanalytic Phenomenology*. Hillsdale, NJ: The Analytic Press.
Friedman, M. (1992) *Dialogue and the Human Image: Beyond Humanistic Psychology*. Newbury Park: Sage.

# 7 The dialogical heart of intersubjectivity

*John Wheway*

This paper sketches the philosophy of dialogue and of intersubjectivity theory and suggests how their integration in psychotherapeutic practice can enable an appropriate working with developmental issues to coexist with fully interhuman relating.

Name? Age? Occupation? Address? . . . Ulrich was being questioned. He felt as though he had got caught up in a machine, which was splitting him into impersonal, general component parts even before there was any mention of his guilt or innocence. His name – those two words that are conceptually the poorest, but emotionally the richest in the language – here counted for nothing. . . .

His face counted only from the point of view of 'description'. He had the feeling that he had never before thought about the fact that his eyes were grey eyes, belonging to one of the four officially recognised kinds of eyes in existence of which there were millions of specimens. His hair was fair, his build tall, his face oval, and his special peculiarities were none, although he himself was of a different opinion on this score. To his own way of feeling he was tall, his shoulders were broad, his chest expanded like a filled sail from the mast, and the joints of his body fastened his muscles off like small links of steel whenever he was angry or quarrelsome or, for instance, had Bonadea clinging to him. On the other hand, he was slim, lightly built, dark, and soft as a jelly-fish floating in water whenever he was reading a book that moved him or was touched by a breath of that great and homeless love whose presence in the world he had never been able to fathom. And so even at this moment he could also appreciate the statistical disenchantment of his person, and the methods of measurement and description applied to him by the police officer aroused his enthusiasm as much as might a love-poem invented by Satan.

(Musil, *The Man Without Qualities*, pp. 185–6)

If we assume that we who 'know' about the mind are possessors of a natural scientist's expertise, we may regard people who do not agree with us as distorting or denying what is 'really' so. We 'know' they are wrong: they are sick, and the cure is exposure to reality. We, by virtue of our professional training, are experts in the real.

This 'fallacy of reification' (Stolorow and Atwood, 1992) leads us to behave as if our concepts referred unproblematically to the facts about human beings. Reification besets the foundation of psychoanalysis in the work of Freud. While Bettelheim (1984) has argued that the English translation of Freud is more responsible than the author himself for creating the impression that Freud regarded psychoanalysis as both a hard science and as a branch of medicine, others (Greenberg and Mitchell, 1983; Hughes, 1989) suggest convincingly that Freud, idealising natural science, saw psychological life as subject to mechanical laws. For example, borrowing the principle of homeostasis, he asserted that pleasure consists in the release of tension, returning the system to a zero point of balance. This system is powered by drives, energy that seeks discharge. If we think this way, psychic distress becomes a failure to manage drives, not the product of difficulties in life. Anxiety becomes a disease to be treated, not the result of the precariousness of being alive.

Intersubjectivity theory (Stolorow and Atwood, 1979) clears up this difficulty bequeathed to psychoanalysis by its founder, employing Dilthey's distinction between natural sciences (*Naturwissenschaften*), which seek explanations, and human sciences, (*Geisteswissenschaften*) which seek understanding. 'We explain nature, we understand mental life' (Dilthey, 1966, p.144). The human sciences develop understanding using the inquirer's experience of living in a social context. The lives of persons, historical periods, the meaning and purpose of social practices are entered and known by sharing in or recreating perspectives other than our own, attempting to grasp them, as it were, from the inside.

Dialogical psychotherapy, developed from the philosophical anthropology of Martin Buber, is based on a distinction between two categories of human relating which run parallel to Dilthey's two kinds of scientific endeavour. 'I–it' relating, in which the other becomes my object, to be used or to be observed, is contrasted with 'I–thou' relating, in which two subjects meet in a fully human way, such meeting being an end in itself.

From two different traditions, the psychoanalytical and the humanistic-existential, the intersubjective and the dialogical approaches thus share a common origin in phenomenology and philosophical hermeneutics. Intersubjective psychoanalysis recasts psychoanalysis within a phenomenological perspective, and brings it close to humanistic-existential approaches such as Gestalt psychotherapy and Person-centred psychotherapy. The stream of thought that includes Dilthey also includes Buber's philosophical anthropology, phenomenology, existentialism; philosophical hermeneutics, and from America, humanistic psychology, identified with 'the introduction of human meanings and values into mainstream psychology' (DeCarvalho, 1990, p.38). Dialogical psychotherapy originates in Buber's *I and Thou*, published in 1922, the same year as Freud's *The Ego and the Id* and Pavlov's *Conditioned Reflexes* (Tarnas, 1996, p. 463). Both intersubjective psychoanalysis and dialogical psychotherapy are relational models: 'the central metaphor of the new psychoanalytic paradigm is the larger relational system or field in which psychological phenomena crystallise and in which experience is continually and mutually shaped' (Stolorow, Atwood and Brandschaft, 1994, p. ix).

It is my view that while intersubjective psychoanalysis provides a theoretical orientation which frees the psychotherapist to relate to the client as one human being to another, it still (perhaps because of the subtle influence of its originating tradition) tends to understand the other by means of a part, rather than as a whole, privileging the organising principles of experience above the living flow of experience that is the client himself. The therapist's understanding of the client is portrayed as the essential act of therapy, and one which the therapist can perform in private, as the result of another private mental act, 'decentering', which, it is held, enables him to set aside the influence of his own subjectivity.

I suggest that in this respect, intersubjective psychoanalysis fails to make the radical movement into the arena of mutual influence and away from the exclusive focus on the client's psyche which it recommends. To underpin such a movement, I believe, we need to go beyond Dilthey to the views of Buber and Gadamer, each of whom developed a dialogical view of understanding based on the model of a meeting between persons.

Buber's thought in particular, focusing on person in relation rather than on interpreter and text, can provide a window into a fuller kind of relating, where the primary object of therapy is not understanding, but meeting, encounter – a living encounter by which each partner is changed.

Dialogical therapy, on the other hand, needs an adequate theory of the development of psychic structure of the sort which intersubjectivity theory provides, to guide the therapist in grasping the client's subjective presence in the context of its history, enabling him to meet the client more fully.

## INTERSUBJECTIVE PSYCHOANALYSIS

Freud developed more than one model of psychic functioning, and continually revised his theories. Each revision, from a positivist viewpoint, would seem to represent progress towards objective knowledge. But from an intersubjectivist perspective, revisions show him trying to respond to shifts in his experience and its meaning in different life situations.

Freud's work, in other words, is one situated human being's attempt to understand psychic health. In their first book, *Faces in a Cloud* (1979) Stolorow and Atwood show how Freud was affected by his own difficulties in life, attempting to deal with his own pain. This is the condition of every theorist of the mind.

Intersubjectivity theory grounds psychoanalysis not in metapsychological concepts and models, but in the world of intersubjective experience, taking a lead from Kohut's self psychology, in which the subject matter of psychology is defined as that which is accessible to empathy and introspection. Both Kohut and the intersubjectivists want to resolve the question of whether psychoanalytical knowledge belongs to natural or human science. They are aware that the reification of mechanical and biological metaphors for human living fails to do justice to the situation of persons. They recognise that persons are constituted and sustained within a matrix of social practices or forms of life.

## Isolated mind: three forms of alienation

Discussing 'isolated mind', Stolorow and Atwood explain how positivist ideology achieved such a powerful grasp on psychological theorising. 'The doctrine of the Isolated Mind', they write, 'envisages the mind . . . [as] radically estranged from an external reality that it either accurately apprehends or distorts' (Stolorow and Atwood, 1992, p.123).

Alienation from nature, life and subjectivity is the consequence. The first leads us to deny the anguish of embodied existence, reifying mind as transcending the body, thus denying the meaning and anguish of our recurrent experience of bodily limitations. Alienation from social life leads us to hold that we can never know, or be known by, another. Personal autonomy is seen as a literal fact, which as a mature being I must be able to confront. For intersubjectivity theory personal autonomy, continuity and agency are produced and sustained by the support of others. (Buber called this 'confirmation'. Rogers spoke of 'respect' and 'prizing' of the client.) Others support, but also restrict what we can be – a further source of anguish. Alienation from subjectivity treats individual experience as an unreliable source of knowledge. Behaviourist psychology represented the polar opposite of a human science in its denial of subjectivity. From the perspective of such a view, human beings are material objects governed by mechanical laws, and are valued as producers and consumers, not as beings.

The procedure of *Faces in a Cloud* discovers the roots of theory in the subjective world of its thinker. Applying this procedure to Sir Isaac Newton, we recognise the development of his model of science as a response to extreme impoverishment in his early relationships. Frank Manuel, his biographer wrote:

> [a] chief source of Newton's desire to know was his anxiety before and his fear of the unknown ... the fact that the world obeyed mathematical law was his security. To force everything in the heavens and on earth into one rigid, tight frame from which the most minuscule detail would not be allowed to escape free and random was an underlying need of this anxiety-ridden man. And with rare exceptions, his fantasy wish was fulfilled during the course of his lifetime. The system was complete in both its physical and historical dimensions. A structuring of the world in so absolutist a manner that every event, the closest and the most remote, fits neatly into an imaginary system has been called a symptom of illness, especially when others refuse to join in the grand obsessive design. It was Newton's fortune that a large portion of his total system was acceptable to European society as a perfect representation of reality, and his name was attached to the age.
>
> (Manuel, 1968, p. 380)

Newton's case illustrates positivism as a defence against unbearable psychic trauma. It shows how rigidity, motivated by threats to emotional stability, might also lead us to objectify others.

Morris Berman writes that this denial of intersubjectivity

> can best be described as disenchantment, nonparticipation, for it insists on a rigid distinction between observer and observed. Scientific consciousness is alienated consciousness; there is no ecstatic merger with nature, but rather total separation from it. Subject and object are always seen in opposition to each other. I am not my experiences, and thus not really a part of the world round me. The logical end point of this world view is a feeling of total reification: everything is an object, alien, not-me; and I am ultimately an object too, an alienated 'thing' in a world of other,

equally meaningless things. This world is not of my own making; the cosmos cares nothing for me, and I do not really feel a sense of belonging to it. What I feel, in fact, is a sickness of the soul.

(Berman, 1981, p. 17)

## Therapeutic approach

Intersubjectivists have provided a rich model of self in its social matrix. Pathology is understood to be due to environmental failures of empathy. The therapist aims to provide empathic attunement, and when he fails, takes responsibility by trying to understand and articulate the impact of his mistake on the client. Such mistakes typically arise from similarities and differences in his and the client's ways of organising experience which, when not brought to awareness, obstruct empathy.

We can understand the intersubjectivist model of the unconscious by using the analogy of a house. The pre-reflective unconscious is like the blueprint, consisting of intersubjectively derived organising principles through which the client will make sense of his experience, past and present. The repressed unconscious, like an attic, is filled with parts of the self unacceptable to the carer, threatening the bond on which development depends. Potentials of the person unconfirmed intersubjectively and unintegrated into the self-structure are relegated to the unvalidated unconscious, like a heap of unused building materials.

Without an empathic other, the sense of self disintegrates, and identity and continuity of being are disrupted. The timely return of an attuned response can restore the self, but where empathy continues to be unavailable, serious trauma results, and compliance and loss of authenticity follow. Unable to have basic self-object needs met, the individual may live in a permanent emotional distress intolerable to awareness because of attendant feelings of shame and disgust.

If we look again at Newton's life, we find that as a boy, in exercise books, Newton wrote:

A little fellow/He is paile/There is noe roome for mee to sit/What imployment is he fit for?/What is hee good for?/He is broken/The ship sinketh/There is a thing which trobeleth mee?He should have been punished/No man understands mee/What will become of me? I will make an end? I cannot but weepe/I know not what to doe.

(Manuel, 1968, pp. 23–67)

This shows Newton profoundly deprived of affect attunement and confirmation.

Therapeutic approaches which require the client, as part of the alliance, to introject his theoretical assumptions, discourage the development of a healthy self-organisation. The client has to comply to safeguard the bond with the therapist. If health requires the confident ability to evoke appropriate empathy and confirmation from others, such approaches reinforce pathological adaptation. We could say that compliance begets a closed system, without initiative, whereas intersubjective health implies an openness to the world, an ability to reach out and meet one's needs. For the intersubjectivist, a true therapeutic alliance validates the client's experience, and illuminates unconscious organising principles, so that subjective life may develop.

Reification amounts to total immersion in I–it relations, while the I–thou is drained of value.

## DIALOGICAL PSYCHOTHERAPY

The passage from Musil quoted at the start of this paper illustrates the difference between Buber's 'I–it' and 'I–thou' modes of relating. Buber holds that healing in psychotherapy is a product of genuine existential meeting between therapist and client (M. Friedman, 1989, pp. 134–6). Such meetings are characterised by inclusion and confirmation: 'A relation between persons that is characterised in more or less degree by the element of inclusion may be termed a dialogical relation' (Buber, 1947, p. 125). Dialogical relating is not simply verbal dialogue.

> Not only is the shared silence of two such persons a dialogue, but also their dialogical life continues, even when they are separated in space, as the continual potential presence of the one to the other, as an unexpressed intercourse. On the other hand, all conversation derives its genuineness only from the consciousness of the element of inclusion.
>
> (Buber, 1947, p. 125)

### Inclusion is not empathy

Practising inclusion, the therapist experiences the living perspective of the other while remaining connected with his own perspective. He may communicate aspects of his experience in order to meet the client fully.

> Empathy means, if anything, to glide with one's own feeling into the dynamic structure of an object, a pillar or a crystal or the branch

of a tree, or even of an animal or a man . . . to 'transpose' oneself
over there and in there. Thus it means the exclusion of one's own
concreteness, the extinguishing of the actual situation of life.

(Buber, 1947, p. 124)

The dialogical therapist does not limit himself to empathy, but is aware
of how he is being touched and affected by the client, and of his own
contribution to the nature of their meeting.

Inclusion . . . is the extension of one's own concreteness, the fulfilment of the actual situation of life, the complete presence of the
reality in which one participates . . . one person without forfeiting
anything of the felt reality of his activity, at the same time lives
through the common event from the standpoint of the other.

(Buber, 1947, p. 124)

This stress on the importance of the therapist's experiencing can be
found in Gestalt, in person-centred therapy, and in the modern object-
relations use of countertransference.

## Inclusion and confirmation

Without confirmation of our being by others our sense of community
is damaged. Therapy attempts to repair such dislocation. Inclusion and
confirmation can lead to moments of authentic meeting in which one's
own wholeness and the wholeness of the other are encountered with
full aliveness. These are I–thou moments.

What is peculiarly characteristic of the human world is above all
that something takes place between one being and another the like
of which can be found nowhere in nature. [This between] is a
sphere which is common to them but which reaches out beyond
the special sphere of each. [We acquire a view of the between] by
no longer localising the relation between human beings . . . either
within individual souls or in a general world which embraces and
determines them, but in actual fact between them.

(Buber, 1947, p. 244)

## I–thou moments and the I–thou process

To combine intersubjectivity theory with the dialogical we need Richard
Hycner's distinction between the I–thou moment and the I–thou

process. The I–thou process – the process of working towards the conditions under which I–thou moments may spontaneously occur – includes the I–it dimension. I–it refers to all the interactions with the other as object. In therapy, such processes include activities involving planning or calculation: assessment; diagnosis; and purposive intervention, which, conducted respectfully, support the conditions for I–thou moments to occur. I–thou moments cannot be purposively achieved, but they can be prepared for – much as a gardener prepares the soil and cares for the plant so that it can grow to its full potential.

## The intrapsychic and the interhuman

The goal of therapy is to enable the individual to contribute to the life of dialogue. The claim that all real living is meeting makes a radical challenge to the almost universal emphasis in psychotherapy on individual autonomy. The intersubjectivist critique of 'the myth of the isolated mind' (Stolorow and Atwood, 1992, ch.1) is consistent with Buber's stress on community.

## TOWARDS INTERSUBJECTIVE DIALOGICAL THERAPY

Both intersubjective psychoanalysis and dialogical psychotherapy see human subjects as created and sustained in a matrix of personal relationships, the failure of which leads to a pathological inability to participate in community. Both see the healing of this condition as requiring an ethical stance that honours and respects the humanness of the client. A healing relationship recognises the common human situation of both parties, in which each one's perspective is brought into play.

Intersubjectivity theory conceptualises the developmental and relational processes associated with lack of inclusion and confirmation. Its critique of reification enables the therapist to place his theories and his training in the context of his subjective world and the meanings central to his history. This is a safeguard – though not a guarantee – against reifying his role as expert and pathologising the client's differences. Intersubjectivity theory underpins ways of therapeutic relating that remain open to the subjective worlds of both therapist and client.

Dialogical theory, in stressing the healing power of the living, concrete encounter between two whole beings, underlines the importance of the existential meeting. In Berman's terms, it opens the possibility of

re-enchantment, beyond alienation. The I–it orientation of intersubjectivity theory might seem inconsistent with its avowed aim of
honouring human experience. Buber, though not untechnical, restores
a poetic sense of the human. Dialogical thinking, in its emphasis on
the primacy of the relational, takes us beyond the intersubjectivist preoccupation with the individual self.

In the quotations from Berman and Musil, we see a world in which
I–it overwhelms and annihilates I–thou. One kind of relating seems to
honour and value the human for itself, while the other reduces the
human to its usefulness, to its materiality. In this view, I–thou is contaminated by I–it. A similar line of thought leads Erich Fromm to
distinguish need-based love from love that prizes the other's being,
(Fromm, 1963, p. 34) and Maslow to say that what he calls 'being-love'
is incompatible with 'deficit-love' (Maslow, 1968, pp. 42–3).

But as Hillman reminds us (1967, p. 18), need is what leads us to a
relationship. Needing, or using, another, does not mean we cannot
relate as beings. There is a world of difference between the use of one
another made by a mother and baby from, say, the use of a concentration camp worker by a Nazi gaoler. The latter intends the destruction
of human identity, while the former may be mutual, the primary source
of the experience of loving in the individual's life. In the thinking of
Fromm and Maslow, confusion seems to arise from stress on the semantic
opposition of love and use rather than their interplay in a process.

With mother and baby, if things go well, we can imagine alternating
sequences of I–it and I–thou relating. As with mother and baby, so
with teacher and pupil, therapist and client. Buber writes:

> many children . . . know that they are unceasingly addressed in a
> dialogue which never breaks off. In face of the lonely night which
> threatens to invade, they lie preserved and guarded, invulnerable,
> clad in the silver mail of trust . . . because this human being exists
> – that is the most inward achievement of the relation in educa-
> tion. Because this human being exists, meaninglessness, however
> hard pressed you are by it, cannot be.
>
> (Buber, 1947, pp. 125–6)

## The limitations of intersubjective psychoanalysis

The literature of intersubjective psychoanalysis lacks any account of
the qualities of human engagement and commitment required in the
therapeutic relationship, preferring instead an instrumental approach,

which sometimes, in its emphasis on theory and method, evokes the very reification against which scepticism is urged. Too often, it can seem that the psychoanalyst attends to his own subjectivity only as a potential source of disruption to the therapy, not valuing his presence as a living being, but only as a careful investigator of the psychic structure of the other. In this way he can seem like the surgeon-analyst of Freud's simile, or of part IV of T.S. Eliot's 'East Coker' (Eliot, 1940).

There are attempts to make good this omission in the work of Donna Orange (1994, 1995). She recognises that intersubjectivists

> are so involved in and devoted to our efforts to get and stay close to the patient's experience that we often forget that we are there too. [This] may prevent us from recognising our contribution to shaping the patient's experience . . . [and] . . . interfere with our recognising that we can understand another's experience only through our own equally subjective experience. [She introduces the term 'cotransference' to refer to] our participation with the patient in the intersubjective field or playspace of the psychoanalytic dialogue.
>
> (Orange, 1994, p. 180)

Yet her reason for inventing this term is to avoid the adversarial connotations of the more usual term, 'countertransference'. Once again, this seems to be an attempt to restrict the engagement of the therapist with the client. There is no room for a creative engagement between the two protagonists in therapy. She commends Gadamer's view of hermeneutics as a dialogue in which the 'risking and testing' of prejudices is 'the path to understanding', yet the relation between therapist and client is still treated as if it were the relation between interpreter and text. However sophisticated this conception may become, however enriched by hermeneutics, it still implies that the act of interpretation of the client by the therapist is *the* therapeutic act. Buber, himself a distinguished theologian and interpreter of religious texts, went beyond this to recognise that not only do client and therapist have different ways of *understanding* the world, they are two different *beings*. Where this is not recognised, 'that which is ineffable has not been acknowledged, and patients may now believe that self-regulating or narcissistically relevant elements intrinsic to all relatedness, is all that there is to relatedness' (Hycner and Jacobs, 1995, p. 221).

Buber wrote:

> [b]ecause this human being exists: therefore he must be really there, really facing the child, not merely there in spirit. He may not let

himself be represented by a phantom: the death of the phantom would be a catastrophe for the child's pristine soul. He need possess none of the perfections which the child may dream he possesses; but he must be really there. In order to be and to remain truly present to the child he must have gathered the child's presence into his own store as one of the bearers of his communion with the world, one of the focuses of his responsibilities for the world. . . . Then there is reality between them, there is mutuality.

(Buber, 1947, pp. 125–6)

Intersubjectivity theorists shift from 'the mechanistic language of Freudian metapsychology', and apply to therapeutic work Dilthey's hermeneutic method of historical understanding, 'achieved through a process of "re-experiencing"' (Atwood and Stolorow, 1984, p. 2). But Buber's 'inclusion' goes further. It sometimes seems as if, like Dilthey, while trying to free themselves from the attitudes of natural science, the intersubjectivists still cannot quite get away from the belief that the human factor in understanding humans must be sanitised by method.

According to Gadamer, this is the delusion of historicism, 'trying to displace our prejudices with methods in order to make something like certainty and objectivity possible in the human sciences' (Grondin, 1994, p. 111). By 'prejudice' Gadamer means the historically limited perspective from which no human being can escape. For Gadamer, knowledge, including so-called objective propositional knowledge, is necessarily embedded in a dialogical situation 'which is the only place it has any meaning' (Grondin, 1994, p. 118)

No abstraction can stand independently of the concrete situation in which human beings meet and try to understand one another. The therapeutic dialogue as a particular case is a meeting of two people embedded in their histories, who see the world and each other through those histories. They cannot do otherwise. Yet in their meeting, the horizon of each may be expanded, if they are open – for prejudice, in Gadamer's sense, allows openness. The child who, in the absence of someone who is open to him and his experience, remains unconfirmed in his being, cannot develop a sense of self, a way of organising experience which has the creative potential for meeting. Compliant with the subjective world of the other, he must continually resist open relating that might destroy the status quo. Because he must reduce the world to the terms of the other, he is unable to participate. To develop that ability, he has to find the mutuality of dialogue.

## The limitations of dialogical psychotherapy

While offering a vital corrective to the neglect of the full, concrete meeting between therapist and client, dialogical psychotherapists such as Rogers and Friedman neglect to show in detail how human development contributes to that meeting. In Rogers (1951, pp. 481–533) there are hints that psychopathology arises as the result of something resembling a true self/false self defensive structuring in response to the fear of the loss of environmental support, and an implication that the conditions for *therapeutic* relating are also the optimum conditions for development in *any* relationship, including a primary one. Intersubjectivity theory as a development of self-psychology, fills out what Rogers merely hints at, that the self develops in stability and complexity throughout life as the consequence of optimum responsiveness in a self-selfobject milieu. Such an elaboration is enormously valuable to the clinician in pinpointing the client's vulnerabilities and needs. Elsewhere, (Rogers, 1990, p. 130) Rogers indicated that he saw no use in transference as a clinical concept; that identification of the point of origin of how the client manifests in the relationship with the therapist is of purely academic interest. He objected to anything that would divert the client from being in full contact with the therapist. Yet if transference is simply the way the client organises experience, past and present, exploring the transference is essential to grasping the client's subjectivity, and of making sense of what he fears, and what he needs, from the therapist.

It seems to me that dialogical therapy can be enhanced by the incorporation of intersubjectivity theory as a theory of development and psychodynamics which aims to focus on the two persons in the therapeutic relationship. Such a theory places the here and now encounter in the context of the partners' historicity, and the histories of their two subjectivities both illuminate and are illuminated by what is between them. But intersubjective psychoanalysis needs to bring in a more inclusive perspective on the therapeutic interaction than it seems to demonstrate, even to its own adherents. Orange asks

> [w]here then, are the discussions of the analyst's organising activity, history and personality in our case reports? Why are many of us still writing as if the analytic patient were the only one organising or reorganising experience?
>
> (Orange, 1994, p. 180)

## Intersubjective dialogue: a stance for practice

If my aim is to support I–thou process, then I will practise inclusion. Combining this with an awareness of intersubjectivity theory, how am I going to be, and to intervene?

| *Will be/do* | *Will not be/do* |
|---|---|
| • Be aware of the field of relationships: the client's and mine | • Exclusive focus on client's history and presence |
| • Be aware of the selfobject dimension | • Behave as scientific observer |
| • Allow for fluid boundary of unconscious, affected by field conditions | • See unconscious as fixed, intrapsychically determined |
| • Allow affect attunement | • Avoid gratifying; be unresponsive |
| • Be available, present | • Neutral/blank screen |
| • See own perceptions, diagnoses as relative to personality, tradition and relational field | • Hold my diagnosis as true, treating client objections as confirmations of pathology |
| • See client experience of our relationship as real for her, affected by me, formed by unconscious organising principles | • Regard client experience as transference distortion |
| • Enter fully into other's perspective, aware of her impact on me, and mine on her | • Empathise with client as my aesthetic object |
| • Offer my formulations of understanding as mine, emerging from our relating, informed by my preferred theory | • Interpret from authority of tradition. |
| • Share my feelings and fantasies where relevant | • Exclude direct communication of my process as 'subjective' |
| • Trust the process (the between) and collaborate with the client | • Disregard the between – value only my detached reflection (isolated mind stance) |
| • Be modest | • Be (with my professional trappings) omnipotent |
| • Participate, collaborate | • Be detached, apply theory |

I am offering this list as a sketch, not as an exhaustive comparison. I think it summarises the essence of the approach I am trying to present. A rule of thumb might be: 'The more certain you feel, the more you need to doubt your view'. It is important to avoid the temptation to see the left hand list as representing 'good', and the right, 'bad', ways of doing therapy. Each column presents a summary of good practice from within a particular perspective. Each set of prescriptions may be practised well or badly.

## The interwovenness of I–it and I–thou

Finally, I want to present a concrete, again fictional, example of how an I–thou process intermingles I–thou and I–it dimensions of relating, and how this culminates in an I–thou meeting.

In Bertolucci's 1996 film *Stealing Beauty* the heroine, a 19-year-old American, Lucy, visits a community of expatriate artists in Tuscany. She has apparently been dispatched there to have her portrait done by a sculptor who had sculpted her now dead mother, in the year Lucy was conceived. She seems to be in search of her mother, her natural father, and a boy on whom she had had a crush during a previous visit to this remote and insular place.

From the beginning of the film, Lucy is observed by others. The view of the other is frequently poised on the borderline between relating and exploiting, between knowing and abusing.

The film opens with the cameraman relentlessly scrutinising the adolescent girl sprawling on her seat alone on a long train journey, sometimes absorbed in her journal, listening to a walkman, sometimes asleep, mouth open, saliva trickling from the corner of her mouth. We see her dirty fingernails, the camera trails over her body, lingering on her lips, her hands, her thighs, between her thighs.

What is happening? Is someone getting to know her, studying her. Or is this prurience, intrusion? Are we being presented with our first glimpse of a human being, or is this an object? Is she being loved, or hated, by the man behind the camera? When she arrives at her destination, we hear this man's voice, English with a middle-aged, Italian timbre, as he prods her awake and tells her he has been watching her for much of the journey, filming her. She hears this in sleepy confusion as she stands on the platform with her luggage at her feet. He makes a gift of the cassette from his camera. She recovers it, when the train has gone, from the tracks where it had fallen. She puts it in her bag. We hear nothing of it again. His giving her the record of his observations changes something. She did not choose to be filmed, but she can choose what to do with the record, with the means of knowing what he saw of her, she is given back something which was usurped.

The sculptor, in their first conversation about the portrait, tells her he will need to look at her a lot, but she won't be aware of his looking. She seems slightly upset, and says she hopes he won't be looking at her all the time. Once again, she is being observed, appraised. The artist is finding out, we can imagine, not only about her as she is revealed visually, but also about his experiencing of her, and in this way he prepares to make the portrait. In later drawing sessions, we see him sketching intensely, staring, discarding drawings, heaping up one graphic assessment after another as he searches for the sense of her that will enable him to reach the stage of beginning his sculpture.

A dying, middle-aged writer who has a room next door to hers invites himself into her company late one night by asking to smoke some of her grass. He is curious about her, fascinated by her beauty. He wants to know about her sex life, discovers that she is a virgin. He touches her, fondling her bare ankle and foot.

Once again, there is a strange proximity intermingled with dispassionate interest: the need of a dying man to make a connection with youth; fatherliness; sensuality; perhaps barely contained sexual desire. As their relationship develops, it seems that his sexual interest in her is sublimated into protectiveness – concern about her finding the right man with whom to lose her virginity. He reveals to the whole community that she is a virgin, and says his interest in her is because he sees a resemblance between himself and her. She is barely able to tolerate the ensuing middle-aged gossip and speculation about who they could find as a suitable boyfriend for her.

Then, the boy she has waited for arrives, with two friends, and she decides to stay. The boy turns out to be a seducer, trying his skill with every beautiful young woman around. One sees him assessing these young women for their susceptibility to his skills, and assessing Lucy. On the point of losing her virginity to him in an olive grove (perhaps the olive grove where her mother had conceived her) she intuits the wrongness of it. She has loved him – he does not love her, simply wants to conquer her. She extricates herself. Her intuition is subsequently borne out by her discovery that he had been lying to her about his interest, and the evidence accumulates of his callous pursuit of his own desires, indifferent to all but the quality of the beautiful objects he wants to win – or steal.

The title of the film, *Stealing Beauty* frames the themes of assessment, appraisal, scrutiny and discrimination – is all this for the sake of forming a relationship, coming to know a person from a position of respect and prizing, or is it theft?

Lucy's writer–patron goes away to hospital to die. He has pleaded the frivolousness of the dying for his indiscretions with her confidences; he has expressed envy towards a young man who sleeps in her room the night of a party, imagining he is 'the lucky fellow'. And he leaves her by praising her beauty and youth. His last words to all of them are 'If only you could see yourselves'.

The sculptor works on his creation. Eventually, it is revealed that he is Lucy's father – which clarifies an earlier ambiguous retort when she asks to see his work – 'Don't you know that an artist only portrays himself?' All is projection: all that looking, essaying, looking for images, all those false starts, was looking for himself in her.

At the film's end, Lucy gives her virginity to a man who loves her. A shy young man, he has been unable to reveal his love until the last moment, so hopelessly in love and in awe of her is he. There is mutual desire, his reticence at the boundary between them requires her help so that he can penetrate her. For once, there is no hint of exploitation here, no subjugation. Their coming together represents the core of the dialogical moment – unambiguously interhuman. It is not that need is transcended; but it occurs within a human relating, with mutual respect and sensitivity, with meeting, recognition, with complete agreement. We can't help feeling that Lucy's mother's seduction into a reluctant motherhood has been atoned for and healed as a result of her daughter's quest.

This beautiful film, I have tried to suggest, is saturated with images that speak of the issues in coming to know another and whether this takes the form of true dialogue, or is vitiated by the predominance or contamination of an interest characterised by a lack of mutuality, inclusion or confirmation.

## CONCLUSION

I have suggested that what brings clients into therapy is a failure in the conditions for creative relating. We have seen how Newton's passionate pursuit of mathematical certainty served a personal need to deny psychological pain. Francis Bacon, another founder of positivism, said 'We must put nature on the rack and wrest her secrets from her' thus suggesting torture as a way of getting to know the world. Peter Reason (1994) contrasts 'a consciousness that fragments and rips apart, and a consciousness that separates in order to look back and behold with awe and love'.

As therapists, our responses, both 'expert' and personal, if they arise from genuine relating to the client, are vital contributions to healing through meeting. To bring together intersubjectivity theory and the philosophy of dialogue allows us to combine system and spontaneity, I–it and I–thou, in an ordered process of psychotherapeutic relating. Thus, 'therapists can continue to refine their abilities to engage in a dialogue with their patients that is both sensitive to their developmental needs and evocative of their richness as human beings' (Hycner and Jacobs, 1995, p. 233).

I have tried to show that while both intersubjective psychoanalysis and dialogical psychotherapy are concerned to overcome positivistic reductionism in the theory and practice of psychotherapy, and to honour the mutuality of the meeting between psychotherapist and client, each lacks something which the other can supply in order to better achieve these goals. Let me end with Buber again, who seems to me to express the whole of what these approaches are trying to address.

> When two men converse together, the psychological is certainly an important part of the situation, as each listens and each prepares to speak. Yet this is only the hidden accompaniment to the conversation itself . . . whose meaning is to be found neither in one of the two partners nor in both together, but only in their dialogue itself, in this 'between' in which they live together.
>
> (Buber 1965, p. 75)

Substantial parts of this paper were originally published as 'Dialogue and Intersubjectivity in the Therapeutic Relationship', *British Gestalt Journal* 6, 1: 16–28. Permission to reproduce these passages was kindly given by the *British Gestalt Journal*.

# REFERENCES

Berman, M. (1981) *The Re-enchantment of the World* Ithaca and London, Cornell University Press
Bettelheim, B. (1984) *Freud and Man's Soul* New York, Vintage Books
Buber, M. (1922) *I and Thou* Edinburgh, T and T Clark
Buber, M. (1947) *Between Man and Man* London, Collins/Fontana
DeCarvalho, R. (1990) A History of the Third Force in Psychology *Journal of Humanistic Psychology*, Autumn 1990
Dilthey, W. (1966) *Gesammelte Schrifte* Göttingen
Eliot, T.S. (1940) 'East Coker', in *The Complete Poems and Plays of T.S. Eliot*

London, Faber and Faber, 177–183 (1969)

Friedman, M. (1989) *The Healing Dialogue in Psychotherapy* Northvale, NJ, Jason Aronson

Fromm, E. (1963) *The Art of Loving* New York, Bantam

Gadamer, H. (1976) *Philosophical Hermeneutics* (trans. D.E. Linge) Berkeley, University of California Press

Greenberg, J.R. and Mitchell, S.A. (1983) *Object Relations in Psychoanalytic Theory* Cambridge, MA and London, Harvard University Press

Grondin, J. (1994) *Introduction to Philosophical Hermeneutics* New Haven, CT and London, Yale University Press

Hillman, J. (1967) *Insearch* Dallas, TX, Spring Publications

Hughes, J.M. (1989) *Reshaping the Psychoanalytic Domain* Berkeley/Los Angeles/London, University of California Press

Hycner, R. and Jacobs, L. (1995) *The Healing Relationship in Gestalt Psychotherapy* Highland, NY, Gestalt Journal Press

Manuel, F. (1968) *A Portrait of Sir Isaac Newton* Cambridge, MA, Harvard University Press/Belknap Press

Maslow, A. (1968) *Towards a Psychology of Being* New York, Van Nostrand

Orange, D. (1994) *Countertransference, Empathy and the Hermeneutic Circle* in *The Intersubjective Perspective* ed. R. Stolorow, G. Atwood and B. Brandschaft Northvale, NJ/London, Jason Aronson

Orange, D. (1995) *Emotional Understanding* New York, The Guilford Press

Reason, P. (1994) *Participation in Human Inquiry* London, Sage

Rogers, C. (1951) *Client-Centred Therapy* London, Constable

Rogers, C. (1990) *The Carl Rogers Reader*, ed. Kirschenbaum London, Constable

Stolorow, R. and Atwood, G. (1979) *Faces in a Cloud* Northvale, NJ/London, Jason Aronson

Stolorow, R. and Atwood, G. (1992) *Contexts of Being* Hillsdale, NJ/London, The Analytic Press

Stolorow, R., Atwood, G. and Brandschaft, B. (1994) *The Intersubjective Perspective* Northvale, NJ/London, Jason Aronson

Tarnas, R. (1996) *The Passion of the Western Mind* London, Pimlico

Yontef, G. (1993) *Awareness, Dialogue and Process* Highland, NY, Gestalt Journal Press

# Introduction to chapter 8

Wheway's sensitive attention to atmosphere, shared experience and dialogue may enrich experience and practice, while also raising some difficult questions. What, for instance, would be specific to therapeutic experience in this, as opposed to other areas of life? For many people, the distinction cannot be dissociated from some conception of progression and change as a necessary element of the process. There is a need to understand events in temporal relationship to each other that is more than contingent. Sooner or later, the idea of causation, a cornerstone of positivist thinking, asserts itself. The historical emergence of psychotherapy, as psychoanalysis, as a practice with a clear theoretical base was posited on a deterministic model by which thought, behaviour and feeling could all be related through causal sequences. The impossibility of doing so on the basis of introspection led to the elaboration of the unconscious mind as a means of completing such causal chains. Although links in the chain could be represented psychologically in terms of meaning, they had their substrate in the passage of packets of energy across neural networks according to strict physical laws (cf. Wollheim, 1991, especially chapter 2).

Despite withdrawal of attention from such neurological models, Freudian psychology never abandoned this deterministic cast. Although they have lost their immediate connection with therapeutic agendas, models of neural networking that could provide a deterministic account of the most complex mental processes are again enjoying a renaissance. But it is ultimately the idea that change should occur that demands understanding of how far it can be predicted or prompted.

Any rapprochement between the hermeneutic and positivist approaches to psychotherapy requires clearer understanding of the relationship of meaning to cause. This is what Digby Tantam undertakes, in an essay which dissects the differences between causal and semantic links in human explanation. These are brought to bear on therapeutic accounts, indicating both the necessity and the limits of therapeutic action.

## REFERENCES

Wollheim, R. (1991) *Freud* (2nd edition), London: Fontana.

# 8   Can meanings be causes?

*Digby Tantam*

Psychotherapists find themselves in a double bind. This is most concisely expressed as a conflict between the pull of natural science, with its reliance on descriptions of events and their causes, and the contrary pull of the humanities, with their reliance on the meaning of events. Ordinary discourse mixes causes and meanings indiscriminately. Indeed, I shall argue that both the causes of actions and the meanings of actions may be called 'reasons' without raising eyebrows. However, the double bind can only be resolved by disentangling causes and meanings and this paper is intended to be a contribution to that process.

## CAUSES

David Hume's treatment is often taken to be the starting point of scientific conceptions about cause: 'a cause is said to be an object followed by another, where all the objects similar to the first are followed by objects similar to the second, and where, if the first object had not been, the second had not existed' (Hume, 1748:76–77). The principle of 'constant conjunction' underlying the last two propositions remains the foundation of much scientific enquiry, i.e. where there is a first object (the cause) there will always appear a second object (the effect) and effects will never appear without the cause preceding them.

Many questions have been raised about constant conjunction: for example, is it a reflection of regularities governing the behaviour of objects, or are some objects imbued with causal properties, for example imbued with the energy to produce effects? Is it true that it is not possible to imagine a cause which is not followed by an effect (in which case there is a logical connection between the two), or is it simply the case that we always observe an effect following a cause and therefore expect it, as Hume argued, but could imagine it not happening? Do we see objects as causes, or do we discover them to have been causes?

Hume challenged fellow philosophers who wrote about the law of causation to 'produce some instance [of that law], wherein the efficacy is plainly discoverable in the mind, and its operations obvious to our consciousness or sensation'. The conservation of momentum is not 'plainly discoverable in the mind': when, to use the most commonly cited example, a billiard ball travels across a billiard table and strikes another ball which is thereby impelled to move, there is only the memory of other balls, and what they did in similar circumstances. However there may be other kinds of causation where Hume's challenge can be met. Anscombe (1971) proposes that 'cutting', 'drinking', and 'purring' are instances where the production of the effects is 'plainly discoverable in the mind'. She means, I think, that if I look at something or someone who is cutting, my recognition that they are cutting carries with it an image of how that action will continue and, as it continues, what result it will produce. I see my daughter cutting a slice of bread and I also see the thickness of slice that she will produce.

If Anscombe's examples are instances of causal laws which are 'plainly discoverable in the mind' and if these instances apply to actions and not other events, then we have arrived by a roundabout route at a distinction made by many philosophers between 'agent causation' and other causes. Agents cause their effects by reaching out towards some goal, or intention. Thus, I am caused to cut off a piece of bread by my wish to eat it (Erwin, 1997). Commonsense usage suggests something like this: I might equally well have said, 'My reason for cutting the bread was that I was hungry and wanted to eat it'. According to one view, championed by Davidson (1967), the latter statement is literally true. Bolton and Hill (1997) discuss how this might be realised. A computation is carried on, involving a succession of changing brain states, and then the consequential brain state – the result of the computation – initiates further brain states that correspond to behaviours which result in the bread being cut. I shall argue later that this description does not account for the serendipitous nature of human action, and that we do not know our reasons for doing things until we have done them.

Before considering this, it is important to note one other implication of assimilating reasons to causes, which is that reasons, too, must demonstrate the constant conjunction between the reason and its effect which is to be expected of other causes. And, since reasons are for their part the effect of other causes, such as perceptions, then an action of mind can be traced back to a chain of constantly conjoined causes and effects. If there is such a chain, it follows that my actions now are determined by perceptions, and by actions that I and others have previously taken. If I follow this back for long enough, it is apparent that my own actions become less and less significant and other people's actions on me become more and more significant until there comes some point when I do not act at all, but I am acted on. At that point I have no autonomy, but since all my subsequent actions have been determined by that state and by perceptions and others' actions on me, it follows that I cannot have gained autonomy. If as Erwin argues, autonomy is a paramount value to the psychotherapist, it becomes important to know whether the links in this causal chain are inexorable or whether there is some room for the entry of another, extraneous, cause which in this context is usually called, 'the will'.

Philosophers pose the question more generally, in the following form. Are causes necessary for the production of effects? Anscombe, in the article already cited, considers that Hobbes, Spinoza, Kant and Hume himself (who all thought that an effect could not occur without being preceded by its cause) points out that determination and cause are, to an extent, synonymous. But she also points out that there are many examples of effects which are the result of the accumulation of small causes and which can only be said to occur with high probability.

This type of probabilistic mechanics was first introduced in predicting the behaviour of sub-atomic particles whose paths are sometimes attributed to the operation of a paradoxical causal principle, the 'indeterminacy principle'. This so-called indeterminacy principle has been cited, by Schroedinger for example, as the counter to determinism, and as providing the opportunity for God to influence the operations of nature. Others have seen it as a point at which will can operate. Psychotherapists have sometimes cited the indeterminacy principle as a refutation of scientific determinism and gone on to argue that psychotherapy can therefore justifiably consider that it no longer needs to submit itself to scientific scrutiny. Anscombe argues against these comfortable doctrines, pointing out, for example, that deviation from determinacy is, by its nature, haphazard whilst an intervention by an agent would, also by its nature, be to influence the effect in one particular direction. Moreover in the everyday world, and in ordinary science, there is no practical difference between a very probable event and a certain one. If I press down the brake pedal on the car, I expect the car to stop and, if it does not, I assume that there is a fault. I do not, unless I want a certain reputation, assume that this was one of those improbable, uncaused, events that sooner or later could be expected to occur.

There is a principle of communication in biological, psychological and social systems which tends to counteract indeterminacy and which may account for the robustness of the non-probabilistic explanations of cause and effect. This principle, the threshold, ensures that effects are not manifest until there has been a sufficient accumulation of small causes. When I press my foot down on the brake pedal, I am contracting my leg muscles in a certain way. Nerve endings on the muscle play a necessary part in this process. At each of these nerve endings there is continuous random release of transmitter, but not enough to depolarize the muscle membrane sufficiently to 'fire' a contraction. Pressing my foot down involves an increase in the amount of transmitter released and although there is still a finite possibility that any particular packet of transmitter might be released, or that any particular receptor on the muscle membrane will be occupied by transmitter, there is sufficient redundancy in the system that a large enough amount is released, and a large enough population of receptors are occupied, for depolarization to occur.

An important corollary of Anscombe's argument is the fallacy of inferring new causes from unexpected events. If I come across a person with the same name as me, or I discover that I was born on the same date as the Prime Minister of Britain, it would be fallacious for me to assume that these unexpected and fairly improbable events imply a cause – although they may be a stimulus for a search for meaning, as I will consider below.

Anscombe's example of balls in motion is one in which balls are impelled and affected by many small causes. Hume's examples of causes are of large and obvious single causes. Does the fact that causal happenings in the world co-occur with other happenings which may either weaken, alter or increase effects, undermine the necessity of causation? John Stuart Mill thought not, and other more recent philosophers have agreed with him. Mill defined cause to be 'the sum total of the conditions positive and negative taken together' but went on to say that, once the sum is realised, 'the consequent invariably follows'.

Mill's formulation raised another difficulty, linked to agency, but this time to the responsibility of the agent, not the autonomy. If many causes conspire to produce an effect, can it be said of any one of them that they caused the effect? And if one of these causes is an agent cause, can it be said that the agent is responsible for the effect? Davidson (1967) considers the example given by Mill of a man, say he is called Mr Smith, dying as a result of falling from a ladder. Mill argues that to say Mr Smith's foot slips and that was the cause of him dying leaves out other causal factors such as the fact that Smith was heavy and therefore hit the ground harder.

However, in the psychotherapy clinic, one may want to reassert the importance of multiple causes. When a patient maintains his aggression towards others is caused by their rejection of him, one may want to indicate that his willingness to give way to aggression is the real cause of his problems. The word 'reason' is again called upon to single out the cause which is going to be of interest. The patient might say 'I hit my partner because I couldn't stand her complaining' and the psychotherapist might say 'I think that the reason was not really that, it was that she reminded you of your mother, and you wanted to hit *her*'. Mill might say that the man who was sensitised by maternal rejection hit out because he could not stand his wife's complaints, but conversation proceeds by singling out one reason, on which judgements of responsibility are made.

# REASONS

'No supposition seems to me more natural than that there is no process in the brain correlated with associating or thinking' wrote Wittgenstein (1981). Wittgenstein's rejection of monism is particularly cogent when it comes to how meaning is produced. Wittgenstein's treatment of meaning involves the use of counter factual conditionals, a class of sentences which have in other hands been elaborated into a semantic analysis of causation but which Wittgenstein used mainly as illustration (Budd, 1989). Counter factual conditionals are conditional statements in which the antecedent is a hypothetical one: for example, 'If I had dropped this lighted match into petrol, the petrol would have caught fire'. They have the remarkable property of being true whenever their antecedent is false which, since it is a hypothetical, it can usually be assumed to be. A statement that is always true, a tautology, normally adds nothing, but counter factual conditionals do seem to be saying something about the world. Since that something is obviously not about the logical relations between things, it is suggested, that it is about their causal relations. Wittgenstein envisages a situation in which someone orders a pupil to write the series n + 2. Let us suppose that the pupil wrote '998, 1000, 1003' and that the teacher corrected the pupil for not following instructions, justifying herself by saying that 'I meant him to write 1002 after 1000'. What does this mean? Wittgenstein says that it means something like the counterfactual conditional: 'If I had been asked, when I told the pupil to write down the series, what came after 1000, I should have said 1002' but the teacher did not say this, because the teacher was not asked: what the teacher would have said is, Wittgenstein argues, an assumption or a hypothesis. It is not something present in the teacher's consciousness and, indeed, the teacher may have made a mistake and said 1003 does come after 1000. Wittgenstein is therefore splitting what was in the teacher's mind when she gave the instruction – what caused the instruction – and what the teacher meant by it which was, amongst other things, to write down 1002.

The principle that meaning may be an *a posteriori* hypothesis rather than an *a priori* determinant of what people say may be generalised to other actions, with more notable consequences. Consider this example:

> Fred's analyst is slightly late for Fred's Tuesday session, and Fred comes ten minutes late for his Thursday session. He says that he had no particular reason for being late, it just took longer to get ready and the traffic was bad. The analyst reminds Fred that he, the analyst, had been late for the previous session and wonders if Fred had been paying him back. Fred says that he hadn't remembered the analyst being late, at which the analyst says that Fred was unconsciously paying him back, and not only for that episode of lateness, but for all the indifference that Fred's father had shown Fred which had been transferred by Fred onto the analyst.

Are the reasons that are attributed to Fred causes of his behaviour? Did Fred cast around for ways to pay back his analyst, and come up with the project to be late? I suppose that neither of these statements is plausible in the face of Fred's character, which is not cruel or vengeful, and in the face of his denials. But we would be tempted to say that he may not have thought these things consciously, but did do so unconsciously. Sartre, in his critique of Freud, argued that this use of the term 'unconscious' was one of the main fallacies of Freudian metapsychology, since it attributed to the unconscious even greater powers of ratiocination than the conscious mind possessed and yet, according to Freud's characterisation, the unconscious was a domain in which reasoning about consequences did not take place.

Let us follow the lines of Wittgenstein's argument, rather than that of Sartre, in considering what caused Fred to behave as he did. Let us further suppose that the following additional evidence is given by the analyst concerned: Fred's analyst said that he had known Fred for years, knew him better than Fred knew himself in fact, as evidenced by the fact that on numerous previous occasions an interpretation of the analyst's had eventually come to be accepted by Fred as the truth. In other words, even though Fred could not account for his behaviour at first as if it was caused by the aggressive thoughts attributed to him, other information about his unconscious is available which confirms that his behaviour can be accounted for by these thoughts.

We thus have two possibilities: there were unconscious processes in Fred which represented a sequence of statements and their emotional consequences and which were planned to achieve a certain interpersonal conclusion; or that his actions could be accounted for in these ways, but the causes of them were independent of these accounts. Wittgenstein's argument shows that the latter is possible, but does not demonstrate that it applies here. People could, after all, be like a chess computer which generates all possible moves and selects the one that is most likely to inflict damage on the opponent. However, human reasoning about chess does not seem to work like this. Human computation, like the teacher's in Wittgenstein's example, seems to make greater use of intensive rules and less use of a review of all possible extensive instances.

Searles (1983) gives an account of learning to ski which illustrates non-computational unconscious processes (note that in this passage, Searles uses the word 'rule' as a synonym for 'verbal instruction'):

> [a]s the skier gets better he does not internalize the rules better, but rather the rules become progressively irrelevant. The rules do not become 'wired in' as unconscious intentional contents, but the repeated experiences create physical capacities, presumably as neural pathways, that make the rules simply irrelevant
>
> (Searles, 1983:150)

Searles later suggests that this acquired skiing ability becomes part of the background of capacities which includes 'skills, abilities, preintentional assumptions and presuppositions, stances, and nonrepresentational attitudes' (ibid.:151).

We can now say that the cause of Fred being late was an irritated reluctance to attend the analytic session and we can note that this cause excludes any propositional content. Does this cover what people mean when they say, 'What is the reason for it?' It is true that some people may give as their reasons for acting that they felt 'bored' or 'pissed off', but these are generally considered unsatisfactory explanations. So it seems that more is meant by reason than that. I have already alluded to possible reasons for Fred's behaviour; that it was due to transference (of course these technical terms are not the reasons, either, but shorthand for the reasons). I have also conceded that Fred may later admit that this was his reason. However, I have also tried to demonstrate that it is implausible that these reasons caused Fred to act as he did, and I have also indicated that there is an alternative explanation, which is that accounts and causes are distinct.

Fincham and Jaspars (1980) distinguish between two kinds of accounts that prisoners give for their offence: *excuses* bear on whether they caused the event that led to charges being preferred i.e. whether they are guilty; while *justifications* bear on the meaning that should be placed on their guilt i.e. whether there are mitigating circumstance. I want to suggest that people use 'reason' to cover two quite distinct cases and these bear some similarity to the excuses and justifications of Fincham and Jaspar. Reasons1 are states which dispose to actions: 'I was just pissed off'; 'I was concentrating on what had happened to me in the past' and I think that they are causes of actions. Reasons2 are attributed to actions as justifications, interpretations, idealisations or whatever but, although they may be couched in intentional language, they are not causes of the action, but afterthoughts. Fred taking longer to get ready is a reason1 for his being late and his wanting to pay the analyst back is a reason2 for which he may have the further reason2 as justification that he had been very badly treated by his father and that the analyst very often seemed to behave in much the same way to him as his father did.

I take this account of things to be consistent with Davidson's influential account (1967) in which he argues that some reasons are 'primary': they are attitudes of wanting something coupled with the belief that some action will secure it. Primary attitudes cause behaviour and correspond to reasons1 as I have described them. Other reasons are not primary, but may imply a primary reason. Davidson considers that 'James went to church to please his mother' is not a description of James's reasons because James's attitude is unclear – he may have liked to please his mother, or felt it his duty to do so, for example. But clearly James might legitimately give it as his reason for going to church, that he wants to please his mother. Davidson says that this reason cannot be 'taken to refer to an entity, state, disposition, or event' and we can therefore assume that Davidson would not consider it to be a cause of James's behaviour. James's reason is therefore a non-causal reason – a reason2 in my terms – but having identified that there are such reasons, Davidson does not go on to characterise their particular features. This is, however, what I intend to do in the next section. Before doing so, I want to pick up one more implication of making dispositions the causes of intentional behaviour, as I have argued that they are.

## BACKGROUND AND FLAVOUR

There is no question that I may plan to do something by articulating the goal that I want to achieve, and then filling in the intervening steps according to a fully explicit rationale. I am not concerned with these situations, partly because they are of little interest to the psychotherapist, who is more concerned with actions that seem to have unconscious purposes i.e. where there is no explicit goal or where the explicit goal does not seem to explain the action. Here is an example given as evidence of the therapeutic action of psychoanalysis.

The proponent of psychoanalysis and the writer of the account, Meehle (1983) was on his way to his analysis in the University Hospital when he saw two people whom he took to be parents of a child who had remained in the hospital. From their expression, the author assumed that the child was dead or dying. He himself felt bereft at the sight of their distress and entered the analyst's office in tears. The analyst asked 'Were you harsh with Karen (Meehle's 5-year-old daughter) this morning?' Meehle remembered that he had indeed been, and following the question and his memory of it, his distress ended and his tears dried up.

Meehle's state fits well the background state which leads to intentional behaviour that Searles, Armstrong, and Malcolm and others describe in different ways and there seems to be no need to posit any unconscious phantasy about killing his daughter, conflict with the social norm of preserving life, or conflict anxiety, as Meehle does. It is enough to say that he was experiencing regret about his conduct and that his regret was associated with a focus of his attention on his daughter. The raggedy doll that the bereaved parents were carrying would have stood out as a result of this attentional focus, and his current emotional state would have facilitated the contagion of the parents' feelings to him. But if this is the explanation, what produced the immediate relief?

The explanation that Meehle himself gives is implausible. The propositional content of the analyst's intervention does not seem to offer an avenue of relief. What is remarkable is that the analyst immediately tuned in to Meehle's preoccupation with harm coming to children, and showed extraordinary percipience in knowing that Meehle's distress was linked to regret about his own conduct. It is not possible to know how the analyst arrived at this statement, whether it was some flash of empathic awareness, or derived from previous occasions when Meehle had discussed his lack of patience with his daughter and the second thoughts that he experienced when he encountered the sick children in the hospital. However it may have been, the impact of the statement must surely have been dependent on the tone with which it was spoken. One can imagine it being said as if by a stern parent who sees all transgressions, and calls to account the transgressor; or as if by a kind and omniscient parent who sees the frailty of the heart, and forgives. The impact of the statement and its solace must have resided not in its propositional content but in its implications of the solicitous relationship of the analyst to Meehle.

The implications of the statement, the emotions and action tendencies that it aroused, are a species of background, too. The intent of the analyst's statement is implicit and not explicit. In fact, it seems doubtful that the analyst would have been able to predict the dramatic response to the intervention ahead of time, as a question like this might often be interpreted as a challenge or criticism by a patient. I will call this particular type of background, which is linked to emotional change rather than to action, 'flavour'. In summary, I would say that the therapeutic effect of Meehle's analyst's question was due to its flavour.

The arguments in this section, that many of the actions of interest to the psychotherapist are not caused by propositions but by background factors, can now be extended. For if propositions are not causal in producing actions, then they are not causal in changing actions therapeutically. I have already argued that 'background' as described by Searles, and others, meets the criteria for being the cause of 'unconscious' actions and it follows that 'flavour', already defined to be that type of background which has therapeutic effects, is a therapeutically effective element.

I conceive flavour to be something that arouses a particular emotional response, usually including a feeling, but also the taint left by an emotion. I use emotion in the broad sense to include non-propositional intentions: an example would be the intention 'get close to mother' that belongs with stranger anxiety. However flavour also, as its name suggests, includes aesthetic responses. I see it as the principle by which iconic images are strung together in syntagmata. If I dream of a wheel, one flavour that is evoked is circularity, and it will be more likely that I will dream next of another circular image, say a ball. In a conversation in which there is no strong strategy, the sequence of one utterance will, I suppose, cause the next by virtue of that utterance's flavour.

Here is an illustration, a folk-tale from East Anglia. A Professor of signs was coming to Cambridge to test the mettle of the students. The student body had warning of his coming, and so they posted themselves on his road into the city. As he came, he stopped what he took to be passers-by to ask them various learned questions and, not knowing that these were students, the Professor became rather over-awed by what he took to be the intelligence and education of ordinary inhabitants. He wondered how he could come out on top with such an intelligent bunch, and resolved to challenge the students to a debate without words, using signs only. The student's champion was much put out and told a drinking acquaintance, a one-eyed miller, that he was sure to lose, such was his ignorance of this subject. The miller reassured him, said that he was an expert, and offered to take his place, which he did. The debate was conducted in the full glare of publicity.

The Professor began by holding up an apple. The miller felt around in his pockets, and held up a crust of bread. The Professor then held up a finger, and the miller held up two. The Professor held up three, and the miller held up his fist. The Professor announced the end of the debate by smiling, taking the miller's hand, and expressing his complete satisfaction at its conclusion.

What causal explanation can we give of this dialogue? Obviously the flavour of an apple suggests the flavour of other foods with which it might be eaten, and the miller, being a miller, would naturally associate it with bread. It is not clear why the flavour of bread would have led the Professor to hold up a finger – perhaps, he had often to ask for his own bread in his childhood by holding up a finger – but the miller, who was obviously of the bellicose sort often associated with the profession, perhaps felt admonished by the wagging finger and held up two in the age-old gesture of defiance. One finger, two fingers, three fingers may have been a sequence from a childhood game but it seems a logical, and mindless, action to follow on in this way. The miller had perhaps been blessed by overfed clergy once too often, and the Professor's gesture, which probably had quite a smug flavour, must have evoked an angry response and led to the accompanying gesture of a raised fist.

Of course, this is a hypothetical sequence but I give it to demonstrate the possible scope of flavour. Had the example not been a conversation but the moves in a relationship, or the movements in a symphony, or the succession of jobs in a career, the influence of flavour might have been even more marked. In this particular instance, it was a conversation and therefore irredeemably linked to meaning. As it happens, the meaning of the exchange is given in the tale: 'First', said the Professor, 'I held up an apple to indicate that "By the apple, mankind has fallen". My opponent miller replied with his crust, as if to say "By the Bread of Life, we are all redeemed". I showed one finger, meaning "There is but one God". He showed two, meaning "But we must not forget his son". I held up three fingers to remind him of the Holy Spirit and he assented by shaking his fist, signifying "Together in the Trinity, they are as one". The miller slipped out whilst this explanation was

going on, but when asked later what had transpired, his account was
that the Professor was an aggressive fellow who as soon as he was introduced, picked up an apple as if to say 'I'll throw this at your head if
you don't watch out'. The miller, not to be defeated, could only find
a crust in his pocket but held it up, to show the Professor that if he
threw the apple, he would get the bread in his face. Then the Professor
held up a finger and the miller knew that that meant that he was
threatening to poke out his eye, so he held up two to show that he
would poke out both his. The three fingers, the miller interpreted to
mean 'I'll tear your skin to shreds' and so he could only think to show
him the size of his fist, meaning to warn him that he could pound him
into mincemeat if he tried anything. At that, as the miller expected,
the Professor hastily backtracked, became as nice as pie, and brought
the 'debate' to a hasty end (tale adapted from K. Briggs (1991)).

I find this tale illuminating about psychotherapy. Each party gives his
reasons for doing what he did, but the reasons are completely different.
However, this is only problematic if we consider that these reasons are
the causes of the Professor and the miller's behaviour. In the previous
section I have argued that the reasons that people give for their actions
may not be causally related to those actions, but be justifications.

## ACCOUNTS AND THE CAUSES OF ACTION

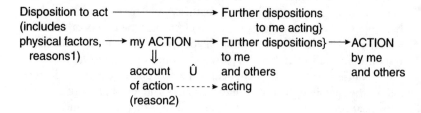

The figure summarises the story so far. The causes of my action include
physical and mental factors, the latter being reasons1. My actions cause
further dispositions on my part and the part of others to act and so. In
addition to this causal chain there is, presumably, a tendency for some
brain states to lead to others directly, and so at least some of my dispositions will cause other dispositions to develop even without my acting.
There remain the questions, if causes in the figure are represented by
the symbol ⟶ : what do the symbols ⇒ and ---➤ represent? Are they
also causal relations?

Donald Davidson's influential view has been that $--\rightarrow$ is a relation which is not causal but accords with the 'constitutive ideal of rationality' (Davidson, 1970:98) i.e. that it is law-like inasmuch as rational argument is law-like, but it is not causal. However, Davidson further argues, that $\Rightarrow$ is not even law-like.

Consider three illustrations:

1 I go to the doctor with a lump, and she performs a number of tests. She tells me that I have cancer, and I begin to weep.
2 I go to the doctor with low mood, and she asks a number of questions about my sleep, concentration and appetite. She tells me that I have a depressive disorder, and I begin to weep.
3 I go to the psychotherapist with symptoms of having nocturnal panics associated with genital pain and with a feeling of being stifled. She asks me about my childhood, and then tells me that I have been sexually abused. I say that it is not possible.

The relation of the statement 'you have cancer' and my having a lump comes close to being causal inasmuch, over the class of fully trained doctors, that symptom would be constantly conjoined with those tests, and the result being what it was would be constantly conjoined with the statement 'you have cancer', or something like it. It is certainly a law-like relation. It is tempting to say that the second illustration is like the first and is therefore a counter-example to Davidson's premise that there can be no law-like relation between brain states and mental descriptions. Illustration 2 is not a counter-example if it is more akin to illustration 3 than to illustration 1, because in illustration 3 it is apparent that the account 'you have been sexually abused' is by no means one that would have been given by everyone, nor would everyone accept that it is the reason2 for the symptoms.

## LINKING REASONS1 AND REASONS2

Whatever the nomological status of some mental descriptions to putative brain states, the accounts that interest psychotherapists are almost all similar to the third illustration. The question is then what is the relation $\Rightarrow$ if it is not causal, or even law-like? One, influential, account is that it is reparative. Reasons2 regulate and, if regulation fails, repair social functioning. One way that they do this by creating potential solutions for otherwise conflictual action sequences.

Young (1989) gives a detailed narrative account of an elderly concentration camp survivor who consults a physician and is examined by him. The examination could have had overtones of Auschwitz and the physical mishandling that Dr Malinowski received from the guards. The physician, like the guards, has a job to do and cannot avoid some degree of intrusiveness, but also allows and even encourages Dr Malinowski to insert his own narrative about his war-time experience into the medical encounter. By sharing this other narrative patient and physician undo the potential harm that the examination could do: 'in the existential context of these stories, what might otherwise be seen as indignities to the body are transmuted into honours: the physician is a man whose touch preserves just those proprieties of the body that are infringed at Auschwitz' (Young, 1989:163).

Young concludes her chapter by referring to the ultimate importance of preserving the proprieties of the body which is that the self needs to be preserved. This, too, is the challenge for the psychotherapist: how to enable a person to become a different self, without ever losing their self. If the normal function of reasons2 is to maintain the self and so to ensure that the person with that self continues to be an effective agent, then getting the reasons2 right is particularly important when a person feels that their self is invalid, as often seems to be the case when a person elects for psychotherapy.

Persons exist as embodied causal agents, and as narrated selves. It would be wrong to suppose that one sort of existence is more real than the other, or even that one is primary. Whilst the baby is in the womb, a body is being assembled and so is a story about the sort of baby that they will be. To confine reasons2 to the function of repairing or regulating causal agency so as to allow social life to occur is to presuppose the primacy of the caused world over the narrative world. From the perspective of the narrative world, stimuli to the generation of new meaning may have an intrinsic value which might broadly be called developmental.

## A parable . . .

The progeny of a grazing creature suffer from the effects of a mutation: their necks grow twice as long. They cannot compete with other grazers in grassland, but move to an area where there are trees and live off leaves instead. After a period of time, because there is little competition for leaves, their numbers increase whilst, because there is much competition for grass, the numbers of their cousins, who did not experience the consequences of the mutation, diminish.

## ... and its interpretation

The causal effects of mutation put the proto-giraffes at a disadvantage, but by widening the meaning of 'grazing' to include leaves as well as grass, the proto-giraffes recovered and, as we know, thrived by being able to adapt into a new ecological niche.

## An illustration from psychotherapy

Jean had been in and out of mental hospital for many years. Her family life was unhappy, and she regularly became depressed. Whilst in hospital, she developed meningitis and very nearly died. On her recovery she seemed to have changed. Her depression had remitted and she had an equanimity about her life that she had never had before. 'I have realised', she said, 'that I am glad to be alive. These problems I have don't seem so important now. I feel that God has given me a second chance, and it's up to me to make the most of it'.

## SUMMARY AND CONCLUSIONS

I tap my quadriceps tendon and, normally, my leg jerks upwards. An observer may infer something about my brain, but I have not meant anything by my leg jerking. The fact that I have had to draw on the unusual circumstances of the consulting room for an example is, I think, an indication that very little of what people do is mere behaviour and almost all of it is action. That is, almost all of what people do is considered to have meaning and to be the attempted realisation of an intention. Failure to grasp this resulted in the failure of naive behaviourism. However, it no longer seems plausible to say that what distinguishes mere behaviour from action is that behaviour is caused, but action is not. Commonsense psychology has no difficulty because it admits of a special class of explanations for action, 'reasons'. The use of reasons is traditionally restricted to human beings of a certain mental capacity.

Most recent philosophers have assumed that actions, like any other event, must be caused. Although it does not follow that the same laws of causality apply as apply to, say, billiard balls, it does seem that any useful causal law should have some minimal requirements and that constant conjunction should be one of them. It seems very improbable that simple mechanical laws are applicable, but what if the brain is a computational machine? Bolton and Hill (1997) argue that this is what most current behavioural and brain scientists assume that the brain is and, according to this model, brain states 'encode' meaning. However they also review a formidable array of philosophical opinion which concludes that 'Cut the pie any way that you like, "meanings" just ain't in the head!' (Puttnam, 1973:705). Quine (1975) invites us to 'construe mind as a system of disposition to behaviour' and that is what I think that Bolton and Hill have done. Dispositions can be encoded computationally, and without reference to goals which 'ain't in the head'.

To the extent that reasons are dispositions, they can be described, as Bolton and Hill correctly point out, by cognitive models, and I have previously given some examples. I call these reasons1 and think that they are causes of behaviour and that in some way they correspond to brain states. However, there is another kind of reason that people give, reasons2, which does not correspond to a cause i.e. an occurrence preceding an action, but is the judgement that people, including the actor, make of the action. Reasons2 are not causes of the action for which they are the reason, but they may cause other consequential actions.

I have panic attacks but panic disorder has not yet been diagnosed. I feel a pain in my chest in the supermarket, and have difficulty breathing. I interpret this to mean that I am having a heart attack, and I say to passers-by, 'Help me, I'm having a heart attack'. They summon an ambulance. On arrival at the hospital, the ambulance men say that the reason for admitting me to the hospital is 'chest pain'. They omit to say 'he said that he was having a heart attack' because the medical nature of the incident requires a causal account. However, the emergency room staff find a normal ECG and my pain remits within minutes of my arrival. The ambulance men are now challenged for their reasons for bringing me in, and this time they do say 'He said that he was having a heart attack'.

It seems likely that had I said 'I am having a panic attack' that I would not have been taken to hospital in an ambulance. Thus the consequences of my chest pain were caused by my account, and not by the pain itself.

Reasons1 and reasons2 are intercalated within the same discourse and are often confused. I argued that psychotherapy research is one casualty of this, amongst many, and I call for a clearer awareness of when reasons1 and reasons2 are being used by psychotherapists. Finally, I have speculated about the value of reasons1 and 2 and concluded that reasons2 modify causal sequences, and that reasons1 stimulate the creation of new meanings.

## ACKNOWLEDGEMENTS

This chapter could not have been written without the encouragement and companionship of Emmy van Deurzen.

## REFERENCES

Anscombe, G. (1971). *Causality and Determination.* Cambridge: Cambridge University Press.

Armstrong, D. and Malcolm, N. (1984). *Consciousness and Causality.* Oxford: Basil Blackwell.

Bolton, D. and Hill, J. (1997). On the causal role of meaning. In M. Power and C. Brewin (eds), *The Transformation of Meaning in Psychological Therapies: integrating theory and practice* (pp. 15–32). Chichester: John Wiley.

Briggs, K.M. (1991) *A Dictionary of British Folk Tales in the English Language: Folk Legends (Part B).* London: Routledge.

Budd, M. (1989). *Wittgenstein's Philosophy of Psychology.* London: Routledge.

Davidson, D. (1967). Causal relations. *Journal of Philosophy,* 68, 426–441.

Davidson, D. (1970). Mental events. In L. Foster and J. Swanson (eds), *Experience and Theory.* London: Duckworth.

Erwin, E. (1997). *Philosophy and Psychotherapy.* London: Sage.

Fincham, F. and Jaspars, J. (1980). Attribution of responsibility: from man-as-scientist to man-as-lawyer. In L. Berkowitz (ed.), *Advances in Experimental Social Psychology* (Vol. 13). New York: Academic Press.

Frijda, N., Mesquita, B., Sonnemans, J. and Van Goozen, S. (1991). The duration of affective phenomena or emotions, sentiments and passions. In K. Strongman (ed.), *International Review of Studies on Emotion* (Vol. 1) (pp. 187–225). Chichester: John Wiley.

Harre, R. and Gillett, G. (1994) *Discursive Mind.* Thousand Oaks: Sage.

Hoagwood, K. (1993) Poststructuralist historicism and the psychological construction of anxiety disorders. [Review]. *Journal of Psychology,* 127, 105–122.

Hume, D. (1748). *Enquiries Concerning Human Understanding and Concerning the Principles of Morals.*

Meehle, P. (1983). Subjectivity in psychoanalytic inference: the nagging persistence of Wilhelm Fliess' Achensee question. In J. Earman (ed.), *Testing Scientific Theories* (Vol. 10, Minnesota Studies in the Philosophy of Science). Minneapolis: University of Minnesota Press.

Power, M. (1997). Conscious and unconscious representations. In M. Power and C. Brewin (eds), *The Transformation of Meaning in Psychological Therapies: integrating theory and practice* (pp. 57–74). Chichester: John Wiley.

Puttnam, H. (1973). Meaning and reference. *Journal of Philosophy,* 70, 699–711.

Quine, W. (1975). Mind and verbal disposition. In S. Guttenplan (ed.), *Mind and Language*. Oxford: Clarendon Press.

Searles, J. (1983). *Intentionality*. Cambridge: Cambridge University Press.

Wittgenstein, L. (1981). *Zettel* (2nd edition, translated by G. Anscombe) G. Anscombe and G. von Wright (eds). Oxford: Basil Blackwell.

Young, K. (1989). Narrative embodiments: enclaves of the self in the realm of medicine. In J. Shotter and K. Gergen (eds), *Texts of Identity* (pp. 152–165). London: Sage.

# Introduction to chapter 9

The following two contributions, while less overtly philosophical than others, illuminate issues key to the present state of psychotherapy. They take up the theme of narrative at a time when it risks being used as a panacea at any moment of philosophical or practical tension. It has been historically important – the hermeneutic approach to psychotherapy, developed by Paul Ricoeur (1970) from a reinterpretation of Freud, was founded on an analogy between the interpretation of literary texts, and the understanding required to enter into another individual's narrative.

As Tantam has illustrated in the previous chapter, emphasis on narrative provides one route by which the experience of agency and of development can be validated without having to concede formal causation. However, it can also be used to square other intricate contradictions in the theory of psychotherapy. Jeremy Holmes provides a lucid introduction to the value placed on narration and capacity to narrate within contemporary attachment theory. This is an approach to psychotherapy that has been rooted in respect for the natural sciences, and a wish to retain the developmental basis of analytic theory. It has also been based in empirical research rather than fantasised recollection, and a distrust of hermeneutically driven models of psychotherapy. The capacity to narrate has been prized in this tradition as a universal marker of attachment status, over and above narrative content, neatly reconciling positivist and hermeneutic interests.

As Holmes illustrates here, attachment theory permits some general rules of therapeutic procedure to be formulated on the basis of its analysis of basic differences in need between people presenting for psychotherapy, and between the responses if different attachment opportunities are offered within a psychotherapeutic frame.

# REFERENCES

Ricoeur, P. (1970) *Freud and Philosophy.* New Haven: Yale

# 9   Narrative, attachment and the therapeutic process

*Jeremy Holmes*

> It still strikes me as strange that the case histories I write should read like short stories and that, as one might say, they lack the serious stamp of science. I must console myself with the reflection that the nature of the subject is evidently responsible for this, rather than any preference of my own.
>
> (Freud 1985 p.160)

The present chapter has two interlocking purposes, one theoretical, the other practical. The first is to show how attachment research can contribute to the debate between science and hermeneutics within psychoanalytic psychotherapy. The second is to explore the therapeutic implications of a narrative stance.

As my opening quotation implies, Freud was troubled by the discrepancy between the novelistic quality of psychoanalytic discourse as it emerged in his writings, and his wish to establish psychoanalysis as a science. But for him there was no fundamental difficulty in reconciling these two facets of his project. He viewed the unconscious rather in the way that today's neuroimaging experts see the brain – an organ that is inaccessible and in many ways mysterious but which, given the right technology, can be clearly illuminated and if necessary manipulated. For him, that technology was the psychoanalytic method: free association, dream interpretation, the analysis of transference. His basic model remained that of dream interpretation, which he devised at the outset of psychoanalysis. The patient brings to treatment an incomplete and incomprehensible story – whether of a dream or a symptom. By reconstructing the underlying unconscious story, psychoanalysis fills in the missing gaps and so rearranges the confusion until it forms a coherent narrative. As in a good detective novel, the culprit – usually unconscious infantile wishes – is finally identified and brought to book.

Phillips (1998) identifies three narrative strands in early psychoanalysis. First is the psychodynamic narrative, in which the patient's
past is retranscribed to include the influence of the unconscious; second,
the developmental narrative, Freud's psychobiological account of
emotional maturation; and third, the narrative of the treatment itself,
the transferential narrative. Freud's grounding in science rested on the
second of these, since he saw his developmental account, and especially
the oedipal story, as a universal framework for understanding normal
and abnormal psychological development. As we shall see, the contribution of attachment theory to a discussion of narrative is a continuation
of this position. But first we must consider other post-Freudian
developments.

As psychoanalysis has evolved, Freud's confidence in the scientific
status of his discipline has been challenged in many ways. For our purposes the most important of these has been the realisation that, for any
given patient, there appears to be no single psychoanalytic narrative.
The proliferation of psychoanalytic schools and tendencies means that
a Kleinian, or a Kohutian, or Kernbergian, or an Interpersonal or a
contemporary Freudian or a Lacanian reading of the patient will each
produce a significantly different story. There is of course 'common
ground' between the different psychoanalytic discourses (Wallerstein
1992), but this is still very different from the situation in the physical
sciences, where, in general, there is little dispute about what constitute
the 'facts' of the situation, even if there may be competing theories
about how best to explain them. Further, it is clear that the 'material'
of psychoanalysis does not arise solely from the patient and the story
she tells; it is a joint product of analyst and patient, and the theories
espoused by the former have a major influence on the shape and meaning
of the treatment.

If there are in fact multiple psychoanalytic narratives, and if these
are inerradicably theory-laden, does this not mean that psychoanalysis
is more closely related to hermeneutic, interpretive disciplines like
history, literary criticism or sociology, than to the physical sciences?
This is the position adopted by authors such as Ricoeur (1970), Shafer
(1992) and Spence (1992). For Spence the historical truth of memory
is always open to question: the memories and imagery which the patient
brings to therapy are selected and shaped by present reality and it is
this that is the real focus for the analyst, whose task is to produce
coherence and aesthetic balance to a patient's view of herself. The
referential status of the patient's story assumes a secondary importance
in this account. Shafer similarly sees the treatment narrative as pre-
eminent. For him the multiple meanings and interpenetration of past

and present in the immediate unconscious milieu between analyst and patient is the cutting edge of change, based on the analyst's hermeneutic capabilities.

This debate within psychoanalysis touches on a wider philosophical debate about the role of narrative in everyday life, in which Alisdair MacIntyre (1981) and Jerome Bruner (1986) are leading exponents. For MacIntyre, personhood and narrative are inseparable. Motives are aims within a historical context. Actions can only be understood within the context of an implicit history or story: 'stories are lived before they are told'. In trying to understand our own behaviour and that of others we seek an underlying story which will explain people's actions. Psychoanalysis is an elaboration of this commonsense folk psychology. Freud's discovery was that seemingly incomprehensible symptoms could be explained if agency was attributable to unconscious motivation – a 'second reality' (Phillips 1998).

Jerome Bruner (1986) is similarly concerned to give narrative its full philosophical due. He argues that there are two kinds of approach to truth:

> [a] good story and a well-formed argument are different natural kinds. Both can be used as a means for convincing another. Yet what they convince of is fundamentally different: arguments convince of their truth, stories of their lifelikeness. The one verifies by eventual appeal to procedures for establishing formal and empirical truth. The other establishes its truth by verisimilitude.

As an advocate of narrative, Bruner's use of the word 'verisimilitude' is risky, given the Oxford English Dictionary definition of it as 'having the appearance of being real or true'. Critics of psychotherapy might argue that this is a concession that the stories elaborated in psychotherapy can lay no more claim to the truth than can myths or fairy stories. How can this charge be answered?

Bruner's response, I believe, would be that there *is* truth in myths and fairy stories – emotional truth rather than factual truth, which can be judged, not by scientific standards, but by such tests as whether the story rings true, feels 'right', is satisfying, coherent, or touches the listener emotionally. Ironically, a play has verisimilitude if it compels the audience to remain in a state of 'suspension of disbelief' for the duration of the performance. Similarly, psychotherapeutic case histories could be Brunerian 'good stories' which have a paradigmatic value in their own right, even though, by the standards of a 'well formed argument', alone they prove nothing.

The criteria of a 'good story' certainly apply to psychotherapy. A psychotherapist is constantly using her intuition to evaluate the patient's narrative, asking herself if it makes sense or hangs together, questioning aspects that don't quite fit, probing clichéd phrases and well worn narratives for what might lie beneath. The quest is always for a more elaborated, all-embracing, spontaneous, individualised and flexible story that encompasses a greater range of experience.

This evaluative activity, akin to Spence's aesthetics, is part of the 'art' of psychotherapy. But can there also be a science of narrative, including one which would encompass the narrative aspects of psychotherapy?

The main drawback of radical narrativism is the implication that a psychotherapeutic narrative is no more or less likely to be true than any other account of the patient's distress, whether religious, narrowly 'organic' in the psychiatric sense, or delusional. The hermeneutic turn in psychotherapy threatens to cut psychotherapy off from aspects of science – especially from evolutionary biology and developmental psychology – where dialogue is both necessary and possible. I shall argue therefore for a partial narrativism, a position which includes both scientific and hermeneutic elements.

## EXAMPLE: HERMENEUSIS AND DEVELOPMENTAL PSYCHOBIOLOGY

A married woman in her thirties presented with feelings of depression and inadequacy. She was a high-flying executive and had handed over the care of her daughter to her house-husband partner. Her depression seems to have started when her husband announced that he was bored with their sex life and inveigled her into group sex activities which she found 'physically satisfying, but emotionally repugnant'. The therapist suggested that there might be a connection with her low self-esteem as a woman and feelings of emotional deprivation as a child, and questioned her about her relationship with her mother. The patient responded by saying 'Oh, we always had boring lunch boxes compared with the other children', and going on to describe an incident on bonfire night when she had been burned by a flying ember from the fire, and how her mother had efficiently brushed it off but had shown little emotional sympathy for the pain and shock which she had experienced.

Here we see the interpenetration of hermenuesis and science. The 'boring lunch box' can be read as a metaphorical expression of the patient's feelings of sexual inadequacy; similarly the 'brushing off' incident, with its concrete and more general meaning, was emblematic of her mother's attitude towards nurturance and linked perhaps with the patient's subsequent renunciation of her emotional needs in favour of a career. All this could only be understood as interpretative narrative analysis. But these observations are not arbitrary. They arise within a framework of scientific understanding based on knowledge of the emotional needs of young children and the patterns of parent–child interaction which can be defined by systematic observation.

I turn now to attachment theory, which provides a set of useful bridging concepts that are relevant to the 'both/and' approach to science and hermenuetics which I am advocating.

## THE CONTRIBUTION OF ATTACHMENT RESEARCH

While the immediate goal of psychotherapy may be to remove symptoms, behind that lie a set of more general and more ambitious objectives – to help an individual to flourish, to foster well being, and so on. These can be seen in terms of the development of a strengthened and more versatile set of selves, for example: a more secure self, a more creative self, a more coping self, a more resilient self, a more autonomous self, a self with a greater capacity for intimacy. In contrast with the Cartesian cogito, narrative theory, according to MacIntyre, sees the 'I' not as a fixed and pre-existing entity, but as an autobiographical self, formed out of the interplay between agency and contingency, needing to be 'told' to another – or storied – before it can come into being (Brockmeier 1997). The telling of a self implies a built-in dialogical structure. There is always an Other to whom the Self is telling his or her story, even if in adults this takes the form of an internal dialogue.

What are the origins of this 'self-story'? How do we begin to learn about ourselves and our feelings? For psychoanalysts Winnicott's notion of maternal mirroring provides a model both of normal development, and of the possible role of therapy. When the mother looks at the baby, according to Winnicott (1967), 'what she looks like [to the baby] is related to what she [the mother] sees there'. This clinical insight has recently been expanded by Gergely and Watson (1996), who suggest that an attuned mother helps her infant identify feelings by mirroring behaviour that has two characteristics. First, the mother's facial expressions of emotion are 'marked' by exaggeration, so that the child can see that they are 'pretend', not real. Second, they are contingent on the child's feelings, so that they arise only when he or she appears to be experiencing a particular emotion, a response which in itself has a soothing function. Here we see the beginnings of a possible representation of, or story about, the self and its feelings. 'Marking' is related to the highlighting effect of narrative. It is as though the mother is saying 'This is you and your feelings that you are looking at, not me'. Contingency is linked with the way in which, unlike the phenomena of 'real life', stories hang together in a coherent way, since the mother makes sure that her responses always follow the baby's lead with, as it were, a beginning, middle and end, in contrast to the unstructured flow of 'normal' responsiveness.

Gergely and Watson's speculations are based on the three decades of research on infant–mother interaction arising from Bowlby's attachment theory (Holmes 1993). Recent developments in attachment research have begun to link this understanding of early life with clinical narrative in adults. The way we tell stories reflects our fundamental stance towards the world. The development of the Adult Attachment Interview (AAI) by Mary Main and her colleagues (Main 1995) in the mid-1980s provided a scientific tool which was sophisticated enough to pick up some of the subtleties of the narratives which are the stuff of clinical reality.

AAI is an audio-taped, semi-structured psychodynamic assessment session, whose aim is to 'surprise the unconscious' into revealing itself by asking detailed questions about relationships with parents and significant others, and about losses and separations and how the subject coped with them.

As a psychometric instrument, the AAI is original in that its scoring system is based not so much on content as on the form and structure of the subject's narrative style. Narratives are classified into one of four categories: 'secure–autonomous', 'insecure–dismissive', 'insecure–preoccupied', and 'disorganised' (or 'unresolved'). The key quality of secure–autonomous narratives is coherence: the subject is able to speak logically and concisely about her past and its vicissitudes, however problematic these may have been. Insecure–dismissive narratives (equivalent to avoidant attachment styles) are unelaborated and unrevealing: the subject may state that she has no memories of her childhood before the age of 11, or that her parents were 'brilliant', without being able to amplify or produce relevant examples. By contrast, in insecure–preoccupied narratives (equivalent to ambivalent attachment styles) the subject appears bogged down in her history, telling rambling and incon-clusive stories as though past pain was still alive today. The unresolved category is rated separately, co-existing with the others, and refering to points in a narrative where the logical flow is interrupted, broken, or disjointed. Main suggests that these narrative fractures may represent the emergence of previously repressed traumatic memories, and may be related clinically to dissociative states.

The AAI was developed within a theoretical framework that predicted that there would be connections between attachment experiences in childhood and narrative style in later life. This hypothesis has been supported by at least two sets of recent studies. First, Main and others have shown that, along with other measures looking at what I have called 'autobiographical competence' (Holmes 1992) such as picture completion and 'tell-a-story' tasks, attachment patterns in infancy are remarkably predictive of adolescents' AAI status when measured some fifteen years later (Benoit and Parker 1994). Fonagy and his co-workers (Fonagy et al. 1991) showed that the outcome of the AAI adminis-tered to prospective parents was, twenty months later, a good predictor of attachment status of their one-year old children. Mothers with secure–autonomous narratives tended to have children who were secure in the Strange Situation, while dismissive parents tended to have inse-cure, avoidant infants.

Even more significantly, Fonagy and his co-workers (1995) found that the capacity to think about oneself in relation to others – a capacity which they call 'reflexive self function' (RSF) – is a key-determinant of whether mothers whose own childhoods were traumatic will have infants who turn out to be insecure in the Strange Situation. The capacity for RSF is a vital protection against psychological vulnerability in the face of environmental difficulty – an important finding for psychotherapists, since a large part of their work could be seen as enhancing RSF in their patients. Clearly too RSF is related to narra-tive competence: in order to tell a story about oneself in relation to others one has to be able to reflect on oneself – to see oneself, partially at least, from the outside, and this in turn depends on the experience of maternal mirroring.

Given their stability and predictive power it is reasonable to assume that attachment status and AAI classification are tapping into some meaningful psychological configuration. Attachment status seems to relate to patterns of parental handling in the first year of life, and is thus clearly an interpersonal phenomenon. Parental responsiveness to infant affect – of which the mirroring function is a central component – is a key determinant of secure attachment. In summary, environments may be consistently responsive, consistently unresponsive, or inconsistently responsive. Mothers of secure infants pick their babies up more quickly when they show signs of distress, play with them more, and generally seem more aware of them and their needs than the parents of insecure children. Parents of children who show the avoidant pattern are more brusque and functional in their handling, while parents of those who show the ambivalent reaction tend to be less attuned to their children's needs, often ignoring them when they are obviously distressed and intruding upon them when they are playing happily. The Strange Situation measures the enactment of the child's relationship to her parents. The AAI by contrast defines individuals' narrative account of their experience – a movement from mechanism to meaning, from attachment behaviour to representation of attachments.

This self-narrative can be disrupted in ways that might correspond with insecure patterns on the AAI. If the parent is unavailable, the child may be so concerned with maintaining proximity to her that she will be unable to play and so find her inner voice, leading to dismissive narratives and difficulty with intimacy. Preoccupied narratives may reflect unmetabolised pain that has not been transmuted into the metaphor of play: the sufferer is searching for a safe container and using whoever happens to be at hand for that purpose. If the parent has been intrusive the child's self-narrative may be contaminated with the parental narrative, always thinking and feeling what is expected rather than what might have emerged had more disinterested parenting been available. Finally, if the environment is traumatising the whole 'containment/self-narrative' envelope may be obliterated, leaving lacunae and discontinuities in the texture of inner reality and its representation in inner speech.

In summary, the findings of attachment research suggest that there may be objective criteria – coherence, succinctness, relevance etc. – by which to evaluate the 'verisimilitude' of a clinical narrative. It also points to powerful links between the 'narrative truth' of the clinical situation and the 'historical truth' of the patient's actual biography.

The autobiographical self can be seen in terms of an inner object with which an individual has a relationship, comparable to 'external' relationships which can be understood in terms of different attachment styles. At a clinical level, the psychological fluidity of the secure–autonomous individual can be contrasted with the relatively static (in psychoanalytic terms 'defended') positions of avoidant or ambivalent attachment.

Gergely and Watson's (1996) ideas suggest that there is a close relationship between the development of the self and secure attachment.

'Marking' enables one to distinguish one's own feelings from those of others, and is thus a bulwark against the excessive use of projective identification. Where 'marking' breaks down, which may be particularly the case in ambivalent attachment, the child may be unable to distinguish her feelings from those of the mother: 'Is it my feelings I am seeing reflected in the maternal mirror, or my mother's?' Contingency is related to the 'truth' of one's feelings, helping one to ensure that there is a correspondence between an emotion and its representation. Here avoidantly attached children may be especially vulnerable, since they have not had the raptness of attention that is needed for them to 'find' their feelings in the mother-mirror.

Those who are securely attached therefore can (a) distinguish between their own experience and that of others, (b) represent and so tell the story of their feelings, and (c) have the capacity to break up their stories and reform them so they are more in keeping with the flux of experience. Ambivalent individuals are so close to their feelings that they cannot achieve the objectification – in White and Epston's (1990) terms, 'externalisation', akin to Gergely and Watson's (1996) 'marking' – needed for a working story. Avoidant people, by contrast, cling to a stereotyped version of themselves and their past and feel threatened by the idea of the constantly updated narrative – again in Gergely and Watson's terms, one that is checked for contingency – that is characteristic of creative living.

## IMPLICATIONS FOR PSYCHOTHERAPY

What is the relevance of all this for therapeutic practice? Patients seek help in a state of uncertainty and confusion. Something is 'wrong', but they do not know what this is, or what to do about it. Footsteps may have to be retraced: a story is needed which will both explain how they arrived where they are and point the way forward. Psychotherapy, like art, 'holds a mirror up to nature'.

The patient learns to put his or her feelings into words; these are then 'reflected back' by the therapist ('marking'); the patient then rechecks this reflection for its congruence/contingency/verisimilitude – whether it 'feels right'; finally a representation, or story is formed.

The narrative approach within psychoanalysis described so far has not gone unchallenged, however. The most powerful critique of narrative has come from Lacan and his followers. Lacan (1978) was consistently and implacably anti-narrative. For him the stories we tell about are lives are unavoidably alienated from the reality of experience, defensive compensations for our helpessness in the face of an imposed linguistic and societal order symbolised by the no(m) du père – the paternal prohibition and 'naming' that takes us away from the primeval maternal experience, that is beyond words and stories.

This uncompromising view has to be seen in the context of Lacan's reaction to American ego-psychology, which he saw as a betrayal of the radicalism of psychoanalytic message. If we turn, as Bollas (1995) has done, to Freud's original model of dream interpretation, an integration of the narrative with Lacan's anti-narrative critique becomes possible. Bollas describes a cycle in which raw, un-narrativised experience is assembled each night in the form of 'day residues' into a dream narrative, and then 'cracked up' each morning as the dream is dispersed and a further set of fresh experiences presents themselves. Bollas (1995) takes this as a general paradigm for the activity of the unconscious which he sees as continuously fashioning lived life into stories, and then dismantling and dispersing those stories in the light of further experience. Unlike the conscious stories which we tell ourselves, dreams are stories shaped by the unconscious. The meaning of the dream or of the self-narrative is a synthesis, reflecting both the rules of narrative logic of the conscious mind, and the shaping influence of unconscious, emotional responsiveness and need. In therapy the patient learns to build up a 'story-telling function' which takes experience from 'below', and in the light of overall meanings 'from above' (which can be seen as themselves stored or condensed stories) supplied by the therapist, fashions a new narrative about her self and her world.

This schema can be compared with the linguistic triad of signified, sign, and the lexicon from which the sign is drawn (Brockmeier 1997). The sign is linked to the referent via the world of language. Similarly, a story is linked to what I am calling 'raw experience' via a world of meanings. It seems likely that the capacity to make this link is a developmental function, mediated by early attachment experience. The attuned mother responds to her infant's affective state, via identification, based on her own 'lexicon' of feelings (Fonagy's RSF). A 'story' is offered to the infant ('Oh you're feeling hungry, cold, bored, cross, wet, tired . . .' etc.) which in turn forms the germ of that child's RSF. If the care-giver is avoidant, the range and complexity of the stories will be limited; if she is intrusive they will fail to match the child's experience. The care-giver does not just soothe her infant, she also symbolises the soothing process. In later life the child in whom this has failed may lack both the capacity for self-soothing (so characteristic of borderline patients), and the ability to talk about, or symbolise their distress. Here we have a model for transgenerational transmission of psychopathology, and a picture of how psychotherapy might help break that cycle.


## NARRATIVE AS A THERAPEUTIC TECHNIQUE

How does the psychotherapist function as an 'assistant autobiographer'? In this concluding section I shall consider some ways in which the narrative principles so far elaborated impinge on the psychotherapeutic process.

The first task of the therapist is to assist the patient to tell her story. The starting point will be some form of distress: desires have been thwarted, or hopes dashed. The attachment research outlined above suggests that secure attachment is marked by coherent stories that convince and hang together, where detail and overall plot are congruent, and where the teller is not so detached that affect is absent, is not dissociated from the content of her story, nor is so overwhelmed that her feelings flow formlessly into every crevice of the dialogue. Insecure attachment, by contrast, is characterised either by stories that are over-elaborated and enmeshed (unmarked), or by dismissive, poorly fleshed-out accounts, that lack contingency-testing. In one it is barely possible to discern a coherent story at all; in the other the story is so schematic or vague that it lacks the detail upon which verisimilitude depends.

Starting with the assessment interview, the therapist will use her narrative competence to help the patient shape the story into a more coherent pattern. With an enmeshed patient the therapist will intro-duce frequent 'shaping' remarks or punctuations such as 'We'll come back to what happened to you as a child in a minute; first let's hear more about what is troubling you right now . . .'. Note the 'We'll . . .', 'Let's . . .' construction in which therapist and patient are brought into an unitary position as joint students of the story. This is the beginnings of objectification, but also a model for an internal observing ego (or self-reflexive self) that can listen to and modulate feelings. Shaping a story is the narrative version of the modulation and responsiveness of the security-transmitting care-giver.

With a dismissive patient the therapist will elicit narrative in a different way, always searching for detailed images, memories and exam-ples that bring perfunctory stories to life. 'What was your mother like . . . ?'; 'Can you remember an incident that illustrates that . . . ?'; 'When did you first start to feel so miserable . . . ?'; 'When you say you feel depressed, what does that feel like . . . ?'; 'Whereabouts in your body do you experience your unhappiness . . . ?'

In both cases, the therapist offers intermittent summarising or 'marking' remarks which serve to demarcate 'the story so far', and to confront the patient with a narrative construction against which to measure the raw material of their experience. Some of these comments may be purely, yet pointedly, descriptive: 'When you were talking about your relationship with your husband you appeared to be apathetic and defeated, yet when you started to tell me about your children you become quite animated!'. Others will be more general and overarching: 'You seem to be confident about your relationships with women, including your mother and girlfriends, but to feel much more uncertain when you come to speak about men . . .'. These kinds of intervention would perhaps be classified as 'pre-interpretations', yet by translating a shared experience into verbal form, they are interpretative in the sense of carrying over experience in one medium ('raw experience', affect) into another (words, narrative conventions). Here again we find a variant of the semiotic triad of signified, sign, and language.

As therapy proceeds, the shaping process becomes less obvious, and is probably most evident in the therapist's rhythms of activity and silence, the balance between verbal interventions and 'mmm . . .'s, grunts, and indrawn breaths. Like an attuned parent, the effective therapist will intuitively sense when the patient needs stimulus and direction to keep the thread of narrative alive, when she needs to be left alone to explore her feelings without intrusion or control. Sometimes, especially when the therapy feels stuck, the therapist may simply describe, or tell the story of what has happened, either in a particular session or sequence of sessions: 'You started off today seeming rather sad, and finding it hard to focus, then you began to talk about how difficult you always find Christmas, then you mentioned your friend's aunt who died suddenly . . .'. This story may well then provoke a realisation, or moment of insight such as 'Oh . . . it was Christmas when my grandmother died, I always feel a bit down at this time of year . . . maybe that is why . . .'. This will mark the end of this narrative sequence; the narrative is dispersed, mingled with new experience, until a new narrative sequence emerges.

In psychoanalytic psychotherapy the transference becomes a 'meta-story' which shapes the overall therapeutic interaction. Each session consists of a number of narrative episodes: what happened on the way to the session, an argument at work, something that happened with a partner, a memory from childhood, and so on. Luborsky (1984) has shown that most therapy sessions contain roughly three such episodes.

Let us say the patient starts the session before a holiday break by talking about an incident at work in which his boss asked him to do a job, but without showing him clearly how it was to be carried out. The therapist might comment: 'There seems to be a story here about being left to fend for yourself without proper support . . . '. This might then prompt the patient to talk about how his parents left him in charge of his younger brother without explanation, and how frightened and angry he felt about this. This in turn may lead to a sudden realisation about how upset he is about the coming break. A core story is emerging about abandonment and the response it evokes.

Implicit in my argument so far is the view that psychological health (closely linked to secure attachment) depends on a dialectic between story-making and story-breaking, between the capacity to form narrative, and to disperse it in the light of new experience. In Main's (1995) evocative phrase, the securely attached child shows a 'fluidity of attentional gaze', and in adult life narrative capacity similarly moves between fluidity and form, between structure and 'de-structuring', construction and deconstruction. This capacity ultimately depends on being able to trust both intimacy and aggression (Holmes 1996) – which form the basis of much psychotherapeutic work. Intimacy provides the closeness needed if meaning and experience are to be woven into narrative; trusting one's aggression enables these stories to be broken up and allowed to reform into new patterns. The attachment perspective I have adopted suggests three prototypical pathologies of narrative capacity: clinging to rigid stories; being overwhelmed by unstoried experience; or being unable to find a narrative strong enough to contain traumatic pain.

## THE ROLE OF THE THERAPIST

Psychotherapeutic work tests not just the skills of the therapist but also her personal strengths. Her moral maturity will be exposed, especially her ability to use her own feelings in the service of the therapy, without allowing them to direct, dominate or intrude upon the patient (Holmes and Lindley 1997). Such maturity would be a goal for a therapist who will inevitably draw on her own experience and preoccupations in her identification with her patients, but at the same time has to find a distance which enables her to allow the patient's imagination to flourish, unimpeded by control or manipulation. Thus the therapist's attachment style, and, *pari passu*, her narrative style will be an all important element in determining the outcome of therapy. Enmeshed therapists tend to

impose their own narrative on patients, or get bogged down in interminable stories that have no end, while those with avoidant styles may
fail to pick up on vital emotional cues, and jump to unwarranted conclusions. The therapist's task is to be attuned while retaining her balance,
a position I have called 'non-attachment' (Holmes 1996). Each story
is there to be revised in the light of new experience, new facets of
memory, new meanings.

In this chapter I have tried to bring to life the cycle of narrative
construction and deconstruction which I believe is central to the therapeutic process. I have argued that narrative has its psychobiological
origins in the 'marking' and contingency of maternal mirroring. I have
traced the links between infant attachment patterns and adult narrative styles. I have tried to show how in psychotherapy the therapist
shapes patients' story-telling and mirrors their affective experience in
a way that leads to a more secure sense of self. My concluding hope is
that some fragments of this story will coalesce in the mind of the reader
to form the building blocks for more tales, as yet untold.

## REFERENCES

Bateman, A. and Holmes, J. (1995). *An Introduction to Psychoanalysis.* London:
Routledge.
Beniot, D. and Parker, K. (1994). Stabilty and transmission of attachment
across three generations. *Child Development,* 65:1444–1456.
Bollas, C. (1995). *Cracking Up.* London: Routledge.
Brockmeier, J. (1998). Autobiography, narrative, and the Freudian conception
of life history. *Philosophy, Psychiatry, Psychology.*
Bruner, J. (1986). *Actual Minds, Possible Worlds.* Cambridge, MA: Harvard
University Press.
Fonagy, P., Steele, M., Steele, H., Leigh, T., et al. (1995). Attachment, the
reflective self, and borderline states: the predictive specificity of the adult
attachment interview and pathological emotional development. In
*Attachment Theory: Social, Developmental and Clinical Significance,* eds S.
Goldberg, R. Muir and J. Kerr. Hillsdale, NJ: Analytic Press.
Fonagy, P., Steele, M., Steele, H. *et al.* (1991). The capacity for understanding
mental states: the reflective self in parent and child and its significance for
security of attachment. *Infant Mental Health Journal,* 12:201–218.
Freud, S. (1985) *The Complete Letters of Sigmund Freud to Wilhelm Fliess:
1887–1905.* Cambridge, MA: Harvard University Press.
Freud, S. (1911). *Formulations On The Two Principles of Mental Functioning.*
Standard Edition, 12:215–217.
Gergely, G. and Watson, J. (1996). The social biofeedback theory of parental
affect-mirroring. *International Journal of Psycho-Analysis,* 77:1181–1212.

Holmes, J. (1992). *Psychotherapy: Between Art and Science*. London: Routledge.

Holmes, J. (1993). *John Bowlby and Attachment Theory*. London: Routledge.

Holmes, J. (1996). *Attachment, Intimacy, Autonomy: Using Attachment Theory in Adult Psychotherapy*. New York: Jason Aronson.

Holmes, J. and Lindley, R. (1997) *The Values of Psychotherapy*. London: Karnac.

Lacan, J. (1978). *The Four Fundamental Concepts of Psychoanalysis*. New York: Norton.

Luborsky, L. (1984). *Principles of Psychoanalytic Psychotherapy*. New York: Basic Books.

MacIntyre, A. (1981). *After Virtue*. Notre Dame: University of Notre Dame Press.

Main, M. (1995). Recent studies of attachment: overview with selected implications for clinical work. In *Attachment Theory: Social, Developmental and Clinical Perspectives*, eds S. Goldberg, R. Muir and J. Kerr. Hillsdale, NJ: Analytic Press.

Phillips, J. (1998). The psychoanalytic narrative. In *Healing Stories: Narrative in Psychiatry and Psychotherapy*, eds G. Roberts and J. Holmes. Oxford: Oxford University Press.

Ricoeur, P. (1970). *Freud and Philosophy: An Essay in Interpretation*. New Haven, CT: Yale University Press.

Schafer, R. (1992). *Retelling a Life: Narration and Dialogue in Psychoanalysis*. New York: Basic Books.

Spence, D. (1992). *Narrative Truth and Historical Truth: Meaning and Interpretation in Psychoanalysis*. New York: Norton.

Wallerstein, R. (ed.) (1992) *The Common Ground of Psychoanalysis*. New York: Jason Aronson.

White, M. and Epston, D. (1990). *Narrative Means to Therapeutic Ends*. New York: Norton.

Winnicott, D. (1967). Mirror-role of mother and family in child development. In *The Predicament of the Family*, ed. P. Lomas. London: Hogarth.

Winnicott, D. (1991). *Playing and Reality*. London: Penguin

# Introduction to chapter 10

Sepping's approach to narrative derives, without apology, from clinical experience and in particular the practical constraints of working with adolescent patients. They are likely to be less responsive than adults to the more confrontational impositions of conventional interpretation. His discussion illustrates how stories are likely to be introduced, deliberately or spontaneously, by client or therapist. As he moves to consider when they are most effective, it is evident that narrative in this context requires co-construction. The process that unfolds appears consistent with post-modern ideals of social constructivism within and outside therapy . . . positing nothing 'inner' at all.

# 10 Narrative and interpretation

*Paul Sepping*

Why was *Sophie's World* (Gaarder, 1994) the only history of philosophy to have ever been in the bestseller lists of fiction? Most observers judge that its clever *narrative* handling brought this often turgidly presented subject to a level of accessibility never previously achieved. If this is true, then is it possible that the therapist's clinical repertoire could well include an element of narrative competence? Eventually, Sophie learned that she was only a character in someone else's story. She had begun by assuming she was real. Now her problem was how to avoid remaining unreal. The end of that story shows her initial efforts to create a story 're-vision' (Parry and Doan, 1994). She had to develop a real story of her own (Freedman and Combs, 1996), i.e. to 'authorise' her own narrative.

Narrative is coming to be used more in the non-analytic aspects of various therapies such as family therapy (Byng-Hall, 1988, and Zimmerman and Dickerson, 1994), in group therapy (Ganns, 1991), in occupational therapy (Fazio, 1992) and in nursing (Wenckus, 1994). In the psychoanalytic tradition, the use of narrative has been largely confined to the therapist's presentation of case histories in professional clinical journals. Freud began the tradition with the use of his considerable literary skills to portray case histories in professional texts, as well as in his critiques of art and artists in the pathographies. More recently the theory and practice of analytic therapy itself has been viewed as a group of narratives not necessarily internally consistent (Schafer, 1993 and Berlin *et al.*, 1991).

## CLIENTS' STORIES

Patients present their therapist with narrative in many different ways which can be classified as follows:

1. The patient's 'problem narrative' and 'life narrative'
2. Their account of another's problem narrative and life narrative, e.g. their mother's, father's, siblings', children's
3. Their account of their own dreams, daydreams and associations
4. Their non-verbal presentations of self in the therapy encounter
5. The patient's reference to a preformed narrative from the media, e.g. TV soap opera, play, poem, novel, song lyrics, myth, folklore, the daily 'news'.

It is often easier for people to exchange these 'third person narratives' (2, 3 and 5) with their therapists than disclosing intimate aspects of their life narrative, at least in the early sessions. In later sessions, reference back to a shared 'story' may also be a shorthand way for a patient to feel 'contained' or 'attached' to the person of the therapist. It is the therapist's nonverbal response which, above all, spells the difference between an enriched deepening of the therapeutic alliance, or a stalling of the joining process (Sepping, 1995).

The following vignettes will illustrate some clinical applications of the principle that verbal discourse between patient and therapist need not be interpretative to be transformative. In fact, it may be that it was *because* the discourse was not interpretative that these adolescent patients found they could 'swallow' the therapy process. It is important to note that when we speak of 'X swallowed the story' we are usually referring to a way of dissembling to a gullible victim. But the practice of clothing a message in a comfortable coating should not be rejected on that account. A good medicine as well as poison can be given a sweet vehicle to aid its consumption.

Alan, a 13-year-old boy, was drawing 'Sylvester the Cat and Tweetie Pie' in the waiting room. The therapist encouraged the boy to bring the drawing into the therapy room. Discussion continued about the personality of the more likeable character, Sylvester, as someone who goes after what he needs (i.e. to eat Tweetie Pie) without guilt. No mention was made of the boy's intractable asthma until later in the session. By that time, the mental set was such that freer discourse occurred about grannies who are mean and grandads who are boring. He 'got things off his chest' in an atmosphere where he could breathe more easily. No interpretation was necessary at this point. Alan was able to come off his deforming steroid medication. In this example, third-person narrative was not 'nothing but' defensive, but can be seen as indirectly revealing. If this is responded to as such, the client may go on to less indirect forms of self-disclosure, revealing fascinations and phobias never previously expressed or perhaps never

previously even admitted into consciousness. Thus without an interpretation ever having been made, the healing process has been
progressed.

Another example was Beatrice, a 17-year-old girl presenting with
ME syndrome ('myalgic encephalomyelitis') who struck up a conversation about her beloved badminton. Therapist and patient conducted a
playful discourse regarding famous players (? heroines) and tactics
(? also referring to the therapeutic encounter) which created a relationship where it was possible to relax and 'toy with' the therapeutic
relationship. The exhaustion experienced in the counter-transference
was not verbalised by the therapist but Beatrice improved, resumed her
badminton, put on weight, continued her advanced school studies, and
did well.

## THERAPISTS' STORIES

From the *therapist's* side, interpretations have themselves been viewed as
the use of narrative (Spence, 1990). Thus, one can regard the therapist's
interpretations as small, discrete steps in deconstructing and reconstructing a story for the patient at the suggestion of the analyst. This new
story might form a variant or alternative narrative to that initially presented by the patient of his/her life history and current relationships.

The exception to the absence of purposive story-telling by analytic
therapists is in the area of child psychotherapy. Pioneering child therapists as long ago as the 1930s (Despert and Potter, 1936) suggested
the use of stories either purely by the therapist or combined with
metaphor suggested by the child patient. Various methods have been
suggested to prompt the child to share story-telling with the therapist
involving the use of cards, icons or role play (Gardner, 1969).
'Prompting' the child might be seen as undesirable in most cases, as
latency age children will usually become expressive in therapy if given
a modicum of time within which to get their bearings. The exception
to this generalisation is the severely deprived child (possibly abused)
who may present as 'frozenly watchful'. Here, 'analytical silence' might
be the response that signals the end of the possibility of a therapeutic
alliance and the precursor of drop-out.

As regards adult psychotherapy, the problem for the analyst is that
the introduction by him/her of a story seems at first sight to conflict
with the basic tenet of the therapist's behaviour being one of evenly
floating attention, whilst encouraging the patient to freely associate.
However, *metaphors* based on material originally provided by the patient

are being used for elaboration in the analytic dyad (McMullen, 1989). This technique has been used by Cox (1987) with offenders in a maximum security institution. His extensive knowledge of Shakespeare provided a rich repertoire of response to inmates' accounts of their own dramatic encounters with their victims.

Bettelheim (1975) has analysed *parent* story-telling but his approach refrained from commenting on story-telling as a *professional* therapeutic manoeuvre in the clinical setting. Similarly, Eifermann (1993) has examined fairytale telling, with regard to the variations of the story introduced by the parent's needs as well as the needs of the child, as follows:

> such story-telling is in fact an interactive process, through which the mother expresses her own unconscious wishes, needs and defences regarding her child . . . one such need consciously denied, is to sometimes expose the child to a certain degree of cruelty and fright through the tale.
>
> (Eifermann, 1993, p.446)

The complications introduced by story-telling at the transference level have been reviewed by Olinick and Tracey (1987) but again these authors have confined themselves to examples of the patient's story-telling. However, this type of examination is useful in principle when the prospect of therapist story-telling comes to be considered, as some of the variables can likewise be applied to the opposite person in the therapeutic dialogue. They state,

> In a psychoanalysis, we see these motives and their transformations in a light that illuminates other story telling as well. Story telling uses its audiences as does the analysand who creates and utilizes a transference figure in the person of the analyst – by enacting verbally and deceptively in order to resolve or circumvent the now symbolized but unfinished, anxious, conflicted experiences of the past. The teller of any tale enlists the reader or listener to act as his agent or deputy, his champion or antagonist, his scapegoat or persecutor. Each assigned role is in collusion and conflict with others contributing to an ambiguity that may be both intriguing and disturbing.
>
> (Olinick and Tracey, 1987, p.320)

The authors here are addressing the more neurotic possibilities of story-telling, whereas the health promoting possibilities have interestingly been omitted.

This negative attitude to the clinical use of fictional stories is characteristic of psychoanalytic criticism. Third person narratives are labelled 'defensive' or as 'nothing but resistance', which calls into question the appropriateness of the psychoanalytic paradigm itself, if one wishes to address the needs of a wide variety of patients.

Critiques by non-analytic observers of the analytic paradigm have come from within the psychiatric discipline. Kirmayer writes,

> [t]his position is based on the conviction that there is an authoritative interpretation of symptoms and symbols that is simply waiting to be discovered by the astute observer. However, if every interpretation of distress is, at root, the invention of metaphors for experience, healing may occur because the metaphorization of distress gives the person room to maneuver, imaginative possibilities, behavioural options, and rhetorical supplies.
>
> (Kirmayer, 1993, p.165)

He has examined the poetics of myth, metaphor and archetype in the healing process as follows, 'metaphoric invention thus occurs both in the acts of speaking and of listening . . . chief among the vices of metaphor is profligacy . . . plurality of meanings induced by the indeterminacy of texts is less obvious in spoken language of discourse'. Kirmayer suggests that myth (which has been created by culture) and archetype (which has been suggested by bodily/brain processes) can be harmonised by the use of metaphor, narrative and ritual.

Other professions allied to the therapeutic task, such as cultural anthropology have also added their insights to the discourse on the nature of the therapist's dialogue with the analytic patient (Levi-Strauss, 1963, 1978). He observed that the decline of traditional myth is coincidental with the rise of the novel and that much of pop psychology may imply that the myths required for modern life can be the result of self-authorisation. This ability to authorise myth may not be a skill of which all are capable.

The implication is that there may be certain people who are by virtue of disposition or training, more mythopoetic, though he does not go as far as to imply that they would come from any particular profession, such as that of psychotherapy.

More recently, the debate has been broadened by the entry of literary philosophers such as Paul Ricoeur (1991).

Ricoeur refers to the worlds of the reader and the text interacting to create 'new modes of being' so that each agent – text and reader – contributes to a 'hermeneutic circle'. Although this point of view derives from the non-clinical situation of literature, Ricoeur points out that the power of myth and story to 'create new worlds' is impressive and makes links to the philosophies of Husserl and Heidegger on the one hand and to Aristotle's *Poetics* on the other. For example, he writes, 'in his *Poetics*, Aristotle paved the way for a generalization of metaphor conceived as heuristic fiction by linking metaphor as a rhetorical trait to the main operation of poetry which is the building of a *mythos*, of a fable' (Ricoeur, 1991, p.84).

## INTERPRETATION

It is clear that we all use the art of interpretation in our everyday discourses within our multiple relationships. Freud's use of *'Die Traumdeutung'* has been translated as *The Interpretation of Dreams* and many of us feel this is a poor translation of *'deutung'* as 'interpretation'. However, interpretation has become the word used by psychoanalysts for the mutative agent among the verbal contributions in the analytic discourse. Literary critics also use the word 'interpretation', as do musicians and artists generally.

What I (as a therapist) 'make of' what you (as a patient) tell me, how I construe it, is one way of giving you feedback about 'where I think you are' *and* of providing you with information about me, and 'where I'm coming from', i.e. it is a jointly revealing response. So is what you are telling me, because it is me you have chosen to tell. The meanings I derive from your story is my interpretation. But these meanings can be offered to you in a direct way (a formal interpretation) or in an indirect way (by way of a narrative), using my conscious and unconscious associations to your story.

Formal psychoanalytic interpretations often include the story of the dyadic analytic encounter (i.e. transference interpretations) as well as the life story that the patient brings to the analyst. However, interpretations can be viewed either as 'telling the truth' (in a positivist sense) to the patient about their predicament, or they can be viewed as intuitive co-constructions (in a post-modernist sense) which, if successful, have a liberating effect on the patient's view of his life, himself and his relationship with the therapist.

Ricoeur proposes that *texts* produce a surplus of meanings each of which is a suggestion of a new way of 'being-in-the-world' (Heidegger) or the *'Lebenswelt'* (or 'life-world') of the community of language-users (Husserl); or if you prefer Wittgenstein to Heidegger, new 'forms of life'. Because Ricoeur is applying his philosophy to literary criticism, it is important in the above quotations (as well as those below) to think of substituting for the word *text* the concept of the patient's verbal and nonverbal communications with the therapist. In thinking about the meaning that is made by a patient of a therapist's communication, Ricoeur writes:

> [i]t implies, instead, a moment of dispossession of the narcissistic *ego*. Only the interpretation which satisfies the injunction of the text, which follows the 'arrow' of meaning and endeavours to 'think in accordance with' it, engenders a new *self*-understanding. By the expression '*self*-understanding', I should like to contrast the *self* which emerges from the understanding of the text to the ego which claims to precede this understanding. It is the text, with its universal power of unveiling, which give a *self* to the ego.
>
> (Ricoeur, 1991, p.97)

Spence (1990) refers to 'the rhetorical voice of psychoanalysis' being in disfavour since Plato mounted his first attack against it. However, he points to the importance of 'keeping the metaphor alive', avoiding reification and defends the use of metaphor because 'there is no other language available'. Therapy, he maintains, should remain true to 'the poetry of Freud's original inspiration' and the 'spirit of the whole adventure'. Whilst he also argues for the safeguarding of the evidential voice of psychoanalysis, he concedes that 'meanings are frequently ambiguous and context determined'. One can argue that the meaning of narrative, in the context of a *particular* clinical dyadic discourse, is not necessarily more indeterminate than the meaning of classical interpretation.

The opposite argument can also be put: namely, that interpretation can very easily sound to the patient like exhortation, whether or not the therapist is conscious of the fact that the patient is hearing it in this way. An illustration of this occurred in a teenagers' group when the therapist said the group was mistrustful of itself. He changed the tone of his voice to indicate irritation when Alison (an anxious and garrulous 16-year-old girl) butted in to protest that she felt the interpretation was wrong. The effect of the interpretation was that Alison became less garrulous because she felt spoken sternly to, but the group missed the intended meaning of the interpretation i.e. that the group members felt anxious about trusting to the group process. Interpretations often have unforeseen effects, as in this example.

On the other hand, Holland (1993, p.330) cautions that 'each of us will find in the literary work the kind of thing we characteristically wish or fear the most . . . because all readers form the fantasy seemingly "in" the work, fantasies that suit their several character structures'. This suggests that, if a therapist shares a story with the group, the story prefigured by the therapist is less critical than the patient's own configuration and refiguration of it. Yet Holland goes on to state: 'the psychoanalytic psychologist can give precision to what the philosophers adumbrated: interpretation recreates identity considered specifically as defence, fantasy and ego style' (Holland, 1993, p.337).

Skura (1993) has made the point that the 'analyst must draw on *all* the ways by which one human being understands another' (p.374, my italics). The situation in analysis however becomes more complex when, by drawing actively on one set of ways, the therapist may disqualify herself from using another set of ways. For instance, the use of story-telling automatically invalidates the encouragement to free association, at least during the time that the story is told. On the other hand, therapists' interpretations also interrupt the flow of free association. Skura goes on to elucidate:

> many analysts themselves are coming to see *exchanges* in the psychoanalytic process as the important part of psychoanalysis, whether their interest is expressed in the Continental philosophy in terms of discourse with the 'other', or in terms of the transference and counter-transference that Freud first described.
>
> (Skura, 1993, p.375)

Unfortunately, Skura does not make it clear whether discourse with the 'other' includes the use of the therapist's narrative or not. She does go on to state that 'the analyst's work is not to make revelations but to find conditions for them'. The way that this problem is stated may be a false dichotomy. In other words, it is not at all clear whether narratives as told by a therapist could qualify as stimulating the conditions for revelations by the patient.

In my limited experience with story-telling, I have found that there are bad and good uses for the technique. Stories that have been artificially contrived by one's conscious planning to hone a tale in response to the patient's creativity are less helpful than stories which are thrown up by the counter-transference. It is these stories (after checking for any obvious contraindication) that I have told to the patient without necessarily understanding the meaning of the story myself.

An illustration of this was when a boy aged 10 was sent to me after his father had spent five years dying of a degenerative disease. Not only had he witnessed his painful and lingering death, but had also to some extent lost the immediate services of his mother who was struggling herself to come to terms with the loss of her husband. Classical psycho-analytic methods seemed to me to be less available and helpful than the use of the story. This involved a boy being shipwrecked when on a journey with his parents and sister at sea. The story involved him being marooned on a desert island whilst the rest of the family continued through the storm on board and eventually arrived safely at their destination. The boy becomes aware of certain things on the island, including a potentially hostile native tribe but eventually by use of a book and some wit, convinces the tribe to help him find his family again. The boy plus his helpers encounter various adventures on the journey by land and sea and the 'odyssey' eventually ends with the reunification of his family.

Contrasted with the very successful response in the boy to this story was a later story (which involved King Arthur and the Vikings) and which seemed to have a far less liberating effect. There was an important reason for this manoeuvre's therapeutic failure. Whilst the content should have been gripping for a latency-age boy (knights, battles, magic), the therapist's inspiration (derived from the patient's partially digested projections), was absent. That is to say, my choice of this story did not arise out of, or at all connect with, my countertransference (a bad and common mistake in the use of narrative-as-therapy), but was one I consciously selected because logically it seemed appropriate.

## INTERPLAY: TO PRODUCE A PLURALITY OF THERAPEUTIC STORIED INTERPRETATIONS

Winnicott's excellent squiggle game is just one possible 'joining' response to the 'frozen' ambivalent child or adolescent. It involves an element of 'exchange' between therapist and patient which in itself can act as a therapeutic factor (Brown and Zinkin, 1994, p.99). Whilst I would not suggest departing from the culture of verbal or written interchange with the patient in the analytical therapies, it is more creative to encourage a certain modicum of play with narrative and metaphor.

The patient of 11 who asks 'if any of the books on your shelf have pictures' can be invited to flip through a book of short tales. He/she can be asked to run his/her eye over a list of titles and choose anything that catches his/her eye. She/he can be given a choice of reading or listening to the story or perhaps sharing the narrative by listening to and reading alternate paragraphs. Most of my patients choose to listen initially and some want to repeat the exercise at the start of each session. Eventually the experience becomes a shared one with listening and reading; then speaking freely from one's own 'internal books' becomes a spontaneous process.

However the most acceptable use of narrative in therapy is when the patient provides a narrative and the therapist responds in an encouraging attentive fashion. Apart from the 'life narrative', the patient may refer to his/her day dreams, his/her friend's dreams or life story; or refer to a publicly available narrative such as a TV 'soap', the lyrics of a song or 'rap', a famous play, film, myth, folk-story or simply the daily news bulletin. The crucial point is how the therapist responds to such offerings from the patient. If the narrative is seen as 'nothing but' a defensive manoeuvre, then valuable insights can be lost and the therapeutic relationship can be silently attenuated.

On the other hand, if uncritical 'applause' is given to the patient, valuable time may be wasted in getting to the heart of his/her ailments. Also the relationship may be handicapped by an unnecessarily seductive element creeping into the patient's image of the therapist.

Steering between these two poles, therefore, is the 'playful response'. It is a way forward with some defensive patients especially when young. Playing with a narrative can not only include getting the patient to associate to a dream but also asking for other possible alternative consequences, altered agencies (e.g. active to passive), and novel endings or conclusions to the story.

Some child therapists will already allow themselves to act out the voices of various stories suggested by the patients. A colleague was asked by a 10-year-old girl to act the part of both the good queen and the bad queen in 'Snow White'. This departure from orthodox child therapy is one step on the way to the full use of narrative.

Such techniques are fraught with dangers I am sure, but may contain some promise in the 'ripe' situation. Fordham (1993, p.128) might provide an indication for when such a clinical occasion is ripe. In his paper 'On Not Knowing Beforehand', he mentions 'a story telling method . . . requiring an extensive knowledge of myth, legend and religion'. He uses the experience of 'digesting the projection', of a 'syntonic countertransference' in a therapist, 'eschewing knowledge, memory and desire', quoting Bion. Although the thrust of his paper is the analyst's need to make interpretations, he advocates the virtues of not accessing the 'filing cabinet' of the case history details.

Classically, of course, it is the child who plays and the therapist who tries her best to give comment or a running narrative to the child's productions in play with, say, the dolls' house or the farm animals. This has the advantage that the therapist uses only the child's stories, or the best approximation that the therapist's interpretation can provide, of the child's 'play-story'. But using tales from a book could be seen as better than no tale at all from the 'frozen child', and has the added bonus of signalling to the patient that a philosophy of narrative exchange is a legitimate activity in the therapy room.

The philosophical underpinnings of the above approach invoke a social constructionist perspective, which sees narrative as constituting the substance of relationships, through the stories we tell ourselves. Geertz comes closest to the idea that positivism may not be so much refutable as irrelevant (in many cases), in the following:

> a challenge is being mounted to some of the central assumptions of mainstream social science. The strict separation of theory and data, the 'brute fact' idea; the effort to create a formal vocabulary of analysis purged of all subjective reference, the 'ideal language' idea; and the claim to moral neutrality and the Olympian view, 'the God's truth' idea – none of these can prosper when explanation comes to be regarded as a matter of connecting action to its sense rather than behavior to its determinates. The refiguration of social theory represents, or will if it continues, a sea change in our notion not so much of what knowledge is but of what it is we want to know.
>
> (Geertz, 1983, p.34)

## BOTH NARRATIVES *AND* INTERPRETATIONS

As Klauber points out, 'Balint stated as early as 1939 that the very possibility of the mirrorlike attitude recommended by Freud was being generally called into question' (Klauber, 1986, p.31). He goes on to state that

> one of the difficulties in the theory of the therapeutic process has been a tendency to see it too much from the point of view of the content of interpretation at the expense of adequate study of the meaning of interpretation in the complex relationship of mutual transference.
>
> (ibid.)

Thus from the time of Strachey's formidable paper in 1934 on 'The Nature of the Therapeutic Action of Psychoanalysis', a sea change has been at work, redefining interpretation from 'militant interpretation' or 'interpretative fervour' (Kohon 1986, p.68) to one which overtly emphasises the subjectivity of the therapist as much as analysing projections of the patient. No longer do the transference interpretations of the 'you mean me' sort (Coltart, quoted in Kohon, 1986, p.72) have such an exclusive claim to be *the* transactions that do the therapeutic work.

On the contrary, Winnicott notes that 'in psychoanalytic practice the positive changes that come about . . . can be profound. They do not depend on interpretative work. They depend on the analyst's survival of the attacks'. He took the view that one reason for using interpretations was to let the patient know that the analyst has not completely understood everything that he/she is thinking. He goes on to say 'the analyst feels like interpreting, but this can spoil the process, and for the patient can seem like a kind of self-defence' (Winnicott, 1971 p.108).

Now it is clear that interpretations *and* narrative can both be used defensively or they can be used creatively as in Symington's 'x-phenomenon'. Symington hypothesised that 'at one level the analyst and patient together make a single system. . . . As the analytical work proceeds the analyst slowly disengages himself from it' (Symington, 1983). He coined the term 'x-phenomenon' for that inner act of freedom that the therapist uses to liberate him/her self from the shared illusion of the therapy process. He defined this x-phenomenon as the transformational object of therapy.

Kohon (1986) thinks of the x-phenomenon as an act of *commitment* by the analyst to her patient. He makes the important addition that an analyst only begins to become an analyst when 'a patient shows signs that I have become an object in his imaginary world . . . the work as an analyst can now start'. In other words, it is first necessary to qualify with the patient as being worthy of introjection. My suggestion, therefore, is that analytical psychotherapists[1] could occasionally avail themselves of the story-telling or 'story co-constructing' mode of response in an attempt to qualify for the patient's consideration as an internal object. I am also suggesting that stories told by the patient *or* the analyst can have a second function; that of analysis itself, i.e. a transformational function.

Therefore, can the term 'interpretation' be redefined to include such a narrative activity on the part of the therapist? Kohon has described the increasingly wide category in which therapists' verbal contributions can be seen as 'interpretations', as follows:

> [i]nterpretations are like swings, the slide, the climbing frame, the sandpit in the playground – a word used by Freud to refer to the

transference situation – in which analysand and analyst are playing. Interpretations are not the dice in a game, but at the same time they can not be considered statements of fact. Interpretations are formed by real words but they constitute an imaginary story. The story is a fiction that takes place in a world created by the mutual working influence of analyst and analysand, with characters borrowed from reality. When we interpret we try to explain, we attempt to elucidate, we would like to make something clear; but we also give our own interpretations, as one does in interpreting a composition in music, a landscape in painting, or a drama in the theatre.

(Kohon, 1986, p.68)

But can one accurately describe a shared narrative (possibly about a fictional hero or heroine or beast) as 'an interpretation'? I think it is unreasonable to do so.

Which leaves us with the hypothesis that there is a new candidate for truly mutative input in the analytical (and other 'dynamic') psychotherapies – the co-constructed story.

Perhaps the occasion on which a shared narrative is helpful occurs when the countertransference inspired story happens to be resonant with the personal myth of the patient (Potamianou, 1988), in a way which is enabling to the patient by virtue of the therapist's partial digestion of the projective identification. Some stories in some dyads seem to have an inner need to be told, as in a birth process the baby needs to be born. These instances can be described as times when a narrative truly comes of age.

## NOTES

1   Coltart's (1982) paper, 'Slouching towards Bethlehem . . . or thinking the unthinkable in psychoanalysis', included in Kohon (1986), rightly draws here a distinction between what is the correct response from a psychoanalyst and from a psychotherapist: 'there is a possible solution or definition here of that controversial problem, the difference between psychotherapy and psychoanalysis'.

## REFERENCES

Berlin, R. et al. (1991) Metaphor and Psychotherapy. *American Journal of Psychotherapy* 45, 3: 359–367.

Berman, E. (ed.) (1993) *Essential Papers on Literature and Psychoanalysis*. New York University Press, New York.

Bettelheim, B. (1975) *The Uses of Enchantment: The Meaning and Importance of Fairy Tales.* Penguin, London.

Brown, D. and Zinkin, L. (1994) *The Psyche and the Social World: Developments in Group Analytic Theory.* Routledge, London.

Byng-Hall, J. (1988) Scripts and Legends in Families and Family Therapy. *Family Process* 27: 167–179.

Cox, M. and Theilgaard, A. (1987) *Mutative Metaphors in Psychotherapy: The Aeolian Mode.* Tavistock Publications, London.

Despert, J.L. and Potter, H.W. (1936) Technical Approaches in the Study and Treatment of Emotional Problems in Childhood. *Psychoanalytic Quarterly* 10: 619–638.

Eifermann, R.R. (1993) Textual Analysis and Related Self-Analysis, in *Essential Papers on Literature and Psychoanalysis*, ed. E. Berman. New York University Press, New York 439–455.

Fazio, L.S. (1992) Tell Me a Story: The Therapeutic Metaphor in the Practice of Paediatric Occupational Therapy. *The American Journal of Occupational Therapy* 46, 2: 112–119.

Fordham, M. (1993) On Not Knowing Beforehand. *Journal of Analytical Psychology* 38, 127–136.

Freedman, J. and Combs, G. (1996) *Narrative Therapy, The Social Construction of Preferred Realities.* Norton, New York.

Gaarder, J. (1994) *Sophie's World: A Novel about the History of Philosophy.* Phoenix, London.

Ganns, J.S. (1991) The Leader's use of Metaphor in Group Psychotherapy. *International Journal of Group Psychotherapy* 41, 2: 127–143.

Gardner, R.A. (1969) Mutual Storytelling as a Technique in Child Psychotherapy and Psychoanalysis. *Science and Psychoanalysis* 14: 23–136.

Geertz, C. (1983) *Local Knowledge, Further Essays in Interpretive Anthropology* New York, Basic Books.

Holland, N.N. (1993) Unity Identity Text Self, in *Essential Papers on Literature and Psychoanalysis*, ed. E Berman. New York University Press, New York 323–340 (1975).

Kirmayer, L. J. (1993) Healing and the Invention of Metaphor: the Effectiveness of Symbols Revisited. *Culture, Medicine and Psychiatry*, 17, 161–195.

Klauber, J. (1981) *Difficulties in the Analytic Encounter.* Free Association Books, London.

Kohon, G. (1986) *The British School of Psychoanalysis: The Independent Tradition.* Free Association Books, London.

Levi-Strauss, C. (1963) *Structural Anthropology.* Basic Books, London.

Levi-Strauss, C. (1978) *Myth and Meaning.* Routledge and Kegan Paul, London

McMullen, L.M. (1989) Uses of Figurative Language in Successful and Unsuccessful Cases of Psychotherapy: Three Comparisons. *Metaphor and Symbolic Activity* 4, 4: 203–226.

Olinick, S.L. and Tracey, L. (1987) Transference Perspectives of Story Telling. *Psychoanalytical Review* 74, 3: 319–331.

Parry, A. and Doan, R.E. (1994) *Narrative Therapy in the Post-Modern World*. Guildford Press, New York/London.

Potamianou, A. (1988) The Personal Myth: Points and Counterpoints. *Psychoanalytic Review* 75, 1: 285–296.

Ricoeur, P. (1991) *A Ricoeur Reader. Reflection and Imagination*, ed. Mario J. Valdes. Harvester Wheatsheaf, London.

Schafer, R. (1993) Narration in the Psychoanalytic Dialogue, in *Essential Papers on Literature and Psychoanalysis*, ed. E. Berman, New York University Press, New York 341–365.

Sepping, P. (1995) Group Therapy Within the NHS II: 'Presence' Precedes 'Performance'. *Group Analysis* 28: 367–376.

Skura, M.A. (1993) Literature as Psychoanalytical Process; Surprise and Self-Consciousness, in *Essential Papers on Literature and Psychoanalysis*, ed. E. Berman, New York University Press, New York 374–402 (1981).

Spence, D.P. (1990) The Rhetorical Voice of Psychoanalysis. *Journal of the American Psychoanalytical Association* 38, 3: 579–603.

Strachey, J. (1934) The Nature of the Therapeutic Action of Psychoanalysis. *International Journal of Psychoanalysis* 15: 127–159. (Reprinted 50: 275–292.)

Symington, N. (1983) The Analyst's Act of Freedom as Agent for Therapeutic Change. *International Review of Psycho-Analysis* 10: 283–291.

Wenckus, E.M. (1994) Storytelling: Using an Ancient Art to Work with Groups. *Journal of Psychosocial Nursing* 32, 7:30–32.

Winnicott, D.W. (1971) *Playing and Reality*. Tavistock, London.

Zimmerman, J.L. and Dickerson, V.C. (1994) Using a Narrative Metaphor: Implications for Theory and Clinical Practice. *Family Process* 33: 233–245.

# Introduction to chapter 11

The theme of narrative has been developed within a philosophical context that is 'post-modernist'. Scepticism about the traditional methods and divisions of philosophy feeds critical attitudes towards the substantiality of entities like mind, self and identity. One of the philosopher's tasks is to articulate the limits of a world that is inherently fragmented and which defies the modernist project of seeking universal, certain truths through the exercise of reason. Rather than ride metaphysical war-horses, the post-modern philosopher explores through new themes and tools. Perhaps fittingly, there is as yet no self-recommending introduction to this landscape.

'Reflexivity' had been a preoccupation of phenomenological philosophers keen to define the universal characteristics of human consciousness. Translated into the lived concept of the mirror, an image emerges that has been of much use to philosophers and psychotherapists alike – indeed, in the hands of Jacques Derrida (in his 'philosophy of reflection') and Jacques Lacan (emphasising the 'mirror stage' in early development) it has been used to redefine their respective tasks. It is not fanciful to suppose that this consciousness has infiltrated psychotherapy, as non-Lacanians from Michael Fordham in analytical psychology to Heinz Kohut in self psychology have also used mirroring as a vehicle for novel ideas about development and its possible failures.

In the following essay, Geraldine Shipton looks at the image that remains to be glimpsed through the mirror after all this activity. What remains of the self? What reports can be offered? The concept of 'heterotopias' allows extension of the possibilities of how we conceive of mental space. They are presented in a way that, in extending ideas of the possible, is ripe with therapeutic promise.

# 11 Self-reflection and the mirror

*Geraldine Shipton*

## INTRODUCTION

The role of the mirror is discussed in relation to understanding the self. A brief history of the mirror introduces the role of the mirror in everyday life and then its use as a metaphor in psychoanalysis. Some psychoanalytic concepts about the mirror as construed by Winnicott, Lacan and Dolto are augmented by the work of Lefebvre and Foucault to show how the mirror functions as a heterotopia. It is proposed that psychoanalytic process operates in a similar way as an 'other space' and that the concept of the self, too, has some heterotopian features.

## HISTORY OF THE MIRROR

The history of the mirror is long and fascinating (see Haubl 1991). It is one of the oldest of everyday tools: there are mirrors dating back to pre-Egyptian times; an engraved mirror from the lost Etruscan world; mirrors made of polished brass, entombed with the Ancient Egyptians; Greek mirrors with handles or on stands dating from 600 BC. Written accounts tell us that Demosthenes practised his speeches in front of the mirror and Seneca describes large mirrors in which the whole body could be reflected. The optics of the mirror were studied by Euclid in 300 BC. Ptolemaeus and Heron of Alexandria studied the laws of reflection. It has been suggested that Archimedes used mirrors to set fire to the Roman fleet.

Glass mirrors were made in Phoenicia though little is clear about the exact timing of their introduction: some say 1000 BC others 600–400 BC. However, metal mirrors were often preferred to glass ones which were not so flat and reflected a different picture. The art of making glass mirrors was lost mysteriously and not rediscovered until the thirteenth century in the Venetian region (though, again, some suggest it could have been as early as 700 AD). The Italians held the monopoly of the glass industry until 1618 when England began to manu-facture plane glass independently. New industrial methods enabled mirrors to be produced cheaply though the coating of mercury remained hazardous and was replaced in the second part of the nineteenth century by silver. From the fifteenth century onwards glass began to take the place of metal in mirrors and elaborate frames were acquired. Mirrors became an important part of interior design especially in the baroque and rococo styles. The fashionable application of mirrors to decorate and beautify has gone from strength to strength with the splendour of mirrored halls in aristocratic residences echoed in the more common-place mirrored walls of the Parisian café in the nineteenth century and the current use of mirrors on the exterior of grand buildings and skyscrapers in the late twentieth century.

An even more prolific spread has occurred when it comes to the use of the mirror as a metaphor (see Grabes 1982). From medieval times until 1500 in England alone there were over three hundred titles including the word 'speculum' in their Latin titles (the vernacular included many more). The next two centuries saw a big increase in vernacular titles in which the words 'speculum', 'mirror', 'glass' and 'looking-glass' figured. In the seventeenth century the mirror was used more frequently in connection with religion than in other centuries. In such works the mirror tended to offer possible models of conduct or spiritual edification.

The mirror is one of our earliest known artefacts and the metaphor of the mirror has been used for centuries to represent the relationship of man and his thinking to nature and to the divine. Plato gives Socrates the following lines in his dialogue with Alcibiades:

> [t]hen if the eye is to see itself, it must look into the eye, and at that part of the eye where sight which is the virtue of the eye resides?. . . . May we say, then, that as mirrors are truer and clearer and brighter than the mirror within the eye, so also is God by His nature a clearer and brighter mirror than the most excellent part of our soul?
>
> (Jowett 1953 132d–e; 133a)

Contemporary philosophers have questioned the validity of both ocular-centric notions of knowledge and of the specific mirror metaphor which flattens and falsifies complex reasoning. Rorty argues that: 'The picture which holds traditional philosophy captive is that of the mind as a great mirror, containing various representations – some accurate, some not – and capable of being studied by pure, nonempirical methods' (Rorty 1980: 12). He challenges the assumption that speech externalises inner representations and that it is itself a representation at all, seeing sentences as connected with other sentences rather than as corresponding to something in the world. Feminist philosophers have considered the plane mirror which posits a separate, unilateral perspective and have criticised the imposition of a phallocentric perspective for understanding women (Irigaray: 1974). Irigaray proposes an alternative concave speculum for women if they are to develop knowledge about and for themselves.

Cultural representations which employ the mirror range from the works mentioned by Grabes, through to contemporary film-makers (see the hilarious satire of the mirror sequence in *Duck Soup* (1933), the macho posturing of Travis Bickle in front of his mirror in *Taxi Driver* (1976) or the eerie scenes in *Carrie* (1976) where the mirror signals occult force). As Grabes (1982) suggests, the mirror functions in four different ways: it reflects things as they are; it shows the way things should or shouldn't be; it shows the way things will be; it shows what exists only in the mirror or the imagination. These are also central concerns in how we understand the phantasies reflected in the patient's discourse.

## THE EVERYDAY USE OF THE MIRROR

The mirror also occupies a special position in everyday life: we look in the mirror in the morning as a matter of routine. This habit itself is interesting. It fulfils a mundane function in terms of making sure the self is presented as normal in the world but also constitutes a daily task which may serve less conscious purposes.

> Habit is a compromise effected between the individual and his environment, or between the individual and his own organic eccentricities, the guarantee of a dull inviolability, the lightning-conductor of his existence. Habit is the ballast that chains the dog to his vomit. Breathing is habit. Life is habit. Or rather life is a succession of habits, since the individual is a succession of individuals; the world being a projection of the individual's consciousness (an objectivation of the individual's will, Schopenhauer would say), the pact must be continually renewed, the letter of safe-conduct brought up to date.
>
> (Beckett 1965: 18–19)

Habit prompts us to look in the mirror each morning. This little ritual punctuates the passage of time and frames a wordless pact we make with ourselves, according to Beckett. Habit stands between the self and awareness of death insulating us from the rawness and temporality of being alive even though the mirror has associations with death – traditionally it was covered over in homes where someone had just died. As Heurtebise, the chauffeur of death tells Orpheus in Cocteau's film *Orphée*: 'I am letting you into the secret of all secrets, mirrors are the gates through which death comes and goes. Moreover, if you observe your whole life in a mirror you will see death at work as you see bees behind the glass in a hive' (Cocteau 1950). Looking in the mirror is the first step in a pact between a subject and an object, tenuously connecting the me 'over here' and the me 'over there' in the mirror. In looking we project and introject our present and future selves and secure a kind of continuity.

A very brief, first-person version of the phenomenology of the mirror as elaborated by the psychologist Romanyshyn (1982) clarifies how this might be experienced consciously. When I confront the mirror as an adult I see a representation of myself as I appear to others: my self incarnate in the material world out there. The appearance in the mirror is not trivial. Yet what is seen is not on the glass, nor quite behind it. The image is as far away on the other side of the mirror as I am on this side. This distance is like the distance between myself and an other, Romanyshyn tells us. But is the figure in the mirror an other or an object? The mirror experience eradicates this distinction. We see a spectre in the mirror which co-exists with us in an uncanny way. We oscillate between the reflected and the reflection, representing a faltering first step towards self-transcendence. We live life and we carry out our therapeutic work in this space which is neither subjective nor objective.

## THE MIRROR IN PSYCHOANALYTIC TECHNIQUE

Psychotherapeutic theory in general is also replete with references to mirrors and mirroring but I wish to concentrate solely on psychoanalytic theory here, in particular as it relates to the self of the analyst or therapist. Freud's first use of the mirror metaphor is in early writings on analytic technique where he recommends the analyst adopt a neutral, reflective stance towards the patient, like a mirror (Freud 1912). Freud has often been accused of encouraging the analyst to adopt a persona which is impenetrable and cold. His comparison of the analyst to a

mirror that reflects nothing but that shown to him and his recommendations to take the surgeon as a model of clinical professionalism
to be emulated by trainee analysts are both commonly cited.

In reading Freud's papers on technique we find a more subtle and
complex picture. Freud was concerned with the analyst's mode of
listening and attending which he tried to distinguish from a conscious
effort to remember and understand. He advised the would-be analyst
to 'withhold all conscious influences from his capacity to attend, and
give himself over completely to his "unconscious memory"' (Freud 1912:
112). The patient's discourse creates an effect in the unconscious of
the analyst. In order to mirror the basic analytic rule of free association for the patient, the analyst must be able to apply the same clinical,
detached approach to his own unconscious.

> To put it in a formula: he must turn his own unconscious like a
> receptive organ towards the transmitting unconscious of the patient.
> He must adjust himself to the patient as a telephone receiver is
> adjusted to the transmitting microphone. Just as the receiver
> converts back into sound waves the electric oscillations in the tele-
> phone line which were set up by sound waves, so the doctor's
> unconscious is able, from the derivatives of the unconscious which
> are communicated to him, to reconstruct that unconscious, which
> has determined the patient's free associations.
>
> (Freud 1912: 115–116)

The analyst does not make frank use of his own unconscious
processing of patient material by sharing his own intimate feelings and
thoughts – a deviation from analytic technique which Freud disapproved
of greatly – but must remain in rôle: '[t]he doctor should be opaque to
his patients and, like a mirror, should show them nothing but what is
shown to him' (Freud 1912: 118). The mirror image is conjured up as
a device to clarify the patient's view of the material that he or she has
produced and is raised in direct connection with a previous recom-
mendation to avoid self-disclosure. The analyst may present himself as
and be a reflective surface to the patient but when he speaks he is
doing so from a position of reflective self-analysis: there has been a
'biphasic' process (see Balint 1968: 344–348). The analyst takes the
viewpoint of the mirror as well as looking in the mirror, as in *Orphée*
– a film where the camera's viewpoint is at times the same as the
mirror's, though at others it shows us the mirror.

Freud assumed at first that an analyst would normally be an uncracked,
non-distorting mirror. However, even at the beginning of psycho-

analysis the idea of the mirror as a container is also present, as well as the mirror as a flat surface. The analyst must receive and reflect upon the patient's projections. A mirror–analyst who can collect and contain projections which are directed at him or her evokes the image of a concave mirror: such a concept raises the problem of distortion. The question of what is central and what is peripheral in the mind of the analyst becomes significant, as does the relative value of the phenomena he or she discovers: what is exaggerated or minimised by the mirror? Furthermore, the analyst becomes aware of what escapes reflection in the mirror, what lies outside and is unrepresented. The literature on countertransference has proliferated in recent publications about psychotherapy and psychoanalysis, with the recognition of the difficulty for the practitioner of having 'a mind of one's own' (Caper 1997) in which to contain projections. A 'mind of one's own' also implies a relationship to internal objects of one's own which help the analyst or therapist be separate and to produce interpretations to the patient; an activity which exposes the patient to an experience of exclusion comparable to a rudimentary oedipal situation.

As well as benefitting from a greater understanding of countertransference since Freud's day, we have many regulations and strictures which have evolved to frame the practice of psychoanalysis and its derivatives: supervision; personal training therapy or analysis; and codes of ethics. Theory itself has developed and is continually being analysed and reconstrued, though, as Fonagy has commented, there is still a problem for psychoanalysts and therapists in knowing how to discard theory which has been found to be invalid (Fonagy 1993: 577). Like Winnicott's transitional object, the infant's first not-me possession, such as a comfort blanket, which represents an overlap between the child's inner world and external reality (Winnicott 1971: 114), and which the child eventually relegates to obscurity, incorrect theory seems not to be given up but to be left somewhere in limbo. Some of the theory about experiences of mirroring relates directly to the concept of the self of the patient, though it is understood very differently by different schools and I prefer not to give up any part of it in favour of another aspect.

## THE MIRROR AND PSYCHOANALYTIC THEORY

### Support to the ego

Winnicott (1967) studied mother–baby interactions and concluded that the mother's gaze upon her infant was a founding experience for the

child's development of a sense of self as a loved and supported individual. The mirroring look establishes a template for the child's ego as
a site for something good and wanted. No special skills are involved
on the part of the mother, she simply holds her baby, both literally
and metaphorically, in a maternal gaze which confirms the child's place
in the world. Gazing back, the infant sees herself reflected in mother's
face as the focus of a pleasurable reverie. Where mother is unable to
reflect back her child in this positive way, Winnicott suggested that
looking could become a process emptied of creative meaning. In other
words, to be able to see creatively, one needs to have been seen lovingly.
As a consequence of mirroring-failure, mirrors become something to
look at rather than into.

## Collusion with the ego

Lacan posited the use of a mirror as central to the formation of the
ego. However, the Lacanian ego is not a gathering together of the self
as described by Winnicott but a perfidious trick effect of the material
mirror which we humans fall for and which traps us in alienated relation to ourselves and to others. Lacan's mirror stage, which he suggests
we all experience in childhood, is about the illusion of the image in
the mirror. The child discovers his or her mirror-image at six to eighteen months. The mirror-image is misleadingly complete and coherent
and encourages the child to mistake who and where she really is in
terms of psychological development, physical maturation, self-mastery,
and space. The image in the mirror is fascinating and fabulous, antic-
ipating a coherence which is lacking in reality. The mirror counterpart
captures the child's imagination and anticipatory expectancy but what
the infant is lacking is masked. The Lacanian subject is always seeking
to make up for the lack of the other which occurs with her entry into
the world at birth and her loss of the mother's body (see Lacan 1966).
Looking in the mirror and seeking what cannot exist there, exempli-
fies the alienation at the core of the Lacanian ego and descibes the
patient's desire to get the analyst or therapist to substitute themselves
for this lack in the transference.

   These two views of the mirror are opposed but related. In both, the
first mirror is the mother, but for Winnicott the maternal gaze embeds
all that follows. For Lacan, the mother is nearly insignificant, the baby
uses mother's eyes as a reflective surface and only gains an independent view of herself when she encounters a real mirror. The
non-maternal mirror is the critical one for Lacan, in both senses of the
word, being an elemental moment of the ego and an introduction to

'méconaissance' (misrecognition). The potential and partial release from this Imaginary world arrives with language and the law of the father which provide the capacity to symbolise and represent the self to others. Nonetheless, the lure of Imaginary identifications with the double in the mirror remains a powerful, regressive force. As therapists we may work with patients who are compliant and whose identifications with phantasies about themselves we just cannot shift. The anorexic patient is a good clinical example: she will commit herself diligently to her therapy without giving up her anorexic project, while her therapist will struggle to maintain analytic thinking in a therapeutic relationship where lack of space between patient and therapist has been identified as a key problem (see Birksted-Breen 1989).

## THE MIRROR AND THE UNCONSCIOUS IMAGE OF THE BODY

Dolto (1984), a French child psychoanalyst who was greatly influenced by Lacan, also saw the mirror stage as the key moment in which the infant grasped the fact of its own gender and the impossibility of returning to non-knowledge of sexual difference or to a state which is prior to sexed identity. At this point the infant's unconscious image of its own body is struck with an excess of the scopic drive (a psycho-sexual drive related to the gaze and to looking) which fixes it forever. Hitherto the unconscious body image has developed as far as the oral and anal stages, but now, for the first time the child sees itself indi-vidualised as others might, as very small, one sex *or* the other, as belonging to *that* body and no other, with *that* sexual identity. Moreover, when the child moves away from the mirror, the image disappears. There is nothing in the language of the child which has prepared him or her for this disappearance and for the discrepancy between what he or she can see and what others can see. If no one humanises the expe-rience by appearing alongside in the mirror or speaking about it, then there is no help in recovering from the shock of seeing this hole into which personal body image disappears. Dolto describes how a little girl who was left alone for hours in a room with a large mirror and no human company, developed a psychosis.

The differences between Lacan and Winnicott on the role of the mirror in the development of the child's identity, involve different levels of narcissism and mirroring. First, the foundational mirror of mother (Winnicott), then later, the self as basis of narcissism (Lacan), in that it is only at this latter point that a 'self' which is not based on mother comes into being. This is the point at which the body image should be formed to take in the whole of the body and the genital zone of difference. Breakdown of coherence or continuity at this point will leave the infant with a fragile body image at a time when phantasies about castration are soon to be aggravated by the dynamics of the Oedipus Complex.

Although we associate the mirror with narcissism in adult life, the mirror can also provide us with links to the future, so long as we are not locked into a phantasy about the self which we cannot alter, nor become besotted with whatever we have projected into the mirror. Freud suggested that self-observation, as it occurs in the uncanny experience of seeing a double (a mirror-other experience), permits an opening onto the future of all kinds of possibilities of the self; 'all the unfulfilled but possible futures to which we still like to cling in phantasy' (Freud 1919: 358). Romanyshyn describes a similar attribute of the mirror: it encourages the calling into being of other versions of ourselves and other stories we could tell about ourselves.

## THE MIRROR AND THE SELF IN SPACE

The special place the mirror occupies is discussed at some length by the French Marxist philosopher Lefebvre in his study of spatiality.

> The mirror is thus at once an object among others and an object different from all others, evanescent, fascinating. In and through the mirror, the traits of other objects in relationship to their spatial environment are brought together; the mirror is an object in space which informs us about space, which speaks of space. In some ways a kind of picture, the mirror too has a frame which specifies it, a frame that can be either emptied or filled. Into that space which is produced first by natural and later by social life the mirror introduces a truly dual spatiality; a space which is imaginary with respect to origin and separation, but also concrete and practical with respect to coexistence and differentiation.
>
> (Lefebvre 1974: 186)

Such a place would be akin to Lefebvre's description of 'topias': 'isotopias, heterotopias, utopias, or in other words analogous places, contrasting places, and the places of what has no place, or no longer has a place – the absolute, the divine, or the possible' (Lefebvre 1974: 163–164).

# Heterotopias

Lefebvre does not explain this term except to describe them as 'contrasting places' (1974: 163) or 'mutually repellent spaces' (1974: 366) and to suggest that a heterotopia can be holy or damned (1974: 294) with prohibitions surrounding its use. Foucault (1984) does not simplify the concept either when he writes about six principles of 'heterotopology' in his own study of spatiality in the contemporary period. The first principle is that all cultures produce heterotopias. In primitive societies there are the crisis heterotopias, a place for those in crisis such as adolescents, pregnant women, menstruating women and the elderly. These are disappearing fast from modern societies but are being replaced by heterotopias of deviation, such as rest homes for the elderly, psychiatric hospitals and prisons. The second principle is that society can alter the function of the heterotopia as is perhaps illustrated in the description above of where the elderly frail might be placed. The third principle is that the heterotopia can accommodate the juxtaposition of sites which are otherwise incompatible, such as the combination of sacred and mundane in the oriental garden. Fourthly, heterotopias are slices of time when 'men' arrive at an absolute break with their traditional time. Again the cemetery illustrates this point. Fifthly, heterotopias cannot be entered freely at any time: they require special gestures to be made or special permission to be sought. Finally, they function to create a space of illusion which exposes real space. An example is the idealisation of spaces in colonised countries where the sound of the church bell ordered the life in the new colony. The prototype space of the old country and its routines, dominated by the factory hooter and the clock, were thus obscured.

Foucault's descriptions are confusing but they do suffice to evoke a sense of another place which has a relationship to what is in the place from which it is extruded. His examples suggest that we can conceive of the analytic setting and process where they function like mirrors as an 'other place', a heterotopia. The analyst or therapist creates a heterotopia in geographical space in the consulting room, gives permission to uncouple speech from its conventional use and also entertains a suspension of linear time while guarding the boundaries of real time very punctually at the beginning and end of a session.

Foucault, however, is caught up in two different views of the mirror:

> [t]he mirror is, after all, a utopia, since it is a placeless place. In the mirror, I see myself there where I am not, in an unreal virtual space that opens up behind the surface; I am over there, there

where I am not, a sort of shadow that gives my own visibility to myself, that enables me to see myself there where I am absent: such is the utopia of the mirror. But it is also a heterotopia in so far as the mirror does exist in reality, where it exerts a sort of counter-action on the position I occupy. From the standpoint of the mirror I discover my absence from the place that I am since I see myself over there. Starting from this gaze that is, as it were, directed toward me, from the ground of this virtual space, that is on the other side of the glass, I come back towards myself; I begin again to direct my eyes towards myself and to reconstitute myself there where I am. The mirror functions as a heterotopia in this respect: it makes this place that I occupy at the moment when I look at myself in the glass at once absolutely real, connected with all the space that surrounds it, and absolutely unreal, since in order to be perceived it has to pass through this virtual point which is over there.

(Foucault 1984: 24)

The mirror is a place where the 'I' hovers between self and other, here and there, lived experience and representation of it, corporeality and disembodiedness: the site through which Lewis Carroll (1872) despatches Alice to looking-glass land and Cocteau transports Orpheus to the underworld. This intersubjective space functions, like psycho-analysis and psychotherapy, through projections, introjections and identifications.

## AN ANTI-MIRROR EFFECT

Lefebvre poses the question of whether or not there is an opposite to the mirror-effect, that is, an anti-mirror effect whereby one could live an experience of blank opacity. Such a state would be tantamount to the predicament of the child who is not mirrored supportively in his or her earliest days as described by Winnicott (1967) and who goes on to experience fragile support for a sense of their identity throughout life. A child who has not benefited from a maternal reflecting gaze will find mother's face is not a mirror and that perception takes the place of: 'that which might have been the beginning of a significant exchange with the world, a two-way process in which self-enrichment alternates with the discovery of meaning in the world of seen things' (Winnicott 1971: 132).

As therapists, when we fail to register, let alone understand, the inner world of the patient it must be like a re-enactment of an earlier kind of anti-mirror effect. Bion might have been meaning something like this when he described early infantile experience of a 'wilfully misun-derstanding object' who returns projections to the child without having contained and understood them, leaving the child with an experience such as Dolto described in her psychotic child patient.

Lefebvre proposes that via the projection of symmetry, the ego recog-nises itself but does not coincide with it, that the self and the sign of the self are present but not identical. Unless we can stop taking what is projected for the actual ego, rather than a mirror effect the result will be devastating:

> The effect is dizzying. Should the 'Ego' fail to reassert its own image, it must welcome Narcissus – or Alice. It will then be in danger of never discovering itself, space *qua* figment will have swallowed it up, and the glacial surface of the mirror will hold it forever captive in its emptiness, in an absence devoid of all conceivable presence or bodily warmth.
>
> (Lefebvre 1974: 185)

Lefebvre concludes that the mirror is both a unifying and disjunc-tive relation between form and content. It is transitional in that it tends towards something else, be it real or unreal. The mirror is thus central to the development of a sense of relatedness to one's own body, another's body, to space and to representation of the body and the self in space as well as to representational space.

## CONCLUSION

Although Rorty (1980) is critical of the use of the mirror metaphor and Irigaray (1974) demands a better mirror that women in particular can use for themselves (a speculum) the mirror idea remains a powerful arterfact for psychotherapists. The mirror gives us ways of thinking about the self and how it may come into being and how it may become an obstacle to living creatively. It helps to conceptualise the subjective experience of the psychotherapist and the intersubjective nature of psychotherapy. As a heterotopia it helps us to take a perspective on what is not strictly there in reality and describes well the process of psychotherapy.

I think some heterotopic qualities can also be attributed to the concept of the self. The self serves to reflect both an internal and external reality, yet its source and its boundaries cannot be found to exist in any concrete way – the body is clearly not the same as the self. In times of crisis, we retreat into the self as a refuge. Without a stable sense of self we are prone to distress and illness: anorexia nervosa has been mentioned as a prime example. How a girl child's sense of self is mirrored may be especially important in the development of this disorder. Irigaray would suggest that how all women are mirrored in the theory of psychoanalysis may be criticised. Winnicott describes a true self which is covered over by a compliant false self. However, this true self is an entity which is purely imaginary. As Khan (1972) has commented, the true self is known only negatively, that is by a sense of dissonance or alienation when it has been deviated from. In this respect, the idea of a self is always in contrast with the not-self. It is a particular extrusion from all that exists in the 'real space' of the inter-subjective world. The self is a 'placeless place' within the personality which is both essential for healthy life and yet an illusion.

## ACKNOWLEDGEMENTS

I am grateful to Ralf Haubl for his generosity and the work he has done on this subject and am indebted to Ursula Stickler for help in trans-lating some of it.

## REFERENCES

Balint, E. (1968) 'Remarks on Freud's metaphors about the "mirror" and the "receiver", *Comprehensive Psychiatry*, 9, 4: 344–348.

Beckett, S. (1965) *Proust and Three Dialogues with Georges Duthuit*, London: John Calder (Publishers) Ltd.; reprinted London: Caldar and Boyars Ltd., 1970.

Birksted-Breen, D. (1989) 'Working with an anorexic patient', *International Journal of Psycho-Analysis*, 70: 29–40.

Caper, R. (1997) 'A mind of one's own', *International Journal of Psycho-Analysis*, 78: 265–278.

Carroll, L. (1872) *Through the Looking Glass*, republished: London: Puffin, 1984.

Cocteau, J. (1950) *Orphée*, Paris: Films du Palais Royal.

de Palma, B. (1976) *Carrie*, USA: MGM-Deluxe.

Dolto, F. (1984) *L'Image Inconsciente Du Corps*, Paris: Editions Du Seuil.

Fonagy, P. (1993) 'Psychoanalytic and empirical approaches to developmental psychopathology: can they be usefully integrated?' *International Journal of Psycho-Analysis*, 86: 577–581.

Foucault, M. (1984) 'Of other spaces', *Architecture-Mouvement-Continuité*, reprinted, *Diacritics*, trans. J. Miskowiec, 1986: 22–27.

Freud, S. (1912) 'Recommendations to physicians practising Psycho-Analysis', in Standard Edition 12, London: Hogarth, 111–120.

—— (1919) 'The uncanny' in *Penguin Freud Library*, Vol. 14, Harmondsworth: Penguin.

Grabes, H. (1982) *The Mutable Glass: Mirror-Imagery in Titles and Texts of the Middle-Ages and the English Renaissance*, Cambridge: Cambridge University Press.

Haubl, R. (1991) *Unter Lauter Spiegelbildern*, Frankfurt: Nexus.

Irigaray, L. (1974) *Speculum of the Other Woman*, trans. G.C. Gill. Ithaca, NY: Cornell University Press, 1985.

Jowett, B. (1953) *The Dialogues of Plato*, Oxford: Oxford University Press.

Khan, M. (1972) 'The finding and becoming of self', in *The Privacy of the Self*, London: Hogarth Press 1974.

Lacan, J. (1966) *Écrits*, Paris: Editions Du Seuil.

Lefebvre, H. (1974) *The Production of Space*, trans. D. Nicholson-Smith. Oxford: Blackwell, 1991, reprinted 1994.

Romanyshyn, R.D. (1982) *Psychological Life: From Science to Metaphor*, Milton Keynes: Open University Press.

Rorty, R. (1980) *Philosophy and The Mirror of Nature*, Oxford: Blackwell.

Scorsese, M. (1976) *Taxi Driver*, USA: Columbia/Italo-Judeo.

Winnicott, D.W. (1967) 'Mirror-role of mother and family in child development', reprinted in *Playing and Reality*, London: Penguin, 1971, reprinted 1986: 130–138.

Winnicott, D.W. (1971) ' The location of cultural experience' in *Playing and Reality*, London: Penguin, 1971, reprinted 1986: 112 –121.

# Introduction to chapter 12

This chapter examines a 'deconstruction' of the self that is still more radical. According to Buddhist thought, any perception of subjective continuity is illusory. Thomas presents some implications of this as conceived within Zen Buddhism, a tradition which, in view of its overt distrust of the intellect, is particularly resistant to theoretical analysis. Although many introductory accounts of Zen are available, the most reliable come from D.T. Suzuki, a scholar and undoubted master who was also conversant with Western needs (Suzuki, 1982).

Given that Zen differs from other Buddhist schools in its emphasis on a sudden realisation or enlightenment that ends discursive or relative modes of thought, it can be thought to have little in common with occidental psychotherapy. Alan Watts (1973) and Eric Fromm (1986) have each compared psychoanalysis with traditional Zen, emphasising common elements of practice and theory. Here, Myra Thomas describes her experience of interacting with a Zen master who has manifestly allowed his methods to fit the circumstances in which he finds himself. She describes how use of a poetic form, the haiku, reveals with great economy and directness the innermost state of each student to a teacher who has already achieved a radically different state of self. These interactions represent a very different model of interpretation from the co-constructed narrations discussed in earlier chapters. Apart from raising questions concerning which aspects of self are the most vital to well-being, the illustration of how radical change of consciousness on the Zen master's part is a prerequisite of effective insight could have far reaching implications for the goals and content of psychotherapists' training.

## REFERENCES

Fromm, E. (1986) *Psychoanalysis and Zen Buddhism*. London: Unwin
Suzuki, D.T. (1982) *Living by Zen*. London: Rider
Watts, A. (1973) *Psychotherapy East and West*. Harmondsworth: Penguin

# 12 Seventeen syllables for the self

*Myra Thomas*

As Suzuki (1973) observes, most people assume that there is a real world of senses and intellect, and a spiritual world which at best is quite separate from ordinary existence and at worst does not exist at all other than in imagination. As Suzuki also points out, this apparently common-sense interpretation is, in Buddhism, seen as quite erroneous.

In Buddhism the sense world is composed of the Five Aggregates of Matter, Sensations, Perceptions, Mental Formulations, and Consciousness. The Buddha taught that the idea of a constant self is an imaginary false belief which is the source of all suffering and craving (Bahm 1958). It is the intellect which constructs the sense world, and what we are accustomed to thinking of as 'I' is not our real self but a mental construction. This mental construction is conditioned by our past experiences and all new experiences are filtered through this conditioned consciousness. Thus in Buddhism it is what we think of as the real world which is illusory, since it is not seen with clarity. We interpret everything we see, hear, feel etc. and judge it in relation to what we perceive as our own best interests.

Many doctrinal disputes arose within Buddhism, (Bahm 1958, Conze 1959) and Zen Buddhism developed along rather different lines from that of orthodox Buddhism. As Suzuki (1973) points out, in Zen the formal teachings of Buddhism, the sutras and sastras, are seen as just so much waste paper, not because they do not contain basic truths, but because the Zen approach cannot be apprehended by the intellect alone and can only be reached through experience. Zen points to the fact that reality can be directly apprehended if the illusory nature of an intellectual and illusory self is seen. The origin of the following declaration is not exactly known, but it is generally regarded as characterising Zen.

> A special transmission outside the scripture;
> No dependence on words or letters;
> Direct pointing at the Mind of man;
> Seeing into one's nature and the attainment of Buddhahood.

Seeing into one's own nature or enlightenment are the terms often given to that state of transcending the apparent contradictions and problems raised by the analytical and intellectual self. However the Zen approach can be profoundly misunderstood unless the term 'self' is used with precision. In everyday life 'self' and 'person' are often used synonymously. In other words 'self' is used as meaning a person or an individual.

Zen, on the other hand, uses the terms 'self' and 'ego' in an interchangeable way, both being psychological constructions which exist as concepts but are not real in any true sense, since the ego is seen as a mental construction which is dropped upon reaching enlightenment. A modern Zen master explains this process as follows,

> at the moment of enlightenment the cognitive structures that maintain our individual egos collapse. The mind is no longer dominated by an abstract sense of 'I' or by goal seeking or time dependent constructs of self. His awareness is centred in the present, attending only to what is, and responding to his perception of what is in a way that makes no mechanistic distinction between self and not-self, cause and effect, social values and personal wishes.
>
> (Hey 1988, p.4)

This loss of self, which as will become evident, is a central part of the psychology of Zen, is perceived very differently in Western philosophy. Exploring the philosophical issues related to the dropping of 'self' Taylor states,

> The agent of radical choice would at the moment of choice have *ex hypothesi* no horizon of evaluation. He would be utterly without identity. He would be a kind of extensionless point, a pure leap into the void. But such a thing is an impossibility, and rather could be only the description of the most terrible mental alienation. The subject of rational choice is another avatar of that recurrent figure which our civilisation aspires to realise, the disembodied ego, the subject who can objectify all being, including his own, and choose in radical freedom. But his promised total self-possession would in fact be the most total self-loss.
>
> (Taylor 1977, p.125)

Taylor's 'pure leap into the void' appears to be precisely what a Zen master tries to invoke. Taylor's assertion that such a thing is impossible is the point at issue. Zen literature makes it plain that is our mental models that preclude our making the leap. Loss of 'self' in this context is therefore seen as 'enlightenment' in Zen and 'mental alienation' in philosophy. This is not some abstruse point which has no relevance in ordinary life. Segal (1996) gives an account of spontaneous enlightenment, which, since she had no religious contacts of any kind, she did not understand. She was treated by a succession of psychiatrists for 'depersonalisation disorder' before coming to terms with her experience.

The Zen view of self is therefore fundamentally different from that of psychodynamic, humanistic, existential and most other schools of therapy. I shall try to summarise this view, relate it to contemporary Western thought, and illustrate how it can make a contribution to cognitive psychology and psychotherapy. The notion that the self is illusory is not confined to Zen. There are many strands of philosophical and psychological thought also coming to this conclusion. And there is now some supporting evidence that the self as normally conceived is not the continuous self that most people imagine controls their thoughts and actions.

The opening sentence of Theodore Mischel's paper, 'Conceptual Issues in The Psychology of the Self' (1977) states that there is at least one issue on which philosophers and psychologists can agree, namely that the self is not some entity other than the person. Would that it were so simple. Contributors to that volume might agree, but there seem exceptions to every rule. In discussing the nature of 'persons' Parfit (1987) explains the difference between 'ego theory' and 'bundle theory'. In ego theory a person's continued existence cannot be explained except as the continued existence of a particular 'ego' or subject of experiences. In other words ego theories assume that 'self' and 'person' can be used synonymously, and that is indeed the way that 'self' is used by Mischel and is used by the average person in everyday life. In Zen however the 'ego' is an illusory structure which stands between the person and life experience, and filters that experience from a perspective of past feeling and knowledge. The aim is neither to confront nor overcome the structure, nor yet to integrate it, but simply to drop it altogether.

The deficiencies of the theoretical position that the self is a continuous entity have been explored extensively by the existential movement in philosophy. Its most famous exponent is no doubt Sartre, who in his *The Transcendence of the Ego* (1972) made it clear that we impute continued existence of a sense of self when logically there is no evidence of continuity. For example, if we say 'I hate Paul' what we mean is that we feel a deep repugnance for Paul at this particular time. We haven't in fact hated Paul for our entire past history, and may or may not continue to hate Paul, depending upon Paul's future behaviour. This feeling is a temporary state. If the 'I' who hates Paul actually changes over time, why do we then posit a continuous 'I' who is in charge, rather than a series of changing 'I's?

The point at issue here is not whether the ego is fragmented into component parts, but whether these have a continuous 'I' or organiser in overall charge. Some may feel that this is just semantic quibbling. Even if 'I' change, 'I' still exist, all that happens is that my personality and opinions change over time. But what philosophers like Parfit are querying is the nature of the 'I' that exists. According to bundle theory we cannot explain either consciousness at any point in time, or over a lifetime, in reference to a person. In a sense, for the bundle theorist the person does not exist. Parfit suggests the first bundle theorist was Buddha, so this viewpoint has obvious relevance here.

As bundle theorists point out, if the 'ego' or subject of experience is synonymous with the person, then it is possible to have subjects of experiences that are not persons, most notably in split-brain personalities. In 'blindsight' research it has been shown that some split brain subjects can 'see' things they are not aware of seeing. Since surgery has separated the two hemispheres of the brain the subject has two separate streams of consciousness, each unaware of the other's field of perception. Likewise in Multiple Personality Disorders (MPD) a number of discrete personalities, apparently unaware of each other's existence, can inhabit one body.

Bundle theorists take the position that ordinary people, at any time, are aware of having several different experiences at once (including being aware of being aware). Thus the separate states of consciousness of the split brain or MPD personality are simply multiple states of awareness, and not separate egos. If that is so, they argue, there are a lot of sub-systems to which we give an 'I' tag when they are in consciousness, hence we are a bundle of I's, but there is no continuous big 'I' in charge. As noted above, awareness of this multiplicity of I's is implicit in many psychological and sociological theories. But as Dennett (1983) points out, even when the theoretical problems of possessing a multiplicity of 'I's' is seen, in practice most people operate in the world as though there were one 'I'.

Many psychological and sociological theories have developed that suppose that the self is not unified but has a number of different components. It seems likely that the pervasiveness of the idea of a conflicted or 'divided self', articulated most notably by R.D. Laing (1960) in the book of that name, is an implicit understanding of the lack of continuity pointed out by bundle theorists. Certainly, these and other models accord with our personal experience of being torn by conflicting aspects of personality. We often seem to be different people at different times depending upon our social roles or personality traits. Such models assume however that our different sub-personalities are continuous and coexist. The difference between that situation and MPD is that we are aware, at least part of the time, of the different parts of ourselves which, however uneasily, make up our total self.

Goffman (1959) in his *Presentation of Self in Everyday Life* likens the various little I's to actors with different roles, whose performances vary depending upon whether they are on or off stage. The Freudian position also sees the person as fragmented, having an id, an ego and a superego. Most psychoanalytic models assume a fragmented self which needs to be understood and integrated into a more harmonious whole. This model has been carried forward in *Psychosynthesis* by Assagioli (1975) with his concepts of sub-personalities and higher and lower selves. Both Freud and Assagioli, in different ways, thought that the healthy person had to integrate their various sub-systems by putting the 'best' fragment in charge of the others.

As Lancaster (1991) observes however, in paradigms of enlightenment, self-knowledge is of a different kind. The paradigm of self-realisation or enlightenment common to many eastern religions, as Lancaster makes clear, is of a much more radical and discontinuous change than the gradual pursuit of greater understanding of one's 'self':

> the importance of self observation in this scheme is not only to gain information about what may be observed, but also to change the centre of gravity of consciousness. Self-knowledge, beloved of the ancients, is not simply a question of one from the multiplicity of 'I's' gaining greater understanding of its fellow actors. It is a state of being which, by comparison, is all-knowing; the view as given from the top of a mountain.
>
> (Lancaster 1991, p.98)

This radical change, which Suzuki (1963) calls the awakening of the conscious in the Unconscious, is contacting the ground of one's being, and has no continuity with any previous concept of self. Suzuki's Unconscious, as he makes clear, is not the unconscious of the empirical mind. The ordinary experience of mind is but a small fragment of a wider consciousness.

Ego theorists have an alternative view which Dennett (1991), while not agreeing with it, puts with his usual admirable clarity. As he points out, psychologists develop models of the structure of the ego but exempt the central concept of self. To do so is to allow the possibility of the dreaded homunculus, which produces the sort of infinite regress abhorred quite rightly by radical behaviourists such as Skinner (1974). How could we be sure that there wasn't another 'I' standing behind the 'I' etc., etc. Even where we think we see that the ego is fragmented and/or illusory, as Dennett points out, we continue to act as though it was real. In other words we may see the theoretical danger, but we do not change our attribution of meaning in our life experience. In effect, regardless of our theoretical orientation we act in accordance with ego theory, as though 'I' take decisions and 'I' act upon them.

But it is not only laymen who make this attribution. In some psychological theories 'I' is regarded as a leader in charge of a troop of sub-personalities. If Dennett, Parfit and Zen are right and there is no central self in charge, then much of Western psychology would appear to be testing psychological constructions e.g. self-control, purpose and intentionality, etc. which are illusory. It is small wonder that the predictive power of many theoretical positions (including Freud's) are so difficult to validate.

Dennett also argues that the continuity we attribute to 'I' and the continuity of consciousness implied by that is totally fallacious. He cites a number of experiments, involving changing computer screens in synchrony with eyeblinks, in which the computer screen appears to ripple to an observer, but cannot be detected by the participant. Such experiments show that there are gaps in consciousness analogous to visual 'blind spots'. If we are unaware of the gaps in our consciousness, and experience consciousness as continuous when it is full of discontinuities, we are similarly unaware that there is no single self in charge of things.

In both cases we attribute a continuity that does not exist. The reason why we do not detect such existing discontinuities is that there are no sentinels in the system for such a purpose. Similar discontinuities in visual processing caused by accident or injury are noticed because there is a difference from what was previously perceived. The gaps Dennett is talking about have no cognitive mechanism to bring them into awareness.

The philosopher Derek Parfit, in his book *Reasons and Persons* (1984), demonstrates that we are not what we believe we are. Most of us have false beliefs about our own nature, and about our identity over time. Some of his arguments concerning 'bundle theory' are discussed above.

However, Parfit also asks the difficult question: does psychological continuity presuppose personal identity? As he points out, we tend to assume
that evidence of a continuous personal identity is provided by memory.
Parfit's book preceded much of the debate in psychology about false
memory syndrome. It is now abundantly plain that the average person
does not have complete recall of all events that ever happened and
that memory is not continuous. What is more difficult to establish is
whether we 'invent' memories. Do we sometimes appear to have memories of something that never happened to us?

I personally find myself doubting my memory when trying to find
something I have mislaid, like keys. When trying to reconstruct in my
mind what I might have done with my keys I produce images which
seem indistinguishable from memory traces, that is I start to 'remember'
doing a number of different things with my keys. In principle I could
verify which of my memories was real and which false when I do eventually find my keys. But how can I be sure that what I remembered was
simply invention, or whether it was a memory trace of some other occasion when I had also lost my keys?

Because we have access only to our own memories and no one else's,
we take this as proof of personal identity. However, as Parfit points out,
Bishop Berkeley exposed the fallacy in this view over two and a half
centuries ago. Continuity of memory cannot, even in part, be what
makes a series of experiences the experiences of a single person, since
the identification of memory within a person presupposes his continued
identity. The argument in fact is circular.

One more relevant strand of thought is the discursive psychology outlined by Harré and Gillett (1994). In this model, mental life is seen as a
dynamic activity, undertaken by rule-following intentional agents.
Psychological constructions such as desires, beliefs, moral attitudes and
intentions are seen as fighting it out against the general background of
mental activity. However, Harré and Gillett also believe that the idea of
a sense of self arising from a string of co-ordinated memories is insufficient as an explanation for a self as a separate entity from the body/brain.
The most fruitful way for psychology to study the sense of identity, in
their view, is to study how selfhood is produced discursively. Looked at
in this way one's sense of a personal identity is constructed as an explanation of who we are when conversing with others. The self is thus a
mental construction. The sense we have that we are agents of our actions,
and responsible to others for them, is something that we acquire through
learning language and the cultural conventions of learning moral responsibility. In effect this paradigm, like that of bundle theory, sees no
central co-ordinating self, and 'I' is simply a linguistic convenience.

Dennett also argues that not only are we unaware of a process of self-deception in regarding the self as a temporary entity, but that we guard and protect that very process and are highly resistant to change. If this change were allowed into consciousness it would fundamentally alter our sense of continuity, and that continuity is simply a mental construction that we are accustomed to calling 'I'. Dennett also has grave doubts about the utility of relying on such an 'I'.

> In fact I think there's lots of evidence, now, and somewhat dis-
> turbing evidence which shows that if there were any homunculus
> in our cognitive committee with which we would be inclined to
> identify the self intuitively, it wouldn't be the boss; it would be
> the director of public relations, the agent in the press office who
> has a very limited and often fallacious idea about what's really going
> on in the system.
>
> (Dennett 1983)

But the system's job, if Dennett is right, is to present itself in the best possible light. Hey, a modern Zen master, agrees when he says,

> [t]he essential elements of ego are consistency, continuity, and
> control. It is an abstract image, but is invested with selfhood as
> though it were real. Virtually all actions and thoughts are condi-
> tioned and controlled in relation to its qualities. . . . It [ego] is blind
> to the paradox of its own existence: that it is in the fundamental
> awareness of ego's existence that selfhood manifests, not in the
> operations of the ego itself.
>
> (Hey 1995, p.28)

This process of constructing meaning by conversing with ourselves about our experience is fundamental to the process of Self Organised Learning developed by Thomas and Harri-Augstein. Such a process is difficult to describe.

> Sometimes we can perform ahead of our explicit understanding.
> The understanding exists in the deep, tacit meanings, but we have
> not conversed sufficiently, or sufficiently well, within ourselves to
> be able to represent this understanding in forms which we can
> recognise and express. . . . If we can learn alternatively to leapfrog
> or bootstrap ourselves forward from understanding to performing
> and from performing to understanding we will have acquired a
> powerful form of learning.
>
> (Harri-Augstein and Thomas 1991)

In Zen the issue is not that this process takes place, but rather who is attributing the meaning as modelling. Hey, in public meetings, often likened this experience to a dog chasing its own tail. Enlightenment arises when the full implications of this position are really felt and the dog realises that the only thing it is chasing is its tail.

I had a unique opportunity to see at first hand how concepts of self intrude on every experience and can be tracked through discourse, during a weekend workshop on creativity lead by Dr Jonathan Hey, the Zen master referred to above. As already noted, Zen is not a body of theory but a living experience which adapts its methods to the needs of the moment. During the weekend Dr Hey provided a living example of someone whose 'self' seemed radically different from those with whom he interacted. This affected interactions in subtle ways and it is possible to demonstrate some of these differences through the rather unlikely medium of the Zen haiku.

Even in the writing of a haiku, which consist of a mere seventeen syllables, it is possible to see how an implicit model of self is produced discursively, illustrating attitudes to the self in a way that no theoretical analysis can. What is more, the haiku show how our perceptions are profoundly affected by our sense of identity.

The workshop had two main themes; how our models of self are inaccurate and thus produce stress, and how this process affects our ability to change and be creative. The first part of the workshop was designed to reveal to participants each individual's personal constructs. The initial exercises were modified repertory grids which showed participants that they had unrealistic ideas of the nature of the self. By building up a picture of each individual's 'ideal self', it was possible to show that this was very different from each participant's actual self. When participants interacted in small groups it became clear that they reverted to roles which affected group performance. Some saw themselves as leaders, others clearly felt that they were more creative than other participants. This process became especially clear once participants attempted to work creatively.

Hey set small groups the task of writing haiku. Each group was given a selection of twenty completed haiku. The purpose of this was primarily to provide examples of the genre, and most were classical haiku from acknowledged Zen masters, although they also included a few written by Hey. Groups were not told anything about haiku, or their traditional form, other than that they normally consisted of seventeen syllables in a 5-7-5 line arrangement. (It was explained that some of the haiku samples were translations and did not always conform exactly to seventeen syllables.)

Each group was also assigned a short Zen story to study. The group task was to reach a consensus of what the story meant, and to write a haiku about it as a group, all within a deadline of twenty minutes. The group then had to appoint a spokesperson to present the meaning of the story and the haiku to the rest of the participants.

The discussion that followed revealed that participants mostly had implicit constructs, that creativity was essentially individual and often involved some form of suffering. The stereotype of the suffering artist was remarkably prevalent and it was agreed that harmonious team working is not often connected with creativity. Having thus participated in workshops which demonstrated to participants that they had unrealistic expectations of themselves, that many overvalued their own contributions and devalued others, and that they could work creatively in harmony as well as in conflict, the exercises moved to individual creativity.

Participants were asked to choose one of the twenty haiku, or a Zen story, and either write a haiku of their own which captured the same inner meaning, or present the meaning of a Zen story of their choice. Each of the nineteen participants then had a ten-minute meeting with Hey to present their offering. As observer to these presentations, I tried to understand what it was Hey was seeing and commenting on. In some of my own past interactions with Hey he had drawn my attention to the viewpoint of the self. Who was judging, thinking, feeling etc.? Looking at the process in this light I thought it was possible to demonstrate via haiku how they showed explicit or implicit self concepts.

Since the examples given to participants were all written by enlightened masters they could presumably be regarded as 'ego-less', since the ego self is dropped on self-realisation. (However the word 'ego' or 'self' had not been mentioned to participants in reference to the haiku or Zen stories.) By contrasting examples of haiku written by participants with those of historical masters such as Basho and Hey himself, it seemed possible to show that our views of self are indeed revealed in discourse, even when only writing the seventeen syllables of a haiku.

## STAGE ONE -- SELF AWARENESS

This stage is where experience is reflected through the obvious presence of an observer:

One never knows
when the deer will leap
out of the forest.

Here the emphasis is on the person who is experiencing rather than
the experience itself. It seems clear that the observer has experienced
seeing deer leaping out of the forest but the event is seen from an
egocentric viewpoint. The haiku also expresses a sense of anticipation,
it is not grounded in the now. Of course I am not arguing here that
haiku have to be dashed off immediately in response to a current event.
But if the quality of observation is remembered with clarity the poem
conveys the quality of the moment.

Hey responded to this haiku with one of his own.

Deer steaming in the
weak-rayed sun.
High moors tawny in the slanting light.

Leaving aside aesthetic considerations, what does this haiku say about
the person? In it a number of things are observed, the deer, the moors
and the quality of the light, but there is no sense of an observer. We
know more about the event and can picture it more clearly than in the
other example. Haiku provide brief snapshots of the quality of observation, but they also indicate the degree of preoccupation with the self. In
the next stage of this process the 'self' is operating at a more subtle level.

## STAGE TWO – INTERPRETATION

Once the obvious presence of the observer has gone, in that references
to I, me, one etc. have been eliminated, the observer viewpoint becomes
more subtle and difficult to spot. Events are described but the events
are given an interpretation. From a Zen point of view a haiku should
be a reflection of life, without interpretation. Two examples of interpretation are discussed below.

One blackbird sings
slicing the night silence
January surprise.

In these veering gales
the weathercock can find
no resting place.

The first example conveys some of the delight that the unexpected song of the blackbird brought to the writer one January night. In fact she wrote a number of versions of this event. But again although the observer is not mentioned it is the surprise of the hidden observer that provides the culminating line. In pure reflection there is no emotional content. Any emotion or opinion implies the presence of an observer who is making judgements on what is perceived. Discussing with Hey how to identify hidden interpretation he said that it often involves stronger language than pure reflection would warrant. In this example the use of the word 'slicing' to convey the sound, is another indication of an interpretation of events.

In the second example the viewpoint has been taken from the observer but given to the weathercock, which in the haiku can find no resting place. This is not reflection, but a rather anthropomorphic interpretation of the event seen. In other words there is too little observation and too much thought in both the above examples.

This interpretative stance is the basis of almost all Western literature and poetry. We tend to admire the ability to interpret perceptions in terms of metaphor – in terms of more complex psychological images. But this process unfortunately is one we carry into our lives. We interpret the present in terms of our own psychological past. In Zen, it is this entire approach which prevents one from experiencing the new. The Zen approach to art is therefore quite different from Western art, which like Western psychology, presupposes the importance of the individual viewpoint. The unrecognised consequence of this is that constant interpretation stands between the person and full appreciation of any current experience. The self subtly closes down the full clarity of what is happening in the now by instantly relating it to some personal past thought or emotion.

Although Hey could have pointed such issues out to participants at the workshop, he preferred to provoke each person's own insight wherever possible. The following is an example of how he did that. Shown the following haiku,

> So obvious now
> among the leafless brambles
> tennis balls thought lost,

Hey responded with

> Nothing lost or found
> Perception is always now;
> Ego seeks itself.

In seventeen short syllables Hey has pointed to the interpretation in the presented haiku, indicated that reflection is always in the present and interpretation in the past, and that the ego sustained a particular ego point of view throughout.

Examples of pure reflection can be found in any number of classical haiku, but another of Hey's haiku is used here to demonstrate the simplicity of an event described without interpretation.

> Now it is raining
> Bedraggled birds are bathing
> In spreading puddles.

## STAGE THREE – IMITATION

It is possible with study to follow the rules of classical haiku and write a very creditable imitation which is difficult for someone not themselves enlightened to distinguish from the real thing. Such haiku often have a theme taken from nature, are closely observed and seem reflective rather than interpretative. The ability to produce a creditable imitation is not easy and no participant did so during the workshop. One participant at the workshop had however written many haiku and was aware of the conventions governing the writing of them. He had sent several to Hey. This example

> The fallen tree by
> the chattering stream
> rain dripping

provoked this response

> Be sure the rain is only outside you
> Do not listen to the chattering mind,
> but to stream alone!
> Their dead do not exist.

## STAGE FOUR – REALISING ZEN

In *Zen and the Fine Arts* Hisamatsu (1982) translates the Japanese term 'zen-ki' as Zen Activity. Zen Activity also partakes of the meanings of wellspring, dynamism, spontaneity, immediacy etc. This quality, as

Hisamatsu makes plain, expresses itself through literature and art when these are performed by one who is awakened or enlightened. It exists also in every act of an enlightened person. Understanding the rules by which great haiku are judged can lead to an error free example. However the haiku of many masters also show a great liveliness of spirit which is more difficult to emulate simply by following rules. Basho's

> Old pond
> leap–splash
> a frog

has a simplicity and panache difficult to copy. (Here the translator has opted for trying to capture the spirit of sudden movement in stillness and has abandoned the seventeen syllable form in order to attain it.)

Just to make things more difficult, realised Zen masters break many of the rules of conventional haiku. In the next example there is a reference to self. However that reference is made flatly as though it were a fact and not a viewpoint.

> Through snow
> lights of homes
> that slammed their gates on me

This is one of my personal favourites as it seems to encapsulate so much in such few syllables. I found when I tried to write it from memory that I changed the last line to '*that slammed their gates against me*'. My memory had dramatised the duality between the lights which could not be prevented from shining, and the gates which had been closed. The real lines do not contain the emotive 'against'. (In translation it is also difficult to be sure whether the rather strong 'slammed' was intended in the way it comes over in English.)

The observations I made earlier about the intrusion of the ego-self on the creative process are intended to reflect the formalisation of a process which I witnessed during the workshop. The use of words denoting the presence of 'self' is not intended to be an infallible guide to judge whether someone is 'self-realised' in the Zen sense. The difficulty which surrounds this issue is that often even those familiar with Zen tend to think of the ego-less state as some calm remote place where no emotion ever stirs. Hey (1988) says of it however,

> [p]re-occupation with self ends and perception turns outward with an intensity and acuity never before experienced. Affect returns

but is profoundly altered: happiness is joy without attachment or sentimentality. . . . It is a dynamic and fluid form of consciousness in which awareness is no longer bound to a particular sense of self.

(Hey 1988, p.60)

The self-realised person in Zen still has a personality, emotions and thoughts, although these are not bound up with the psychological baggage that most of us collect over a lifetime. References to 'self' have a lightness of quality. That sense of freedom and even playfulness is surely what is expressed in the following haiku of Basho

> If I'd the knack
> I'd sing like
> cherry flakes falling

or

> How pleasant
> Just once not to see
> Fuji through mist.

The simple, almost childlike unselfconsciousness of the first of these verses reflects a very different sense of self from that of the strained 'One never knows when a deer, etc.' written at the workshop. The second is not however as simple as it looks. Mount Fuji is often used as a symbol for enlightenment in classical haiku. Basho was therefore commenting on the unenlightened state of 'seeing Fuji through mist' as well as the more straightforward descriptive meaning.

One participant at the workshop who knew something of haiku form and symbolism produced the following final haiku

> You are not far from
> Mount Fuji, this swallow
> will lead you there.

This drew a laugh from Hey who responded with

> Autumn moon,
> tides ebbing
> and flowing to the very gate.

In the first haiku there is imitation, i.e. some of the conventions are followed, but there is also interpretation. The spirit of freedom exemplified by the swallow is still used 'in order to' achieve something. In contrast in Hey's response the symbolism is organic. Tides ebb and flow 'naturally' and suggest that the state aspired to has to be arrived at in a less pointed fashion.

## CONCLUSIONS

Not only do we try to present ourselves to others in discourse in the best possible light, but we also unwittingly reveal deeper models of self-hood in the judgements we make. The fallacy of a continuous self is gradually being investigated by Western psychology and philosophy. But resistance to the notion that the self is illusory is likely to be strong. One of the concerns often raised regarding the position of the existential movement was that when there was no sense of a continuous self, then there would be no moral sense arising out of shared societal values. The implication was that if the self was a social construction which was stripped away, what followed was nihilism and chaos.

In Zen by becoming aware of the self-imposed restrictions of the ego self, there is a realisation of the true nature of the self. This essential self is *more* sensitive to the interconnectedness of all things, and not less, and is therefore less destructive. Once our judgements are untrammelled by our hopes and desires, the resultant clarity allows for action or non-action, whichever is appropriate.

Most people of course are neither aware of, nor trying to achieve, that state of being which is called enlightenment. Many however are unhappy with their lives and some are deeply disturbed. What I have tried to indicate here is that the concepts of self that are embedded in our conscious view of the world affect everything we do. As many participants at the workshop found, it is difficult to express any thought or feeling without interpretation. And this interpretation is carried out by what we think of as our 'self'.

But if this self is illusory, if we collect self concepts as we go along and enshrine them as central to our sense of self worth, then this has profound consequences for Western philosophy, psychology and psychotherapy. Can any decision made by a mental construction be regarded as exercising free will or intentionality? Is the realisation that the self is mentally constructed a symptom of 'depersonalisation disorder' or the start of true personal freedom? If our past experiences condition our thinking, should clients be encouraged to dwell on them in therapy? Unfinished personal business is very much the domain of the ego.

Those participants at the workshop described above came to understand that their concepts of self were idealised and not very accurate.
To take a step further and realise that *all* concepts of self produced by
the ego are equally suspect is difficult. As Dennett notes above, even
when the theoretical danger of relying on a continuous autonomous
self is seen, people go on making the same type of attributions of
meaning. The challenge of Zen is to find some other way of being.

## REFERENCES

Assagioli, (1975) *Psychosynthesis*, Penguin, Harmondsworth
Bahm, A.J. (1958) *Philosophy of the Buddha*, Asian Humanities Press, Berkeley,
    California
Basho (1995) *Haiku*, Penguin Books, London
Conze, E. (1959) *Buddhist Scriptures*, Penguin Books, London
Dennett, D.C. (1983) 'Artificial Intelligence and the Strategies of Psychological
    Investigation, in Miller, J. (ed.) *Conversations with Psychological Investigators*,
    BBC, London
Dennett, D.C. (1991) *Consciousness Explained*, Allen Lane, The Penguin Press,
    London
Goffman, E. (1959) *Presentation of Self in Everyday Life*, Penguin, Harmondsworth
Harre, R. and Gillett, G. (1994) *The Discursive Mind*, Sage Publications,
    California
Harri-Augstein, S. and Thomas, L. (1991) *Learning Conversations*, Routledge,
    London
Hey, J. (1988) *The 'I' of Zen* unpublished manuscript, copyright The Zen
    Foundation
Hey, J. (1995) *The Zen Game* unpublished manuscript, copyright The Zen
    Foundation
Hisamatsu, S. (1982) *Zen and the Fine Arts*, Kodansha International Ltd., Tokyo
Laing, R.D. (1965) *The Divided Self*, Penguin, London
Lancaster, B. (1991) *Mind, Brain and Human Potential – The Quest for the
    Understanding of Self*, Element Books, Shaftesbury, Dorset
Mischel, T. (1977) 'Conceptual Issues in the Psychology of Self', in Mischel,
    T. (ed.) *The Self – Psychological and Philosophical Issues*, Basil Blackwell,
    Oxford
Parfit, D. (1984) *Reasons and Persons*, Clarendon Press, Oxford
Parfit, D. (1987) 'Divided Minds and the Nature of Persons', in Blakemore, C.
    and Greenfield, S. (eds) *Mindwaves*, Basil Blackwell, Oxford
Sartre, J.P. (1972) *The Transcendence of the Ego*, Octagon Books, New York
Segal, S. (1996) *Collision with the Infinite*, Blue Dove Press, San Diego, California
Skinner, B.F. (1974) *About Behaviourism*, Jonathan Cape, London
Suzuki, D.T. (1969) *The Zen Doctrine of No Mind*, Rider, London

Suzuki, D.T. (1973) *The Essentials of Zen Buddhism*, Greenwood Press, Westport, Connecticut

Taylor, C. (1977) 'What is Human Agency?' in Mischel, T. (ed.) *The Self – Psychological and Philosophical Issues*, Basil Blackwell, Oxford

Thomas, L. and Harri-Augstein, S. (1985) *Self-Organised Learning – Foundations of a Conversational Science for Psychology*, Routledge and Kegan Paul, London

# Introduction to chapter 13

Existentialism, a movement usually identified with Kierkegaard, Nietzsche, Heidegger and a group of French thinkers among whom Sartre remains the best known, has been influential in many fields including theology, literature and politics. No longer at the zenith of fashion, Warnock's introduction (1970) remains a useful overview of its most characteristic features. Its concern with how people are situated in the world in the widest sense lends it to therapeutic application. More recently, several distinct attempts have been made to describe psychotherapies claiming to be 'existential' either because they emphasise key existentialist themes, such as the creation of meaning or assumption of personal responsibility, or because they claim descent from a particular school. Some instances where the links have been even closer will be considered in the final chapter of this book. A comprehensive historical guide to the principal currents of existentialism and psychotherapies linked to them has been provided by the author of this chapter (van Deurzen-Smith, 1997).

In the present chapter, an attempt is made to distil recurrent themes from the existential therapies, to present an ideal type. This not only provides a touchstone of whether it would be fair to see a therapy as 'existential', but, in illuminating the interdependence of these themes, provides a practical indication of where explorations in therapy may need to go once this territory is entered.

## REFERENCES

Van Deurzen-Smith, E. (1997) *Everyday Mysteries*. London: Routledge.
Warnock, M. (1970) *Existentialism*. Oxford: Oxford University Press.

# 13 Existentialism and existential psychotherapy

*Emmy van Deurzen*

## INTRODUCTION

### Philosophy and psychotherapy

It is somewhat surprising that philosophy and psychotherapy do not have a more distinguished history of co-operation. Both disciplines are concerned with human well being and human living, the one in a theoretical manner, the other in a much more pragmatic way. One would expect psychotherapists to have noted the central importance of philosophy to the practice of their own profession and to draw on philosophy as a source for understanding their clients' predicaments. Unfortunately this has not been the case. Psychotherapists have on the whole neglected the study of philosophy, which they have frequently dismissed as irrelevant, and they have turned to medicine and psychology as the disciplines of theoretical reference for their domain. This may well be because of the aridity and high level of abstraction of much of Western philosophy. This is rather ironic, as Hellenistic philosophy several millennia ago set out as a disciplined search for the well lived human life, or *eudaimonia*. Philosophy then proposed a form of dialectical debate where individuals were encouraged to seek to clarify their beliefs about the world in order to come to a better understanding of their conflicts and the objectives of their everyday existence (Nussbaum 1994, Vlastos 1991).

Philosophy to a large extent lost track of its own mission to understand, clarify and sustain the concrete realities of ordinary people and as it spawned the sciences, became increasingly abstract and detached from its former objectives. This is particularly evident in logical positivism. Nevertheless there has always been a strand of philosophy that concerned itself with human issues, which is that of ethical philosophy. There are a number of philosophers, like Kant, Rousseau, Spinoza, Hume and Hegel· who have made important contributions in this way and they should be essential reading for trainee psychotherapists. It is however with the new impulse of the philosophies of existence, particularly those of Kierkegaard (1844, 1846, 1855) and Nietzsche (1881, 1882, 1886, 1887, 1888) that philosophers themselves became directly interested again in the concrete questions of human existence. The philosophies of Kierkegaard and Nietzsche draw attention to the subjective life of the individual and in this way provide an excellent basis for the kind of philosophy that can inform the practice of psychotherapy. With the advent of Husserl's phenomenology (Husserl 1900, 1913, 1925, 1929) a more concrete methodology of investigation of human issues was proposed enabling existentialism to come into its own with the work of philosophers such as Heidegger (1927, 1954, 1957), Sartre (1939, 1943a, 1943b, 1948) and Merleau Ponty (1945, 1964, 1968).

Existentialism became a popular movement as people reclaimed philosophy as being of personal relevance. Here at last was an approach that would give them a handle on the moral choices, existential crises and constant challenges of daily reality. Philosophy was shown to be capable of providing a forum for debate where light could be thrown on the far-reaching changes that humanity was having to negotiate in the modern and post-modern era. It was therefore predictable that existentialism should also generate a new form of psychotherapy in which medical considerations were replaced with wider human ones and where a person's particular problems were set against the background of a general existential perspective.

## Existential psychotherapy

Existential psychotherapy is the only established form of psychotherapy that is directly based in philosophy rather than in psychology. It was founded at the beginning of the century, on the one hand by the original work of Karl Jaspers in Germany, (1951, 1963, 1964) which itself influenced Heidegger's thinking and on the other hand by the work of two Swiss psychiatrists, Ludwig Binswanger (1946, 1963) and Medard Boss (1957, 1962, 1979, 1988), who were in turn inspired by the work of Heidegger to create an alternative method of dealing with emotional and mental distress. All three turned from psychiatry to philosophy, in an attempt to understand the human predicament, paradoxes and conflicts of their patients. These early applications of existentialist philosophy to psychotherapy have been followed by a number of other and varied attempts, as for instance in the work of Frankl (1946, 1955, 1967), May (May, Angel and Ellenburger, 1958; May, 1969, 1983),

Laing (1960, 1961, 1967; Laing and Esterson, 1964), Szasz (1961, 1965, 1992) Yalom (1980, 1989) and van Deurzen-Smith (1984, 1988, 1992, 1997, 1998).

There has however continued to be great diversity between these and other authors as no official or formal rendering of existential psychotherapy has ever been agreed. To confuse matters further, existential principles have also been applied more indirectly to psychotherapy as part of the humanistic psychology movement, for instance in person-centred and Gestalt approaches to psychotherapy, which often pride themselves on their existential origins. Personal-construct therapies also have a basis in the phenomenological approach and there are a number of psychoanalytic writers who take existential ideas into account as well. All of these approaches however tend to focus on the intra-personal dimensions of human existence and they have formulated psychological theories that do not allow the philosophical dimension to come to the fore or to be central. Radical existential psychotherapy focuses on the inter-personal and supra-personal dimensions, as it tries to capture and question people's world-views. Such existential work aims at clarifying and understanding personal values and beliefs, making explicit what was previously implicit and unsaid. Its practice is primarily philosophical and seeks to enable a person to live more deliberately, more authentically and more purposefully, whilst accepting the limitations and contradictions of human existence. It has much in common with the newly developed practice of philosophical consultancy, which is just finding its feet in Germany, the Netherlands, Israel and the United States (Lahav and Venza Tillmanns 1995, Achenbach 1984, Hoogendijk 1991).

There continues to be a lack of systematic theorizing about existential psychotherapy and a lack of research to demonstrate the effectiveness of this kind of work. This is mostly because the existential approach resists formalisation and opposes the fabrication of a method that can be taught as a technique and followed automatically. Existential psychotherapy has to be reinvented and recreated by every therapist and with every new client. It is essentially about investigating human existence and the particular preoccupations of one individual and this has to be done without preconceptions or set ways of proceeding. There has to be complete openness to the individual situation and an attitude of wonder that will allow the specific circumstances and experiences to unfold in their own right. We can however distinguish a number of themes that will predictably emerge in this process. The following list of existential issues is a personal selection based on the compilation of the work of the major philosophers of existence.

The order in which the issues are presented and discussed is based on my experience of teaching trainee psychotherapists some of the predictable patterns that emerge when clients in psychotherapy present their concerns and begin to examine their lives in a philosophical manner. Of course life is a great deal more complex than this list suggests and one can look at the same issues in many different ways. What follows is a brief description of my particular pathway towards clarity. It is important to remember that existential psychotherapists aim to assist their clients in finding their own.

## EXISTENTIAL ISSUES

### Ontological description

The first thing to keep in mind when applying philosophy to psychotherapeutic practice is that when philosophers think about human living they do so not as anthropologists or psychologists. They do not primarily preoccupy themselves with concrete experiences, but they rather allow themselves to build theories about human living in an abstract sense. They are concerned to describe the ontological dimension of life and only secondarily come to the concrete experience of the individual. They try to pinpoint what it is that makes human living possible and difficult in the first place. Ontological descriptions are thus descriptions that tell us what is the *sine qua non* of human existence. They sketch out the conditions without which there would be no real human life. It is extremely useful to ask oneself what the basic foundations of human living are. Heidegger's book *Being and Time* (1927) is just such an attempt at describing the essential being in the world of humans. His consideration of human beings as *Dasein*, or being-in-the-world, redefines questions of self and psychology as questions of living and philosophy. His sharp thinking about what makes human being possible provides a useful map of existence, which can certainly be argued with and revised, but which nevertheless asks important questions about people in general, allowing for a closer examination of the particular individual life afterwards. Of course there are many such possible maps and ontological theories to be found in philosophy. Existential philosophy is particularly focused on the predictable dilemmas of human living that will be regularly encountered when doing psychotherapy.

## Meaning of life

According to Heidegger the most fundamental philosophical question is: 'Why is there something rather than nothing?' We do not actually know the answer to this question, but it remains a fundamental question to ask ourselves if we are going to be serious about examining human living from scratch. Clients ask themselves this question regularly and in particular they are unclear about the meaning of their own life. Philosophers have shown such questioning to be necessary in order to become a self-reflective human being. Doubts about the meaning of life are the beginning of all philosophy. Doubt and wonder enable us to rediscover the miracle of being. Children have not lost this ability to wonder and they ask the question 'why' at the most inopportune moments. Adults tend to wonder about the meaning of life most particularly when things are difficult and no longer self-evident. Once upon a time the meaning of life was given by religion or by social rule. These days meaning is often looked at in a far more sceptical manner (see Tantam, this volume). It is therefore not surprising that people often find themselves in what can be called a vacuum of meaning (Frankl 1946, 1955). The experience of meaninglessness becomes a major problem in many people's lives and it may lead to a number of concrete difficulties, which may look like personality problems or other forms of pathology. Psychotherapists, psychologists or psychiatrists often have considerable difficulties in recognizing the validity of philosophical questioning. They are reluctant to engage in theoretical discussions with clients and patients who are seemingly disturbed, but who actually may be in search of meaning. We can only engage in such discussions if we have been willing to question our own lives and can recognise that anxieties and doubts about meaning do not have to be equated with personal pathology or mental illness (Szasz 1961, 1965, 1992).

It is by no means easy to be truly available to help others in finding meaning in their lives when their existence is in crisis. The meaning of life is never given and can not be transmitted unless a person is willing to search for it independently. Phenomenologists recognised that meaning making is one of the defining characteristics of human consciousness. It could therefore be argued that the meaning of human living is to learn to give it meaning. In order to come to a position from which we can learn to give meaning we have to first come to a point of doubt and a realization of the lack of intrinsic meaning in our lives. Frankl (1946) spoke of three sources of meaning. First through taking from the world what is there, learning to savour and appreciate what is already given to us, as in aesthetic enjoyment of nature or the pleasures of the senses. Second to give to the world and add new enjoyments to it through acts of our own creativity and by giving to others in this way as well. Third by suffering, which is to endure the harsh conditions we may be exposed to. If there is no alternative to our suffering, it is always possible to find an attitude of human dignity by enduring the hard labour, pain and disappointments, Frankl argues, even when we have to face up to extremes of torture and deprivation.

## Existential anxiety

The experience of meaninglessness and the creation of meaning are closely related to the experience of Angst or existential anxiety. This occurs against the backdrop of the personal realization that I am ultimately alone in the world and that I have to contend with my mortality and other limitations, taking responsibility for myself in the face of endless challenges and confusions. This crisis of meaning was first described by Kierkegaard (1844, 1855), who thought that it was a great deal preferable to begin to feel anxious about life and question it, than to live in the despair of those who deny the need to think for themselves. Kierkegaard thought that human beings would only gradually become capable of such questioning. He believed that people are vegetative to begin with, not taking much notice of the meaning of anything at first. They then grow sentient as they are beginning to follow their senses and relate more intensely to the world. After this they grow conscious of the world around them and as they begin to form judgements about things, eventually they become knowing about some of what is. Out of knowing can grow self-knowing as we apply the ability to think and recognise, compare and judge for ourselves. Out of self-knowing can come a self-awareness that leads to autonomy and the ability to make choices and decisions for oneself. This process plunges us into Angst, or existential anxiety, likened by Kierkegaard to a dizziness of freedom. He thought that experiencing Angst was the *sine qua non* of us assuming our responsibility as individuals and that without it we could never come face to face with the demands our life makes on us.

Anxiety or Angst is a core concept in existential philosophy, which sees it as the basic ingredient of vitality. Learning to be anxious in the right way, i.e. not too much or too little, is the key to living a reflective, meaningful human life. As Kierkegaard put it, 'Whoever has learnt to be anxious in the right way has learnt the ultimate' (Kierkegaard 1844:155).

Anxiety has to be distinguished from fear. The former is a generalised feeling of *Unheimlichkeit* (Heidegger 1927), of not being at ease, or at home in one's world, whereas the latter has a concrete object. It is anxiety that allows us to define ourselves as separate persons and to become responsive and responsible as well as aware and alert. Although we may become overwhelmed with anxiety, so that it becomes counterproductive, on the whole anxiety is to be seen as a positive breakthrough towards the goal of the fully lived human life.

## How are we to live our lives?

In this sense existential psychotherapy does not reassure people when they come to talk about the predicaments and conflicts in their lives. They are encouraged to consider their anxiety and their problems as a valid starting point for the work that has to be done. When people wonder what is wrong with their life it is tempting to treat such questioning as symptomatic of emotional problems, but existential psychotherapy sees it as an attempt at coming to grips with philosophical dilemmas. Most of us are likely to encounter such dilemmas sooner or later and people should be assisted in getting clarity on how they want to live when such issues arise. People easily lose their sense of direction. Moral and ethical issues are increasingly obscure in the world we live in today. It may be helpful to turn to Nietzsche's challenge (Nietzsche 1883) that we should re-value all values. He insisted that our thinking had gone astray and that much that people took for granted had to be reconsidered. He thought it crucial to consider afresh what a good human life consists of. In order to do so it is useful to turn to the map of human existence that can be pieced together from the writings of existential philosophers, so that we can find our way through the obstacles of human living without losing our bearings.

## Intentionality

The linchpin of human existence is the concept of intentionality. It was Husserl's phenomenology that established intentionality as its new foundation, following Brentano's original idea (Husserl 1900, 1913, 1929). Phenomenology posits that human consciousness is essentially transparent and in this sense is always and necessarily connected to a world. It is never independent and always has an object. As we are non-substantial, transparent beings, we cannot but reach out to a world. We are always in relation. Through us the world comes to light. We always, think, do, desire, imagine something. There always is some content to our mind. It is possible to set aside our automatic ways of intending things and judging things and take heed of our tendency to do so. We can learn to be disciplined about our intentionality and through the phenomenological reduction question all the automatic judgements we normally take for granted. Husserl called this process 'coming to things themselves' and it is often referred to as the *epoche*. It consists of putting our usual assumptions about the world in brackets. This does not mean that we get rid of them or pretend they do not exist, but rather that we deal with them separately so that we can describe the situation, object of our attention or other person we are dealing with fairly and as it really is. To make oneself consistently query one's assumptions about the world and reconsider it with a cleared attitude of openness is obviously extremely relevant to the practice of psychotherapy. What we find when we apply this manner of observing other people is that they themselves are always in a relationship of intentionality to the world they live in. It is their mode of being in the world that we need to turn to next.

## Lived world

Husserl spoke of the *Lebenswelt* or lived world to describe the sort of universe that we live in. Everyone has their own perspective on the world, their own particular point of reference their own atmosphere and outlook. The lived world of the cat is obviously different from that of the dog or the bird for instance. When a cat comes into a room it may seek out cosy hiding places, while a dog may orientate himself by his sense of smell, looking for good spots to lift a leg on, whereas a bird might be focused on finding high places to perch on. The same room would seem a very different place to different people. In an even more complex manner they have a world of their own. This world determines where people go and what they want and do. Heidegger (1927) described the human world in quite a lot of detail, showing it always to have a horizon, a home ground and a foreign ground. We are always at a certain distance from things, although our relation to things might be determined by our intentional stance towards them more than by the actual space that separates us. When I run for the bus for instance, it seems closer to me than the ground that I run over. I see it as near and if it suddenly pulls out, the severance that I experience and the sudden distance between me and the object of my desire may plunge me into confusion and disappointment. To describe the experiences of my world as completely as possible and without the usual assumption that I already know what I am describing leads to new insights into what human living entails.

## Situations

We discover immediately that people are always connected to the world in a number of concrete ways. Heidegger in this context spoke of our 'thrownness'. He said that we are always thrown into a world that is already there to start with and into which we are simply inserted. It is important to recognise the factual situations that we are confronted with. We are part of a certain culture, a certain environment with a particular climate and history, a certain society and a specific situation. It is only within the givens of that situation that we can exercise our own choices. Sartre (1943a) called this our 'facticity' and he recognised that we can never release ourselves from this, even though we can choose our position in relation to it. In terms of psychotherapy it also means that it may be necessary to look at people's problems in a structural way. Instead of seeing everything as the person's personal, emotional or internal problem, problems can be seen as part of an overall situation. Context is crucial and has to be taken into account.

## Limit situations

Of all the situations in which we can find ourselves there are certain ones that are irrevocable. These situations have to be accepted. We cannot avoid them or overcome them: we have to learn to live with them. Heidegger emphasised the importance of death as a marker of our finite nature. Death in this sense is not to be taken as something happening to us at some point later, but as something that is relevant to us right now. The realities of our mortality and of our incompleteness have to be faced for us to become aware of and true to our nature, which is to be finite. Heidegger considered that the reality of our death is that it completes us. The recognition of the inevitability of death gives us a certainty that nothing else can give us. The fear in the face of death allows us to claim back our individuality, our authentic being, as we are inevitably alone in death and find ourselves much sobered and humbled by the knowledge of our mortality. Death, according to Heidegger 'amounts to the disclosedness of the fact that *Dasein* exists as thrown being towards its end' (Heidegger 1927: 251). In other words: death is part of me and to accept my living towards this end gives my life back to me in a new way.

Jaspers (1951, 1971) spoke of limit situations as those situations which define our humanity. Sooner or later we inevitably come up against guilt, death, pain, suffering and failure. The philosophical take on this is that we should encourage people to come to terms with some of the inevitable conflicts and problems of living whilst also asking themselves how they can move forward in a new and desirable direction. Limit situations are what bring us into confrontation with ourselves in a decisive and fundamentally disturbing way. They evoke anxiety and therefore release us from our tendency to be untrue and evasive about ourselves and our lives.

## Self-deception

Sartre was particularly adamant that as human beings we try to pretend that we are solid and definite in the way that objects are. People do not like to face up to their fundamental nothingness and mortality. We think we can pretend to be like a stone or a solid thing, but in fact in doing so we are deceiving ourselves, reinventing ourselves in bad faith (Sartre 1943a). To be in bad faith is an almost unavoidable state of play for human beings as we seem to find it particularly difficult to face up to the implications of our freedom as consciousness. One of the objectives of human living is to become increasingly aware of our ability to choose to live deliberately rather than by default and to diminish the extent to which we seek to tell ourselves false stories about ourselves. Sartre said that the only choice we do not have is not to choose because not to choose involves a choice as well. 'In fact we are a freedom which chooses, but we do not choose to be free' (Sartre 1943:485). The coward is fulfilling the project of cowardice, in the same way in which the hero is fulfilling the project of heroism. They can both either choose to take responsibility for their choice or pretend that it just happened to them and is not open to question.

Heidegger saw the existence of other people, with whom we are fallen into a world where the anonymous 'They' decides about our actions and our identity, as the major obstacle to authenticity. He recognized, as Sartre did, that human beings are condemned to living inauthentically for much of the time, but that we should nevertheless aim to retrieve ourselves from inauthenticity. It is the anxiety of our possible death, and our discovery that we are alone in the face of our own fate and destiny that allow us ultimately to take ourselves seriously and posit ourselves firmly, resolutely, as individuals facing death.

## Time

This is when it also becomes possible to become more aware of the dimension of time, which is a crucial category of human living. It is always today and not tomorrow or yesterday. I am always no longer and not yet. We orientate ourselves in relation to the various ways in which we stand out in time. Our lives are a constant process of transformation that we cannot stop. Heidegger spoke of the three ec-stasies of time (Heidegger 1927:329), which are the ways in which we stand out in the past, in the present and in the future. We go back to ourselves in terms of remembering the past. We let ourselves be encountered by the world in the present and we reach out towards ourselves in the future. The past (*Erbe*) is the legacy we go forward with and which we can recollect in different ways. This means that we can re-present the past to ourselves in a new and creative manner. The present is our fate (*Schiksal*), which we have the task to live out as fully as possible, obviously drawing on the legacy of the past and making ourselves present to our own fate by facing our limitations rather than hiding away in inauthenticity. The future is our destiny (*Geschick*) and the destination that we choose for ourselves in relation to what is available to us. Our destination is thus created from our legacy and our fate. All of my actions are full of the awareness of my temporal change. There is decay and development around me. Life consists of movement, transformation and action. All of these are only possible in time. My existence is historic. It creates a story. How I create this story is of utmost importance. Existential psychotherapy is about retracing the story and reorienting a person in time.

## The fragile self

The way in which I tell my story is the way in which I create a self. Existential philosophy does not posit the notion of a fixed and determined self. There is no such thing as an essential solid self, only intentionality and being in the world. Sartre used to say that existence preceded essence. I come into the world first and exist and only after that do I create a self for myself out of my actions. The self is a window on the world; out of our living in time and standing out in the world we become what we are. Sartre went as far as to say that people were the sum of their actions. Therefore the choices we make are constitutive of the sort of person we become. We are constantly in the process of creating a self, yet when we try to capture this self, we realise it is as if we were trying to catch our shadow: it moves away from us and changes as we try to fix it. We cannot be a definitive something. Our stories change as we live and so we are changed too. As we saw before, the only way in which we can believe in a self is by being in bad faith, i.e. by using self-deception. Any image we create of ourselves is in a sense a lie: it never tells the full story about who we are or could be.

We have to re-create ourselves every day and to become aware of this is to become authentic and true to the self which is not one. We are thus doomed to feel a sense of incompleteness as life requires us to try ever harder to be equal to what we are capable of, even though we can never achieve it.

## Existential guilt

Most of us will therefore have a frequent sensation of unease with ourselves. The awareness that we are not true to our full human ability and that we live inauthentically will lead to the experience of existential guilt. In existential guilt we hear the voice of our conscience and this must be taken extremely seriously. We are not guilty because we have fallen short by other people's standards or because we have behaved badly, but simply because we fall short as human beings. It is important to note that most existential philosophers assume that human living will inevitably expose us to falling short and therefore to feeling existential guilt. We are always indebted to life. We are always capable of being more alive, more open, more true to the potential of human consciousness than we actually are. We are therefore condemned to feel existential guilt, as we are condemned to feel existential anxiety; largely because we are, as Sartre said, condemned to be free. Heidegger greatly valued the call of conscience which he believed warned us of our existential guilt, thus bringing us back into confrontation with our human fate, allowing us to rediscover our authentic being. 'The call is the call of care. Being guilty constitutes the Being to which we give the name of "care"' (Heidegger 1927:332–3).

To become authentic requires us to take into account our essential ways of existing and conduct ourselves accordingly. All of these modalities of existence, which Heidegger refers to as the existentialia are consequences of our intentional nature.

## Care

Our intentional nature, and the nature of our consciousness as the place where being comes to light, as Heidegger put it, makes us care. People are the custodians of Being because they are nothing in themselves but need to reflect something, in order to exist fully. As transparent entities human beings are therefore condemned to care. The world always matters to us and we have to take account of our care for the world, which manifests in many different ways. It is therefore not the question whether we care, but how. Care is not to be understood as a negative or a positive, but rather as the inevitable mode of our relating to a world that is of importance to us. Heidegger speaks of care as manifesting as our concern for things and our solicitude for people. But our care also manifests in some specific ways in which we are in the world and relate to it.

## Mood

The fact that the world always matters to us is evident in the way in which we are always in a mood. We cannot be separate from the world, but always respond to it in a particular state of mind. Heidegger (1927: 134) called this *Befindlichkeit*, or the way in which I find myself. This state of mind is a response to the atmosphere created between the world, and me by my care for what is happening in it. *Stimmung*, or attunement, is the way in which I respond to the atmospheres, the way in which, like a musical instrument I am attuned in a particular way to the world around me. Through my resonance with the world I disclose the world in a particular way. My mood colours the world as it is also coloured by it. My own being is disclosed in my moods at the same time as it discloses the world. Moods are therefore invaluable indicators of what is happening between my world and me. We can never not be in a mood and we cannot just stop a mood. We can only get out of one mood by getting into another. Sartre elaborated on this idea of the central position of mood or mode of being by describing emotions as active rather than passive. He spoke of emotion as a kind of magic by which I alter the world and therefore myself in one blow (Sartre 1939).

## Understanding

As human beings we can respond to the world through our emotions, but we can also, through our emotions and our ability to reflect on them, come to grasp things in a new way. This new way of understanding (*verstehen*) is not just about human intelligence and the capacity for calculating things in the world. Heidegger makes the distinction between *Vernunft* (rational mind) and *Verstand* (understanding) which is our ability to see the whole of what is rather than analyse things with our mind (Heidegger 1927:144). Understanding discloses the potential of our being, as it shows us what we are capable of. In his later work he made the distinction between calculative thinking and meditative thinking (Heidegger 1954). He showed how important it was to learn to think again in this more encompassing meditative manner where we are open to the world and receive it with gratitude for what is, rather than trying to subject it to the analysis and manipulations that our calculative mind imposes. Heidegger suggests that we use *Sicht*, or vision, to understand the world and our relation to it. *Umsicht*, or the vision of looking around one, applies to objects and we need to approach objects with the care of circumspection. We use *Rucksicht*, which suggests a kind of withholding, in relation to other people, which manifests as considerateness. Finally, and perhaps most importantly, we employ *Durchsicht*, or seeing through things in relation to ourselves. It is thus transparency that brings into being careful understanding of ourselves.

## Discourse

Language is an essential vehicle for understanding our modes of being. Heidegger speaks of discourse as the third essential mode of being (together with mood and understanding). Discourse is a broader concept than language and includes it. Although discourse is obviously linked to language it can also manifest as silence. We have to struggle to retrieve valuable discourse out of all the possible misuses of talking. Speech can turn to idle talk (*Gerede* rather than *Rede*). Discourse can flounder in curiosity, which is a moving across the surface of things, distracted by their novelty, as we collect and accumulate useless information. In this way we drown in existence and we go under in ambiguity (Merleau Ponty 1945). Discourse is to be used carefully for it to become a valuable resource for the manifestation of being. In language or in silent thought we can capture and express ourselves in relation to life and begin to come to terms with our essential function of being the shepherds of being.

## Communication

The mastery of language makes human communication possible. However communication is a lot more complex than simple speech. Heidegger was aware that *Mitsein*, or being with others, was part of our essential nature. He also described people as at the mercy of the anonymous other who defines their being-in-the-world. Authentic being is only possible when we set ourselves aside from others. Sartre described our struggle with others as a desperate attempt at survival and at gaining a false sense of security. He saw human communication, which is by no means only about language, as taking place either in a sadistic, a masochistic or an indifferent way. We can try to dominate the other or we can submit or withdraw from communication altogether. In sharp contrast to Sartre's pessimistic view of human relations and human communication, the philosopher Martin Buber (1923, 1929) saw the possibility of a more positive way of human interaction. He distinguished between I–it and I–Thou modes of relating. He noted that the way we relate to others determines what kind of person we become. In the I–It mode of relating I treat the other as an object and become an object myself. In this mode I see the other only for part of what the other is capable of and at the same time become partial myself. In the I–Thou mode I relate to the other for all the other is capable of and I relate thus with my whole being as well. The I–Thou mode of relating has a spiritual dimension. Buber described the way in which we create a space between others and ourselves. In this space human communication becomes a reality. He called this space the in-between. True dialogue can be created in this space when we release our self-reserve and reach out to the other with our whole being. 'Where un-reserve has ruled, even wordlessly, between men, the word of dialogue has happened sacramentally' (Buber 1929:3–4).

## Mastered irony

Kierkegaard believed that language should be used with what he calls mastered irony. This requires the ability to detach oneself sufficiently from one's situation to be able to see oneself in some perspective. He claims that those who lack irony do not have even the beginning of a personal life. To have a personal life and be able to be objective about oneself and subjective about others is to Kierkegaard a primary objective. 'Most men are subjective toward themselves and objective toward all others, frightfully objective sometimes – but the task is precisely to be objective toward oneself and subjective toward all others' (Kierkegaard 1967: IV 4542).

He distinguishes fanatics, who cling to certain beliefs from nihilists who deny all beliefs, but sees them both as lacking in courage. In mastered irony one questions one's own beliefs while still being committed to them. As usual, the challenge is to be able to live in the tension between opposites.

## Paradox

This idea that human living takes place in the tension between opposing forces is present throughout existential philosophy. Most obviously this is represented by Heidegger's (1927) description of the tension between life and death, or by Sartre's descriptions of the tension between being and nothingness, expressed in the tension between being-for-itself (the being of consciousness) and being-in-itself (the being of objects) (Sartre 1943a). Kierkegaard, for his part, described this tension as one between the infinite and the finite. He claimed that one can be too much drawn into either the finite or the infinite and that the challenge of living is to maintain the right sort of tension between both. The person who is immersed in the finite gets caught up in the dangers of concrete living. The person who gets too immersed in the infinite is the dreamer, who merges with the universe and becomes either overwhelmed and terrified or depressed by it, ending up feeling alienated from everyday reality. Kierkegaard thought it was important to be capable of modulating between the two extremes. Merleau Ponty was equally aware of the paradoxical nature of human living and he firmly believed that we have to live with what amounts to an essential ambiguity (Merleau Ponty 1945, 1968).

## The four-dimensional force field

In this force field of opposites there are a number of different dimensions of experience. Systematic descriptions of human experience have outlined four dimensions. Heidegger spoke of the different dimensions as those of earth, world, man, and gods (Heidegger 1957). Binswanger (1946, 1963) spoke of the *Umwelt* (environment), *Mitwelt* (world with others) and *Eigenwelt* (personal world), whilst a spiritual dimension (*überwelt*) is also implied in his work (van Deurzen-Smith 1984). In essence philosophers have recognised that human experience is multiple and complex and takes place on a number of different levels. First there is our involvement in a physical world of objects, where we struggle between survival and death. Second there is our activity in a social world of other people, where we struggle with the contradictions between our need to belong and the possibility of our isolation. Third there is a personal dimension where we grapple with the tension between integrity and disintegration. Finally there is a spiritual dimension where we seek to find meaning against the threat of meaninglessness. On each of these dimensions we have to learn to stand in the tension between opposites, discovering that we cannot have life without death, love without hate, identity without confusion, and wisdom without doubt. As Paul Tillich once said, 'The courage of confidence takes the anxiety of fate as well as the anxiety of guilt into itself' (Tillich 1952: 163).

# CONCLUSION

## A dialectical approach

Approaching psychotherapy from an existential perspective is to see
that a dialectical process manages all these tensions of human existence. Conflicts are constantly generated and then overcome, only to
be reasserted in a new form. Paradoxes are inevitable and life flows
out of contradictory forces working against and with each other. The
existential psychotherapist has as primary task to recognise together
with the client the specific tensions that are at work in the client's life.
This requires a process of careful scrutiny and description of the client's
experience and a gradually growing familiarity with the client's particular situation and stance in the world. To understand the worldview
and the states of mind that this generates is to grapple with the way
the client makes meaning, which involves a coming to know of clients'
values and beliefs. The particular circumstances of the client's life are
recognised, as is their wider context. The psychotherapeutic process
of existential therapy is then to elicit, clarify and put into perspective
all the current issues and contradictions that are problematic. Part of
the work consists in enabling the client to come to terms with the
inherent contradictions of human living. Another part of it is to help
clients find a satisfactory direction for their future life with a full recognition of the paradoxes that have to be faced in the process. Ultimately
the therapeutic search is about allowing the client to reclaim personal
freedom and a willingness and ability to be open to the world in
all its complexity. Authentic living with courage (Tillich 1952) and
in humility would be a suitable existential objective. Learning to reflect
for oneself and communicate effectively with others is another (Buber
1923, 1929). As mentioned before, existential psychotherapy can take
many different shapes and forms, but it always requires a philosophical exploration of what is true for the client. When this exploration
is conducted satisfactorily and fully it often leads to a greater recognition of what is true for human beings in general, affording the beginning
of a genuinely philosophical stance, which may make it easier to tackle
life's inevitable darkness and adversity. In time it may even lead to that
elusive objective of all philosophy that makes everything worthwhile,
ordinary, hard earned, human wisdom.

Existentialism and existential psychotherapy 233

# REFERENCES

Achenbach B.G. (1984) *Philosophische Praxis*, Köln: Jurgen Dinter.
Binswanger, L. (1946) 'The Existential Analysis school of thought', in *Existence*, ed. May, R., Angel, E. and Ellenberger, H.F. (1958) New York: Basic Books.
Binswanger, L. (1963) *Being-in-the-World*, transl. Needleman, J., New York: Basic Books.
Boss, M. (1957) *Psychoanalysis and Daseinsanalysis*, transl. Lefebre, J.B., New York: Basic Books.
Boss, M. (1962) 'Anxiety, guilt and psychotherapeutic liberation', *Review of Existential Psychology and Psychiatry*, vol 11, no. 3, Sept.
Boss, M. (1979) *Existential Foundations of Medicine and Psychology*, New York, Jason Aronson.
Boss, M. (1988) 'Martin Heidegger's Zollikon Seminars', in *Review of Existential Psychology and Psychiatry* ed. Hoeller, K. Vol 16.
Buber, M. (1923) *I and Thou*, transl. Kaufman, W., Edinburgh: T and T Clark, 1970.
Buber, M. (1929) *Between Man and Man*, transl. Smith, R.G., London: Kegan Paul, 1947.
Deurzen, E. van (1998) *Paradox and Passion in Psychotherapy*, Chichester: Wiley.
Deurzen-Smith, E. van (1984) 'Existential therapy', in *Individual Therapy in Britain*, ed. Dryden, W., London: Harper and Row.
Deurzen-Smith, E. van (1988) *Existential Counselling in Practice*, London: Sage Publications.
Deurzen-Smith, E. van, (1992) in *Hard-earned Lessons for Counselling in Action*, ed. Dryden, W., London: Sage Publications.
Deurzen-Smith, E. van (1997) *Everyday Mysteries: Existential Dimensions of Psychotherapy*, London: Routledge.
Frankl, V.E. (1946) *Man's Search for Meaning*, London: Hodder and Stoughton, 1964.
Frankl, V.E. (1955) *The Doctor and the Soul*, New York: Knopf.
Frankl, V.E. (1967) *Psychotherapy and Existentialism*, Harmondsworth: Penguin.
Heidegger, M. (1927) *Being and Time*, transl. Macquarrie, J. and Robinson, E.S., Oxford: Blackwell, 1963.
Heidegger, M. (1954) *What is Called Thinking?*, transl. Scanlon, J., The Hague: Nijhoff, 1977.
Heidegger, M. (1957) *Vorträge und Aufsätze*, Pfullingen: Neske.
Hoogendijk, A. (1991) *Spreekuur bij een Filosoof*, Utrecht: Veen.
Husserl, E. (1900) *Logical Investigations*, transl. Findlay, J.N., London: Routledge.
Husserl, E. (1913) *Ideas*, transl. Boyce Gibson, W.R., New York: Macmillan.
Husserl, E. (1925) *Phenomenological Psychology*, transl. Scanlon J., The Hague: Nijhoff, 1977.
Husserl, E. (1929) *Cartesian Meditations*, The Hague: Nijhoff, 1960.
Jaspers, K. (1951 ) *The Way to Wisdom*, trans. Manheim, R., New Haven: Yale University Press.

234 *Emmy van Deurzen*

Jaspers, K. (1963) *General Psychopathology*, Chicago: University of Chicago Press.

Jaspers, K. (1964) *The Nature of Psychotherapy*, Chicago: University of Chicago Press.

Jaspers, K. (1971) *Philosophy of Existence*, transl. Grabau, R.F., Oxford: Blackwell.

Kierkegaard, S. (1841) *The Concept of Irony*, Bloomington: Indiana University Press, 1965.

Kierkegaard, S. (1844a) *The Concept of Anxiety*, transl. Thomte, R., Princeton, Princeton University Press, 1980.

Kierkegaard, S. (1844b) *The Concept of Dread*, transl. Lowrie, W., Princeton: Princeton University Press.

Kierkegaard, S. (1846) *Concluding Unscientific Postscript*, transl. Swenson, D.F. and Lowrie, W., Princeton: Princeton University Press, 1941.

Kierkegaard, S. (1855) *The Sickness unto Death*, transl. Lowrie, W., Princeton: Princeton University Press, 1941.

Kierkegaard, S. (1967) *Journals and Papers*, Bloomington: Indiana University Press.

Lahav, R. and Venza Tillmanns, M. da (1995) *Essays on Philosophical Counselling*, Lanham: University Press of Maryland.

Laing, R.D. (1960) *The Divided Self*, London: Tavistock Publications.

Laing, R.D. (1961) *Self and Others*, Harmondsworth: Penguin.

Laing, R.D. (1967) *The Politics of Experience*, London: Tavistock Publications.

Laing, R.D. and Esterson, A. (1964) *Sanity, Madness and the Family*, Harmondsworth: Penguin.

May, R. (1969) *Existential Psychology*, New York: Random House.

May, R. (1983) *The Discovery of Being*, New York: Norton and Co.

May, R., Angel, E. and Ellenberger, H.F. (1958) *Existence*, New York: Basic Books.

Merleau Ponty, M. (1945) *Phenomenology of Perception*, transl. Smith, C., London: Routledge.

Merleau Ponty, M. (1964) *Sense and Non-Sense*, transl. Dreyfus, H. and Dreyfus, P., Evanston: Northwestern University Press.

Merleau Ponty, M. (1968) *The Visible and the Invisible*, transl. Lingis, A., Evanston: Northwestern University Press.

Nietzsche, F. (1878) *Human All Too Human: A Book For Free Spirits*, transl. Hollingdale, R.J., Cambridge: Cambridge University Press, 1986.

Nietzsche, F. (1881) *Daybreak: Thoughts on the prejudices of morality*, transl. Hollingdale, R.J., Cambridge: Cambridge University Press, 1987.

Nietzsche, F. (1882) *The Gay Science*, transl. Kaufman, W., New York: Vintage Books, 1974.

Nietzsche, F. (1883) *Thus Spoke Zarathustra*, transl. Tille, A., New York: Dutton, 1933.

Nietzsche, F. (1886) *Beyond Good and Evil*, New York: Vintage Books, 1966.

Nietzsche, F. (1887) *On the Genealogy of Morals*, transl. Kaufman, W. and Hollingdale, R.J. New York: Vintage Books, 1969.

Nietzsche, F. (1888) *Twilight of the Idols*, transl. Hollingdale, R.J., Harmonds-worth: Penguin, 1969.

Nussbaum, M.C. (1994) *The Therapy of Desire: Theory and Practice in Hellenistic Ethics*, Princeton: Princeton University Press.

Sartre, J.P. (1943a) *Being and Nothingness: An Essay on Phenomenological Ontology*, transl. Barnes, H., London: Methuen, 1956.

Sartre, J.P. (1943b) *No Exit*, transl. Gilbert, S., New York: Knopf, 1947.

Sartre J.P. (1948) *Anti-Semite and Jew*, New York: Shocken Books.

Sartre, J.P. (1939) *Sketch for a Theory of the Emotions*, London: Methuen and Co, 1962.

Szasz, T.S. (1961) *The Myth of Mental Illness*, NewYork: Hoeber-Harper.

Szasz, T.S. (1965) *The Ethics of Psychoanalysis: The Theory and Method of Autonomous Psychotherapy*, Syracuse: Syracuse University Press, 1988.

Szasz, T.S. (1992) 'Taking dialogue as therapy seriously', *Journal of the Society for Existential Analysis*, vol 3.

Tillich, P. (1952) *The Courage to Be*, New Haven: Yale University Press.

Tillich, P. (1954) *Love, Power and Justice*, Oxford: Oxford University Press.

Vlastos, G. (1991) *Socrates: Ironist and Moral Philosopher*, Cambridge: Cambridge University Press.

Yalom, I. (1980) *Existential Psychotherapy*, New York: Basic Books.

Yalom, I. (1989) *Love's Executioner and Other Tales of Psychotherapy*, London: Bloomsbury Publications.

# Introduction to chapter 14

Quoting two key figures from chapter 13, Heidegger and Kierkegaard, Joan Hurd explores the vicissitudes of faith and desire in a wide-ranging exploration of the nature of commitment in therapy as well as the limitations of theory. She examines the forms desire has taken in Kierkegaard, and in its analogues in the superficially diverse work of popular chronicler of Yaqui mysticism, Carlos Castaneda and the psychoanalytic anti-hero, Jacques Lacan.

The clinical arena is therefore approached via searching introspection, and an idiosyncratic teacher. Once there, the contradictions of desire are understood as a personal rather than a philosophical challenge. They cannot be hidden or accepted as immutable. In particular, one can benefit from Lacan's analysis without subscribing to nihilism. The task of therapy is to free passion rather than explain it.

# 14 Leaping beyond theory

*Joan Hurd*

Is there any way in which we psychotherapists can prepare ourselves for the therapeutic encounter, if not by arming ourselves with theory?

## THINKING, THERAPY AND THEORY

I would like to start with some quotations. The first quotation comes from *What is Called Thinking?* by Martin Heidegger. This is the text of a course of lectures given by Heidegger at the University of Freiburg, the last before his retirement and the first following his association with the Nazis.

> [W]e are attempting to learn thinking. The way is long. We dare take only a few steps. If all goes well, they will take us to the foothills of thought. But they will take us to places which we must explore to reach the point where only the leap will help further. The leap alone takes us abruptly to where everything is different, so different that it strikes us as strange. . . . To keep clear of prejudice, we must be ready and willing to listen. Such readiness allows us to surmount the boundaries in which all customary views are confined, and to reach more open territory.
>
> (Heidegger 1968 p. 12)

In 1904, Raine Maria Rilke, a poet noted for his symbolic imagery and his spiritual reflections, wrote the following when, as R.D. Laing in his paper 'Hatred of health' puts it, he was 'an old, young man of twenty-eight'.

> We must accept our reality as vastly as we possibly can, everything, even the unprecedented must be possible within it. This is in the

end the only kind of courage that is required of us: the courage to face the strangest, most unusual, most inexplicable experiences that can beset us. . . . But the fear of the inexplicable has not only impoverished the reality of the individual; it has also narrowed the relationship between one human being and another, which has, as it were, been lifted out of the riverbed of infinite possibilities and set down in a fallow place on the bank where nothing happens. For it is not only indolence that causes human relationships to be repeated from case to case with such unspeakable monotony and boredom; it is timidity before any new, inconceivable experience, which we don't think we can deal with.

(Rilke 1987 pp. 88–90)

In his paper Laing asks 'Do we take this seriously in theory and in practice?' (Laing 1987 p. 79).

Alexander Solzhenitsyn in the speech he made in 1973 after being awarded the Nobel Prize for literature in 1970 said

Not everything has a name. Some things lead us into the realm beyond words. . . . It is like that small mirror in the fairy tales – you glance in it and what you see is not yourself, for an instant you glimpse the inaccessible, where no horse or magic carpet can take you. And the soul cries out for it.

(Solzhenitsyn 1973 p. 11)

None of these quotations is about therapy, or psychoanalytic theory. They all, however, speak to me of therapy and of the nature of therapy. They all speak of a place, or places, that defy theorization, places described in terms of 'where everything is different, so different that it strikes us as strange' (Heidegger 1968 p. 12) or 'the riverbed of infinite possibilities' (Rilke 1987 p. 89) and the 'realm beyond words . . . where no horse or magic carpet can take you' (Solzhenitsyn 1973 p. 11). They speak of surmounting boundaries, not of creating boundaries through formulating a theoretical framework within which therapy may take place. These places, are they the stuff of mere speculation or idealization, or do they approach, in some way, the complexity of the therapeutic situation? For allowing possibilities and recognizing complexity both seem to be central to the practice of psychotherapy. Where do the boundaries of the therapeutic encounter come from? Boundaries do appear in our therapeutic and analytic encounters, whether we are aware of what informs these boundaries or not.

Like others, when I first started my own therapy, I was afraid to think. What thinking I did was very much directed to not thinking. Not thinking, that is, in the way Heidegger speaks of thinking. Thinking, if we follow what Heidegger says about thinking, allows thoughts to come alive, allows the person to come alive. Heidegger illustrates this by quoting from the poem 'Socrates and Alcibiades', written by Hoelderlin, an eighteenth century lyric poet, 'Who has most deeply thought, loves what is most alive' (Heidegger 1968 p. 20).

As a therapist, at first I sit and listen. That listening generates thoughts. Those thoughts generate the words I choose to say. Without going further, this could be a description of any conversation, not necessarily a therapeutic one. The quality of my listening is one mark of the quality of my presence as a therapist. Does my listening allow me to hear difference that 'strikes. ... as strange' (Heidegger 1968 p. 12)? Am I listening for what Heidegger would term the most thought-provoking, or am I listening for what might fit in most easily with patterns that I am already familiar with? Does my listening allow for a range of possibilities? In her book *The Other Side of Language: A Philosophy of Listening*, Gemma Fiumara speaks of a cultural 'aversion – almost – towards listening to the rich multiplicity of reality' which, she says,

> seems to be linked with a background of profound fears and to the resulting defensive postures that express themselves in a tendency to reduce knowledge in general to a set of principles from which nothing can escape.
>
> (Fiumara 1990 p. 21)

She also says, 'It might be fruitful ... to train ourselves in detecting those ways of thinking that are able to parody the values of hominization and yet are unable to develop them' (Fiumara 1990 p. 10).

Thoughtlessly applied theory and untested speculation may be able to parody the values that are about being human and humane but that is not the same as being human and humane. Theory in therapy easily becomes a trap. A trap that takes the theory to be the way the world is and not simply how we have structured it for ourselves to make life easier for ourselves. Isn't it very easy for us to slip into the madness that actually believes in the truth of the theory? It is certainly easier to do that than to accept the challenge of the French psychoanalyst, Roustang. In his book *Dire Mastery* (1982), Roustang challenges us to examine our transference onto the theories that we hold or adhere to.

Submitting to the already constructed theory of another by trying to make it one's own is a way of drowning one's own ability to fantasize in rationality, or in a rationalization that corresponds to the fantasies or desires of another or to the fantasies and desires other than one's own. One is therefore ignoring one's own fantasies, or repressing them, but more fundamentally, one is ignoring the fact that the other's theory is based on fantasizing; or what I call in the broad sense delirium. One then slips back into the foreclosure of the subject, essential to scientific productions, while an analytic theory must stay as close as possible to theoretical formulations in connection with the unconscious. . . . In order to question analysis, one must first stop being fascinated by theory and analyse the fantasies or desires that give rise to it; one must analyse theory as the text of dream or myth.

(Roustang 1982 p. 57)

The theory can no more be a *tabula rasa* than, as Freud came to discover, can the therapist or analyst.

What is the difference between sessions where the relationship between therapist and patient becomes 'set down in a fallow place where nothing happens' (Rilke 1987 p. 90) and sessions that visit 'the riverbed of infinite possibilities' (Rilke 1987 p. 89), where there is a leap which 'takes us abruptly to where everything is different'? (Heidegger 1968 p. 12)? How can we enter that area where 'abruptly . . . everything is different, so different that it strikes us as strange' (Heidegger 1968 p. 12) where we can listen to 'the rich multiplicity of "reality"' (Fiumara 1990 p. 21) and allow ourselves to be led 'into the realm beyond words' (Solzhenitsyn 1973 p. 11) where we may 'accept our reality as vastly as we possibly can' (Rilke 1987 p. 88)? Is there indeed any way in which we can prepare ourselves for the therapeutic encounter, if not by arming ourselves with theory? Perhaps we can learn from three very different thinkers.

## SOREN KIERKEGAARD AND THE KNIGHT OF FAITH

In *Fear and Trembling* (1983) Kierkegaard considers the story of Abraham and his son, Isaac. In the discussion of faith arising from this story, Kierkegaard introduces the 'knight of faith'. This is the name given by Kierkegaard to those who are able to 'make the movement of faith' (Kierkegaard 1983 p. 34) by being able to 'plunge confidently into the absurd' (Kierkegaard 1983 p. 34) in such a way 'that one does not lose the finite but gain it whole and intact' (Kierkegaard 1983 p. 37). The knight of faith has 'resigned everything infinitely, and . . . grasped every-thing again by virtue of the absurd' (Kierkegaard 1983 p. 40). Kierke-gaard says of the knight: 'Let me say frankly that I have never, in the course of my experience, seen a reliable example of the knight of faith' (Kierkegaard 1946 p. 40).

However, he goes on to describe the knight of faith in a number of different situations; going home to his wife from work, falling in love with a princess. One example repeats the metaphor, already encoun-tered, of the leap.

> The most difficult feat which a dancer can attempt is said to be to leap and take up a definite attitude, so that at no particular moment does he appear to be trying to take up this position, but assumes the position as he leaps. Perhaps there are no dancers who can perform this feat – but the knight performed it . . . [those who are not knights of faith] make the upward movement and fall down again; and this posture has much to recommend itself and is not unpleasing to the eye. But every time they fall down, they cannot immediately take up their positions, they falter for a moment and their faltering shows that they are strangers in the world. . . . To be able to fall in such a way as to appear at once standing and walking, to be able to trans-form the leap of life into normal gait, to be able to express perfectly the sublime in terms of the pedestrian – only the knight can do this – and this is the single miracle . . . the knight has the strength to be able to concentrate the whole content of his life and the whole sig-nificance of reality into a single desire. If a man lacks this concen-tration, this determination, his soul from the beginning is scattered in the manifold. . . . Every infinite movement is effected through pas-sion, and no reflection can ever produce such a movement. . . . Even to make the famous Socratic distinction between what is understood and what is not understood, passion is necessary, and it is still more necessary of course to those who want to make the real Socratic movement, which is that of ignorance. What is lacking in our times is not reflection but passion.
>
> (Kierkegaard 1946 pp. 44–47)

## CASTENEDA – A WOULD-BE KNIGHT OF FAITH?

Carlos Casteneda was a graduate student in anthropology at the Uni-versity of California, Los Angeles, gathering information on various medicinal herbs used by the Indians in Sonora, Mexico, when he met the old Yaqui Indian, Don Juan. Don Juan was believed by those living locally to be a 'brujo', which means a medicine man, curer, witch or sorcerer (usually one with evil powers). Casteneda describes how he became an apprentice to Don Juan and how he attempted, under Don Juan's tutelage, to become a 'man of knowledge'. A 'man of knowledge', according to Don Juan, needs an 'ally', who can be met by following very precise steps both in the preparation of the drug mixture to be taken and in the preparation of the individual to become a spot-less warrior, able to take the preparation without harm. There is much evidence documented by Richard de Mille in his two books, *Casteneda's Journey: The Power and the Allegory* (De Mille 1976) and *The Don Juan Papers: Further Casteneda Controversies* (De Mille 1980), that the works of Casteneda are imaginal and not based on field work as he claimed. The similarities of his ideas with other people's writings are used to support this accusation. Agehananda Bharati, in *The Don Juan Papers*, says:

> [t]here is nothing in Casteneda's mysticism that you cannot find, sometimes in nearly the same words, in Hindu and Buddhist tantrism or in the official Patanjali yoga. . . . To me the glaring sign of Don Juan's illegitimacy is his intercontinental eclecticism. . . . Stir together bits of Blavatsky, dollops of David-Neel, gobs of Gurdjieff, sops of Ouspensky, snatches of Govinda, yards of tangled American folklore, and a series of programmatic LSD trips, and you have the Don–Carlos idiom.
>
> (de Mille 1980 p. 148)

Kierkegaard's knight of faith is not cited in the evidence that de Mille amasses; however there does seem to be a resemblance between the 'knight of faith' and the 'man of knowledge'. There are similarities between the descriptions of Carlos Casteneda's search for an 'ally' in his books about his apprenticeship with Don Juan and Kierkegaard's descriptions of the knight of faith. One significant similarity is the encounter with death that is involved in both. Kierkegaard, whose name means graveyard, was obsessed with death and with the tenuousness of existence, also with the paradox that life can only be understood by the discovery of death as subjective truth. It is the ability to live a paradox, to 'plunge . . . into the absurd' (Kierkegaard 1983 p. 34) that characterizes the knight of faith.

Casteneda faces death, as he faces the ally. Death has to be faced in the pursuit of a richer existence. After one encounter with the ally, Casteneda says 'The ally had not killed me . . . I had succeeded . . .

I jumped up and down with delight' (Casteneda 1972 p. 306). Casteneda maintained that Don Juan 'tricked' him into learning. In turn Casteneda is accused of attempting to trick his readers by claiming that his writings are not fiction. Mary Coleman Nelson, editor of the *Psychoanalytic Review*, in her paper 'Paths of power: psychoanalysis and sorcery', refers to Kierkegaard as a non-scientist, like Casteneda, who tricked us into learning by his dialectical role-playing and his journalistic disguises. There are similarities too between the descriptions of extraordinary reality, which Casteneda explored and the place, or places, mentioned earlier, that defy theorization. Don Juan repeatedly presented Casteneda with a world which was not representable in words, a world, which for Casteneda, did not exist. Wittgenstein, talking about the sense of words, says 'One thinks that one is tracing the outline of the things in nature over and over again, and one is merely tracing around the frame through which we look at it' (Wittgenstein 1969 p. 48).

By the time Casteneda had committed himself to an apprenticeship with don Juan, however, he had passed beyond the point where, to speak in Heideggerian language, what is incomprehensible remains merely offensive to be able to give it acknowledgement and respect. Those who know the stories of Casteneda, in which he describes being led by Don Juan into other realities where 'everything is different' (Heidegger 1968 p. 12), where he was subject to the 'fear of the inexplicable' (Rilke 1987 p. 89), might ask themselves whether they allowed their own apprenticeship, during their own training as therapists, to be as arduous and challenging as Casteneda's was. We, perhaps, begin to recollect the enormity of what we take on as therapists and the impossible task we have set ourselves. In our own therapy, if we are lucky, we learn, among other things, how and when to disarm ourselves; how to search for our own words and language to speak for ourselves; how to live with our passions; how to think about what has been unthinkable. We do indeed get glimpses of that other world, which our soul cries out for.

I search for a way of speaking of myself as a therapist that lies somewhere other than through the reduction of the world that occurs by applying theories; a way that lies somewhere other than in the world of speculation, which has no prescribed boundaries or limitations. How can we acknowledge and address boundaries and limitations that exist, neither creating false boundaries nor assuming that there are none? How can we tolerate our fear of the inexplicable, accepting our reality as vastly as we possibly can without becoming hopelessly lost? How do we come up against our own boundaries and the boundaries of the other?

Kierkegaard's knight of faith is a knight by virtue of having the 'strength to be able to concentrate the whole significance of reality into a single desire' (Kierkegaard 1946 p. 47), the alternative being that our soul is 'scattered in the manifold' (Kierkegaard 1946 p. 48). This surely means more than as a therapist remaining focused on what is happening in the therapy, rather than thinking about what to have for supper or what our patient was saying in the last session, or what to do about. . . . Kierkegaard says that he has never seen a knight of faith. The knight of faith has every fibre of his being committed totally to a single desire, a single aim. Is it the nature of desire, the therapist's desire, the patient's desire, the scattering or the concentration of those desires that begins to generate those boundaries that already exist; that also generates the ethics of our everyday lives, as well as our lives as psycho-therapists or analysts? Recently, a patient was speaking of never knowing what she wants and of not being able to hold onto her own values, always being drowned out by the other's opinion. She said 'you know those drawing pads for children made with iron filings where you use a stick to draw the filings so that they're all lined up in one direction to make a picture? That's what happens when I come here but when you go away it stops working'. When I go away and, to a lesser extent, between sessions, her desire is indeed 'scattered in the manifold' (Kierkegaard 1946 p. 48), the iron filings of her picture lie higgledy-piggledy, not 'all lined up in one direction'.

So Kierkegaard names desire and the concentration of desire as that which separates those who are strangers in the world from those who are not; that which separates those able to 'plunge . . . into the absurd' (Kierkegaard 1983 p. 34) from those who cannot. What is called for in the therapist or analyst, perhaps, is an embodiment of the paradox of being at home with being a stranger in the world. Casteneda in his apprenticeship writes of an attempt to embody what Kierkegaard speaks of, whether he was aware of Kierkegaard's knight of faith, or not. Lacan, an analyst, brings those themes of desire, of death, and of the paradox that life can only be understood by the discovery of death as a subjective truth, into the realm of psychoanalysis.

The miracle of the knight of faith is to be able to concentrate the whole content of life and the whole significance of reality into one desire. Is it, then, unconscious desire that is the main bounding force in psychotherapy: the unconscious desire of the therapist and the unconscious desire of the patient and what goes on when those two desires come up against each other, mingle with each other, coalesce with each other?

## LACAN AND DESIRE

Schneiderman, who was in training analysis with Jacques Lacan, wrote a book about Lacan, following Lacan's death in 1981. In this book, Schneiderman illustrates how these themes of life and death and the paradox they present come together in the work of Lacan. First, 'Man's humanity "comes to light" only in (his) risking his life to satisfy his human Desire – that is, his Desire directed toward another Desire' (Schneiderman 1983 p. 7) and then,

> [t]he theme of the desire for death is clear and unmistakable in Lacan's work. It organizes the third section of his essay 'Function and Field of Speech and Language' ... the desire to die does not translate into suicide ... one ought to sustain desire ... the desire to die is best enacted when death is kept at a distance.
>
> (Schneiderman 1983 pp. 22/23)

Lacan's notion of desire has two origins: that of the desire that dreams tend to satisfy and that of desire as a life force. Desire is characteristic of the unconscious and unrelated to objects in the external world. Desire for Lacan is the loftiest expression of the truth of the subject. It is desire, as a continuous force, that Lacan has put at the centre of his psychoanalytic theory. Desire is defined by its cause the '*objet petit a*', that is, by lack and void. It appears when the mother refuses to respond to the demand for love, whereby demand sees the object it was seeking disappear, and finds itself confronted with the void. It is this void that transforms demand into desire, and causes desire. Lacan says: 'Relations between human beings are really established before one gets to the domain of consciousness. It is desire which achieves the primitive structuration of the human world, desire as unconscious' (Lacan 1992 p. 224). In his discussion of the paradoxes of ethics, Lacan brings desire into the analytic domain, 'I propose then that, from an analytic point of view, the only thing of which one can be guilty is of having given ground relative to one's desire' (Lacan 1992 p. 319).

What does Lacan mean when he says that 'the only thing of which one can be guilty is of having given ground relative to one's desire' (Lacan 1992 p. 319)? In the same way as Kierkegaard has not met a knight of faith, no one can have the 'strength to be able to concentrate the whole significance of reality into a single desire' (Kierkegaard 1946 p. 47). There is surely no one, no therapist, no analyst who is not persistently guilty of having given ground relative to their desire. To be true to our desire in this way demands a passion, which is almost always beyond us. So, although Lacan says this is the only thing of which we can be guilty, we therapists are, nevertheless, all constantly guilty in this way.

Whereas Freud structured the psyche in terms of the superego, the ego and the id, Lacan talks of three registers, the real, the imaginary and the symbolic. Within the symbolic register, Lacan speaks of the gap, the inevitable gap between the symbol and what is signified by that symbol. Lacan locates that symbolic register in language.

In tracing the path of my desire in these thoughts, meanderings, the gaps, leaps are perhaps more important than the destination. There is a gap in language between what we say and the desire that generates what we say, a gap where unconscious desire lurks. There is a gap between having the 'strength to be able to concentrate the whole significance of reality into a single desire' (Kierkegaard 1946 p. 47) and the way we are 'scattered in the manifold' (Kierkegaard 1946 p. 48). There is a gap between our desire and what we are able and willing to articulate relative to that desire. There is a gap between the way our desire manifests itself and our recognition of ourselves in that desire.

These are areas that perhaps depend more on our own analysis or therapy than on our training. We all get lost and diluted along that chain of Lacanian signifiers between unconscious desires and what appears in our speech. This happens all the time, even when we talk about how we work as therapists, which is, perhaps, about having faith that every so often we will accidentally make that life-changing leap with our patients.

## LEAPING BEYOND THEORY

By looking at a selection of the writings of Heidegger, Rilke, Solzhenitsyn and Fiumara, I have presented thinking and thoughts (in the Heideggerian sense) as being compatible with the psychotherapeutic experience in a way that theorizing and theory frequently are not. The theoretician, as we hear from Roustang, rarely gives thought to the fantasies and desires that give rise to the theory. Initially, I turned to Kierkegaard's 'knight of faith' to examine the difference between therapy where nothing much happens and therapy as a life-changing experience. The life-changing leap referred to is deceptive for, as Kierkegaard indicates, the knight is an ordinary person to an observer 'I do not for a moment deny that every other man may be such a knight' (Kierkegaard 1946 p. 40). What for the therapist and patient may seem like hurtling from one swinging trapeze to another, in the most daring of acts, to the observer may seem as uneventful as any other moment. Trapeze artists do not learn their art from the writings of other artists but by engaging in the practice under the supervision of one who is an artist himself. Perhaps the same principle applies to both the therapist and the patient in their pursuit of the art of living. Casteneda, by describing Don Juan's attempts to get him to let go of his hide-bound frame of reference in order to be able to see through another frame, attempts to persuade the reader to do the same. Therapy 'works', when it does work, in that moment between one 'trapeze' and another, in that moment between letting go of one frame of reference and taking up another. Kierkegaard's example of the dancer, however, warns us that it is not the movement in itself, but some quality embodied in that movement that makes the difference; that quality being the 'strength to be able to concentrate the whole significance of reality into a single desire' (Kierkegaard 1946 p. 47). Casteneda describes his struggles to embody the teaching of don Juan, his struggle to experience what, to begin with, he cannot even imagine. Casteneda's adventures purport to have been real, for the reader they are necessarily imaginary. Lacanian theory posits the symbolic, in addition to the 'real' and the 'imaginary', the symbolic and with it the 'gap', where we have no option but to 'leap', as the prerequisite of desire.

For the person whose desire has been simultaneously contained and obscured in the fantasy of being famous, for whom living in the world (rather than in fantasy) has been too painful, for that person to walk down the street and to be an ordinary person, among other ordinary people, performing a seemingly mundane act, is a truly extraordinary event. The life-changing leap, a moment of contact between patient and therapist, is an everyday act of human contact, but one in which the patient risks yet another life-threatening fall and in which the therapist risks yet another outburst of scorn and contempt. To the observer it is an unremarkable incident with an equally unremarkable outcome; to the participants it is a memorable occasion, a truly remarkable life-changing leap.

## REFERENCES

Casteneda, C. (1972) *Journey to Ixtlan: The Lessons of Don Juan*, London: Penguin Books

De Mille, R. (1976) *Casteneda's Journey: The Power and the Allegory*, Santa Barbara: Capra

De Mille, R. (1980) *The Don Juan Papers: Further Casteneda Controversies*, Santa Barbara: Ross-Erikson

Fiumara, G.C. (1990) *The Other Side of Language: A Philosophy of Listening*, London: Routledge

Heidegger, M. (1968) *What is Called Thinking?*, New York: Harper and Row

Kierkegaard, S. (1946) *Fear and Trembling: A Dialectical Lyric by Johannes de Silentio* trans. Robert Payne, London: Geoffrey Cumberlege/Oxford University Press

Kierkegaard, S. (1983) *Fear and Trembling/Repetition* ed. and trans. H.V. Hong and E.H. Hong, Princeton: Princeton University Press

Lacan, J. (1988) *The Seminar of Jacques Lacan: Book 2 The Ego in Freud's Theory and in the Technique of Psychoanalysis 1954–1955* ed. Jacques-Alain Miller, trans. Sylvana Tomaselli, Cambridge: Cambridge University Press

Lacan, J. (1992) *The Ethics of Psychoanalysis 1959–1960: The Seminar of Jacques Lacan* ed. Jacques-Alain Miller, trans. with notes by D. Potter, London: Routledge

Laing, R.D. (1987) 'Hatred of health', *Journal of Contemplative Psychotherapy*, Vol. IV, 77–86

Nelson, M.C. (1976) 'Paths of power: psychoanalysis and sorcery', *Psychoanalytic Review*, 63(3), 333–8

Rilke, R.M. (1987) *Letters to a Young Poet*, New York: Vantage

Roustang, F. (1982) *Dire Mastery*, trans. N. Lukacher, London: John Hopkins University Press

Schneiderman, S. (1983) *Jacques Lacan: The Death of an Intellectual Hero*, Cambridge, Massachusetts: Harvard University Press

Solzhenitsyn, A. (1973) *Lecture*, trans. Nicholas Bethell, London: Stenvalley Press

Wittgenstein, L. (1969) *Philosophical Investigations*, Oxford: Blackwell

# Introduction to chapter 15

Talking and thinking are operations that become highly developed in psychotherapy and education, which are now also the main institutions through which people attempt personal change and growth. It is important to know not only what their limits are, and how psychotherapy might itself be taught, but how, if at all, they can properly be combined. Catherine Wieder's own work is able to address these questions in the light of her considerable experience in working across boundaries in a way that is generally unfamiliar in English-speaking cultures.

Wieder's use of thought here challenges many assumptions about the boundaries of situations and of the mind. She illustrates the cathartic effect of introducing philosophical reading that touches directly on clients' personal predicaments. Her particular interest in adolescents echoes that of Sepping, and suggests that such methods, if not yet orthodox, may be particularly appealing and effective with this group.

# 15 Thinking as a healing process

*Catherine Wieder*

## PHILOSOPHICAL COUNSELLING: BETWEEN PEDAGOGY AND WILD THERAPY?

> The discourse of the philosopher that wouldn't cure any human affection is indeed an empty one. Similarly, a medicine that wouldn't wipe out the body's illness would be of no use, neither would philosophy were it not wiping out the soul's affection.
>
> Epicurus (*Us*, 221)

> If happiness were obtained by recording discourses, it would then be possible to reach such a goal without having either to choose one's food or achieve some acts. But, since we must change our present life for some other life by cleansing us both through discourses and through actions, let us examine which discourses and which actions predispose us towards such a new life.
>
> Porphyrus (*On Abstinence*, I, 29, 6)

Being both a Freudian psychoanalyst and a professor of the history of ideas in a small provincial university, I have come across a very typical French Socratic issue: when one teaches philosophy to first-year university students in psychology, one cannot avoid a question they all raise – 'since you are an analyst teaching us philosophy, by listening to your lectures and through quite a few face to face interviews in the course of workshops, don't you help in some kind of a philosophical counselling (I would add: "thus enabling us to avoid the costly experience of the couch")?'

My purpose here will not be to offer a definite theory of either psychoanalysis or philosophical counselling, but rather to question both topics as a means to 'help' young adolescents suffering from temporary thought inhibition. I shall be considering in what ways a psychoanalyst might benefit an adolescent patient, and in what ways be of less benefit to him, by departing from the classical use of interpretation and the requirement of free association, through use of philosophical metaphors and epistemology in a phenomenologically biased 'philosophical counselling'.

This is a subject I have studied through a research programme shared between philosophers, psychologists and literature specialists entitled 'to think in order to heal', or 'the therapy of thought, through thought processes'. My task as leader of this group consists in helping postgraduate students to write their PhDs on the topic of thought difficulties with reference to clinical data and projective psychological tests. My official 'hat' in that research group is that of what we call in French a 'psychopedagogue'. To be a university professor within such a context obliges me to teach, to engender research programmes in the form of clinical workshops and to gather the material in the form of synthesizing publications (a book on the topic of 'thinking as a healing process' will be soon published in French).

In France an adolescent is introduced to philosophical concepts for the first time in his syllabus, in his Upper Fifth form (i.e. just a few months before the Baccalaureat (= 'A' Level). If, though succeeding very well at school, he suffers from some kind of temporary inhibition of thought, he may under the French health system, seek the 'help' of a 'psychopedagogue', i.e. a teacher of philosophy, who also has some competence in 'counselling' and who will use those very philosophical texts to give him back self-confidence.

In this research I try to reach a few truths about the way 'thought' works and, more specifically, on the evolution of thought processes in a counsellor's mind when, in the role of psychopedagogue, he or she is confronted with bright adolescents suffering from thought difficulties. Since the ethic of the psychoanalyst is 'never intervene', whilst that of the pedagogue is 'never let school fail when you can force the adolescent to more positive strategies', this is an ethically peculiar situation.

As leader, I had to give a title a couple of years ago to this research; I hesitated between two subtitles for it: either 'teaching philosophy, psychoanalytic cure and psychoanalytic psychopedagogy' or 'could psychoanalytical psychopedagogy be a therapy of one's thought?' The latter has the double meaning of 'through' thought and 'about' thought processes, which is my question here. In the end, I decided to use the French pun on 'penser' and 'panser', i.e. to think (*penser*) in order to heal (*panser*).

My hesitation signified some difficulty in focusing properly on the object of my own personal quest, and in confronting my identity in the three 'hats' of psychoanalyst, teacher and group leader. Am I a 'clinician', a 'pedagogue', or both? Normally, I solve this problem by claiming the status of 'translator', in that I always try to translate the world and the words of my elders in philosophy and those of my adolescent patients or students (whether in amphitheatres, in cafés or behind the couch). My question about personal identity becomes: 'Is the psychopedagogue an avatar of a professor of philosophy? Or is he or she just a psychoanalytic psychotherapist who uses philosophical texts as tools in the same way as Winnicott used his "squiggle games" with children?' A wide array of unsolved identifications appear.

Thinking about 'psychopedagogy' compels me to experience a kind of dialogue between internal images of pedagogue and analyst, as if these were representatives, different yet linked, of my ideal self – against which I may find myself falling short in some way or other. It is indeed a 'matter' of identity and, may be too a 'problem' of identity in so far as it compels me to try and find out the 'vertex'[1] to be adopted in reflecting about psychoanalytic psychopedagogy and philosophical counselling.

## PEDAGOGY AND PSYCHOANALYSIS

What do we mean by thought processes in the case of the adolescent 'patients' we deal with here? Our approach of 'thought' and thinking is also a theory about knowing, about learning from experience and its disturbances. Here we take into account the theory according to which all knowledge has its origin in primitive emotional experiences related to the absence of the object.[2] Characteristics inherent in this emotional experience sometimes intervene in an attenuated form in the later experiences of discovery, learning, and formulation of new ideas in any field, whether scientific, aesthetic, or psychoanalytic.

We believe in the existence of similar configurations in very dissimilar experiences, i.e. in pointing out invariants or equivalent structures every time the individual, group or society is faced with a problem of knowledge. Hence, with Bion (1962), we assume that the ultimate reality of the object is unknowable in the Kantian sense of the term. The object of knowledge in psychoanalysis is one's own or another person's psychic reality. Investigation of it poses various problems. One of the main problems is related to the fact that this object of knowledge, psychic reality, is not an object in the physical sense. The basic emotions the psychoanalyst deals with – anxiety, love, fear, hate – cannot be apprehended with the sense organs (they cannot be touched, heard or seen), but verbal and bodily transformations of them can be discriminated. The problem posed by psychoanalytic experience is, in a sense, the lack of an adequate terminology to describe such events. It resembles the problem that Aristotle solved by supposing that mathematics dealt with mathematical objects.

Bion suggested that it is convenient to assume that the psychoanalyst deals with 'psychoanalytic objects'. In the course of psychoanalytic treatment and through successive abstractions and transformations the psychoanalyst tries to detect a way of communicating the nature of these objects. This process of intuition, abstraction and transformation is similar in some of its characteristics to the process of discovery and abstraction that Bion assumes takes place in the infant's mind during development. Thanks to his 'alpha function',[3] the infant deduces from his first emotional experiences the models and concepts he will use as hypotheses in his contact with internal and external reality. From constant evolutive interplay his conceptions, concepts, vocabulary and language, will arise and intervene in the modulation of other developments.

The relationship between psychoanalysis and teaching has never been easy. It has never been easy to navigate between them, unless, as I do today on a 'scholarly' basis, one tries to be a kind of 'go-between'. Psychoanalysis always compels analysts to fear more than anything any 'unconscious desire to teach' as a substitute for investigation of the content of communication. Could there be a 'pure' psychoanalysis, deprived of any unconscious superego attitudes lurking in the background, but always referring to some kind of ultra-pedagogical, nay, magical, philosophical omnipotence?

We have at least quite a few good reasons to practise and exercise philosophy if we wish to learn how to live, to learn how to pursue true dialogue, how to die and, last but not least, how to read. Let us note that each of these goals refers to what is obvious for every one of us, and which we should turn into action, i.e. that we are all living creatures aiming at living better, speaking and communicating creatures wanting to understand the world better, reading creatures and, certainly bound to die. Now my aim becomes the restoration of a 'space' for thought, conceived as a privileged field for the psychopedagogue and a focused, new, listening approach to thought deficiencies.

## THOUGHT IN THERAPY

Clinicians will expect that such a new philosophical counselling might lead to both pedagogical and therapeutical benefits. But when I insist

on its being grounded, like psychoanalysis, on an ethical and seman-
tical background of neutrality, I refer to the historical dictionary of the
French language that gives us the following definitions: 'Therapy' comes
from the Greek '*therapeia*' which means 'care'. Before 1473, it referred
to the Greek '*therapeutikos*', with reference to 'the person who takes
care of another one' and with reference to ' the means used in order
to take care'. A derivative is to be found in the term '*therapeuien*', 'to
take care' but also 'to be the servant, a warrior's squire', and the 'thera-
pon' in Homer's works is 'the rider's squire' too. 'Pedagogue' comes from
the Greek '*paidagogos*', i.e. 'the slave in charge of taking the children
to school' and 'a private tutor'.

'*Penser*' in French (i.e. 'to think'), comes from the Latin '*pensare*', 'to
weigh', a similar origin as '*panser*', 'to heal', with reference to expressions like 'to take care of someone', 'to put bandages on the wounds',
or the French '*pensement*' (1188) meaning 'a bandage'. Such etymo-
logical references compel us to stress that

- both therapist and pedagogue are some kind of 'slave', i.e. 'at the
  service of someone'
- at the same time, this is 'bandaged' with a 'healing' dimension.

If I refer to the expression 'therapy of thought', I must at the same
time stress that it means a discursive, secondary thought process.[4] The
expression becomes even more problematical, when one refers to fantasies and dreams. Not only does it become ambiguous (a therapy for
thought or a thought therapy?) and paradoxical (since there may be a
therapy only of the specific concrete individual, whilst thought is always
universal and abstract), but also it can become doubly scandalous for any
philosopher. He not only commits a crime in believing there may be a
'pathology' of thought and a medicalisation of the intellect, but in psychoanalytic terms offends by this intellectualisation of the unconscious.

Can a subject's thought be taken care of and healed? Should it be
healed? Wouldn't we here be practising some kind of orthopaedics of
the intellectual functioning? Would there thus be a sane thought, a
straight, correct thought as opposed to a twined one meant to become
straight again? Could there be a thought that wouldn't be right? Of
course, it all depends on one's definition of thought.

I have previously said that 'thought processes imply a communication task between representations and to think means introducing
changes within spontaneous links between representations' (representations of things and representations of words) (Wieder, 1994). Thought
would then be defined as a linking activity, unbinding and binding

at the same time, examples of 'thought diseases' being 'bad' links (dys-functionings), or an 'absence' of links (repressions, inhibitions, etc.), or 'an attack on linking': 'dangerous liaisons', in other words (all terms in quotations follow Bion (1974, 1975)).

To think would then be not just a matter of intelligence, but at least a matter of one's free will, that is, once more, a matter of ethics of the subject's freedom even to think 'incorrectly' (as in the expression 'polit-ically correct' too often used nowadays) when the counsellor (whether a therapist or not) should keep always neutral, a task that only the psychoanalyst can adhere to.

The French philosopher Pascal (1962) indeed urged us to 'think well', adding that 'such was the principle of morality'. He too would prob-ably today use the term 'politically correctly'. This is what philosophers might argue about. And that is most probably the reason why so many philosophy professors are doctrinally opposed both to pedagogy and to psychoanalysis as therapeutic approaches and processes. The psychoan-alyst in this situation remains caught within mediation itself and practises some kind of cognitive training, or teaching, but never therapy as such. The psychopedagogue who is a psychoanalyst may insist that, while working on the level of conscious secondary psychical processes, he takes into account the level of unconscious primary processes.

Through the mediation of working from the difficulties in thought training, a task promoting the use of cultural objects as transitory spaces, this kind of psychopedagogue aims at a global psychological change in the subject. But in doing this, doesn't a psychopedagogue who is also a psychoanalyst practise instead some kind of 'Jungism'? Doesn't he eschew the dimension of the unconscious and infantile sexuality while claiming at the same time it represents his very reference? Doesn't he risk getting lost altogether in the mediation by using this roundabout approach?

## ANALYTICAL PSYCHOPEDAGOGY

Analytical psychopedagogy, formerly labelled 'curative pedagogy' and now 'therapy through cultural mediation' (Méry, 1978), is in fact a manifold approach. It is not simply a crucible remelting Freud's pure gold, but also an alloy of several important contradictions promoted by his disciples. To stress the specific character of analytical psychopeda-gogy and its affiliations, it may be helpful to question it with reference both to philosophical teaching and to counselling and psychoanalysis as a means of cure. In this way we may derive new approaches to thought processes through shared thought, i.e. co-thought. Thus analytical psychopedagogy would locate itself between thought processes as therapy and therapy as thought process.

It may seem a kind of simplistic caricature to talk of therapy when one mentions philosophical counselling and philosophical approaches to life when one talks of the psychoanalytic cure. Yet, I would like to vindicate this comparison without wishing to reduce one to the other, but rather, to enable binding, linking and unbinding all at once of the various components of such approaches.

Philosophy, as much as psychoanalysis, has always been, both a theoretical activity and a practice: there is no philosophy, indeed, without some kind of teaching that represents 'thought in process and acting'. This is what the historian Pierre Hadot showed about Classical philosophy in his 'Spiritual exercises and antique philosophy' (Hadot, 1987).

The world of unconscious communication between people is strange and often awesome. It may also be complicated and confusing. This has led to a regrettable divide between specialists in the unconscious, who have developed an esoteric language with which they speak to each other more precisely, and the majority of non-specialists who feel excluded by this.

There is a common myth that the experienced analyst understands the bright student swiftly and unerringly. Although some patients try to oppose this, risking the retort that they are 'resisting', other patients do expect this. Perhaps it satisfies a wish to find certainty. Some analysts also appear to expect it of themselves; perhaps to gratify an unacknowledged wish to be knowledgeable or powerful. It is not surprising, therefore, how often, during the years of our training – particularly in France, where philosophy is the major topic of study when one is a lay analyst – we have imagined that immediate philosophical understanding was required from us and our supervisors. This has always created a pressure to philosophise, hence, to know, in order to appear competent. Interpretations offered to patients may then be taken 'off the peg', culled from the writings and teachings of our masters, who, in turn, have accepted such formulations as time-honoured, even though overuse rapidly degrades these insights into analytical clichés.

Let me first give an example of how it sometimes takes place. My focus throughout is normally more on technique than on theory. But I do not wish to define or to prescribe ways of working which others should follow. Instead I raise issues and questions, the answers to which will often lie in the work experience of the individual practitioner.

Jeremy was 16 when I met him for the first time. He had been sent to me by a psychoanalyst who was concerned about his school achievements, compared with his excellent IQ results. It took eighteen months before any form of positive transference could be reached. Whenever I suggested reading a text or asked him to bring me one of his own choice, it never worked. He was never really aggressive but not willing to help 'me', strangely enough. I suggested the very same activities which had been successful with other adolescents suffering from the same problems. For example, knowing that he was very fond of games, I suggested he should freely associate with a list of words he would find in the Greek texts he had to study, e.g. Plato's Republic, IV, and play on these words, then asked him to write a story that would use these very words. The text in itself was most uninteresting. Then, all of a sudden, he told me about a childhood event: 'once, the house shook and we thought it was a landslide', but then he added, as a strong denial of the traumatic character of the event: 'it wasn't all that devastating, but we thought it could jolly well have been'.

Why did Jeremy mention the 'landslide' in the same manner as quite a few adolescents I had taken care of? Like him, they had had to live through traumatic family events in the course of their childhood? For these young people, *movement* would not refer to the mastery of one's body and to the pleasure that might be linked with it, but, rather, to the earth crumbling under their feet and the risk of being swallowed by the void.

A few days later, Jeremy came back with Golding's *Lord of the Flies* and Bachelard's *The Wafer*. For the very first time, we could 'share' the horror and fascination evoked by these masterpieces. I could suddenly join him in understanding how 'thought objects' can be understood both in terms of sadistic oral drives and of a pleasure derived from 'tasting' something both appetizing and beautiful. Bachelard writes: 'I was eating fire, I was eating gold, I was eating its smell and crackling whilst the burning wafer was being crumbled in my palate'. Though Jeremy might not have understood the depth of such a text, I couldn't help reading him the lines that followed the passage he had selected: 'The conquest of the superfluous gives a greater spiritual excitement than the conquest of what is necessary. Man is a creation of desire and no creation of need'.

Jeremy had been brought up by his grandmother (who was always cooking wafers for him when he came back from school), since his mother was unmarried, and, at the age of ten – not knowing at all who his father was – had one day met a man who had rung at the door and had said: 'Here I am, I am your daddy'. Needless to say, Jeremy might have felt then the earth was cracking under his feet, with the fear of being swallowed by it.

There are many paradoxes in such counselling, as practised by a psychoanalyst dressed in the garments of a university professor, doing philosophy both consciously and unconsciously! I will mention just a few, following in this Patrick Casement's approach in *On Learning From the Patient* (1986). For each person, there are always two realities – external and internal. External reality is experienced in terms of the individual's internal reality, which, in turn, is shaped by past experience and a steady tendency to see the present in terms of the past. Analysts therefore have to find ways of acknowledging both realities and the constant interplay between them.

There are many ways of remembering, when one does not stick to analytic couch associations. In everyday life, memory is usually thought of as conscious recall. When unconscious memory is operating, another kind of remembering is sometimes encountered – vivid details of past experience being re-lived in the present. This repetition of the past is by no means confined to good times remembered, as in nostalgia. More often it is what has been fearful in the past that is re-experienced in the course of analysis. This is believed to be so because of an unconscious search for mastery over those anxieties which had earlier been unmanageable.

Nobody can know his or her unconscious and be a counsellor, without help from some other person. Repression maintains a resistance to what has been warded off from conscious awareness; and yet, clues to unconscious conflict still emerge in derivative forms which another person may be able to recognise. If this unconscious communication can be interpreted in a meaningful and tolerable way to a patient, what previously had been dealt with solely by repression can begin to enter conscious awareness, and become subject to conscious control or adaptation: 'Where id was, there ego shall be', as Freud said.

It is usual for analysts to see themselves as trying to understand the unconscious of the patient. What is not always acknowledged is that adolescent patients in particular also read the unconscious of the analyst, knowingly or unknowingly. Analysts can no longer claim to be the blank screen or unblemished mirror, advocated by Freud, because they, too, are people and no person can be blank or unblemished. Every analyst communicates far more to the patient about himself or herself than is usually realised. Though I will not develop this point in detail, it is important to take this clinical fact into account.

Analysts try not to make mistakes, or to get caught in defensive behaviour of their own. (Even this wish of mine here to try and analyse philosophisability and philosophical counselling may be one. There will, nevertheless, be numerous occasions when this happens. Frequently patients – and bright adolescents in particular – make unconscious use of these mistakes in ways that throw new light on the therapeutic process. The ensuing work with the adolescent is often enriched by the experience of the analyst being able to learn from these mistakes. In this way the help is restored from what might otherwise have become seriously disruptive.

Before wondering whether 'philosophising everything' in the form of a philosophical counselling is possible, one should question whether 'saying everything' is possible. Freud said to his patients: 'say everything that comes into your mind without any form of selection'. We all know this is an almost impossible task, thus, a highly paradoxical message. And some yet go even so far as to decide that, when all is said, i.e. when every simple thing has been said, then one is sure the analysis is terminated!

When we refer to 'free association' as the process of what is at stake on the couch and elsewhere in counselling, we must not forget that we use the adjective 'free' in that expression. 'Freedom': that's quite a good ideal, isn't it? It appears to be one of the major goals aimed at by any analytic cure, and it should consist in giving the adolescent, however trapped he may be in his compulsion to repeat and in his fixation to his beloved symptoms, the 'freedom' of his choices and new goals. In other words, isn't it precisely for that, that officially all these adolescents come to consult us?

## IS EVERYTHING ANALYSABLE?

Are we allowed to analyse only what surges in the course of the transference neurosis, i.e. only strictly within the traditional framework of the analytic cure? What happens precisely during 'philosophical counselling'? Does it help us to understand the limits of psychoanalysis? What do we do with borderline cases and psychosomatic patients, with the rocks of passivity, of narcissism, of character neurosis, of the compulsion to repeat? What happens when adolescent patients compel us to interpret nothing, and yet they have been assessed as analysable? In other words, it could also lead us to wonder whether there might be an 'outside of the psyche'. Can we imagine any thought – because it cannot be psychoanalysed – that is outside the psyche?

These indeed are difficult questions, which my colleague analysts so often avoid because they are at the crossroads of philosophy, the neurosciences and psychoanalysis. In other words, does the totality of mental life coincide strictly with the Freudian description of the psychological apparatus? Wouldn't such a vision be a terribly scaled-down one? I know I am being frightfully provocative and yet I am a strictly orthodox Freudian most of the time – but also one trained in England despite my being French, and that does make a difference! Therefore, does any psychoanalyst, in 1998, consider himself or herself as a specific, all-knowing, sharp-pointed technician of psychopathology, or an expert qualified in examining any human action? Here we are, and megalomania is lurking. We should add: are we psychoanalysts only within the strict setting of the psychoanalytic cure? What about our constant interpretation of art and the rest (in France, there is even a psychoanalyst who regularly comes on television to interpret any minor detail about our political leaders)? Are we doomed to be analysts twenty-four hours a day or, on the contrary, can we claim we are analysts only when sitting behind the couch?

And when we ask the question 'is everything analysable?', what remains to be analysed after all these long years of analysis not only for our patients but also for ourselves? What has precisely made us become analysts if not those 'remains'? When I told some friends how I saw, in a psychiatric ward, people dribbling and grumbling like animals as a result of being too severely lobotomised, a colleague said that one day there would also be wards for those who would have been too severely analysed, for too long, and too thoroughly. Like the white tornado of Ajax, full of chlorine bleach, analysis would thus cleanse everything, metapsychology being but an innocent witch, whereas analytical practice, and interpretation in particular, would be like a plague of locusts dashing over the plains of fantasies, our attention being no longer able to float free.

When we find ourselves using similar forms of megalomania through interpretation, with several different patients, it is probable that we are becoming stereotyped, repetitive and sterilising. And when this repetition develops into cliché interpreting, it is likely to promote an intellectualisation of the analytic experience. How then can we recover that freshness of insight which alone can promote therapeutic change?

We cannot always avoid interpreting in ways that have been frequently used before (by others and by ourselves) but the effectiveness of such interpretations is easily dulled through overuse. Also, when we rely on what has come to be regarded as universal truths, we can lose touch with the individual. Therefore, when some stereotyped interpretation is foremost in our thinking, it is often better to wait before speaking and to look for some less focussed comment that can lead towards subsequent interpretation.

I am not thinking only of the danger that actual interpretations become clichés because of their familiar form. I am also concerned with the stereotyped thinking that entails this: for instance the notion that everything should be interpreted in terms of transference, or in terms of the adolescent's current regression in the transference relationship. The danger then is that we will notice only what our theoretical assumptions prompt us to look for, and our preconceptions begin to be imposed upon what we see. Let us remember Wittgenstein, '*worüber man nicht sprechen kann, darüber muss man schweigen*'.[5]

What I am trying to illustrate in this caricature of interpretation, also often to be found – though much less manifest – in philosophical counselling, is that, when any assumption is held to be beyond question, interpretations can too easily be imposed upon whatever appears to fit in with that assumption. Clinically, we must always be wary of this tendency to think that we are seeing evidence of what we are expecting to find, particularly as we are all inclined to relate to the familiar as if it were universal. Hence the positiveness of the universality of philosophical references. We do not have to be so prone as to use old insights when we can learn to tolerate longer exposure to what we do not yet understand. And, when we do think we recognise something familiar in a patient, we still need to be receptive to that which is different and new.

Analysts and professors sometimes have to tolerate extended periods during which they feel ignorant and helpless. 'The only thing I know is that I know nothing.' In this sense our students are privileged: they have licence not to know, though many still succumb to pressures that prompt them to strive to appear certain, as if this were a mark of competence. The experienced analyst, by contrast, has to make an effort to preserve an adequate state of not-knowing if he is to remain open to fresh understanding.

Bion, perhaps more than anyone, was explicit about the need for openness to the unknown in every individual. He did not advocate any comfort in knowing. Instead, he was clear about the anxiety with which we can react when we are genuinely faced by the unknown. He said: 'In every consulting room there ought to be two rather frightened people; the patient and the psycho-analyst. If they are not, one wonders why they are bothering to find out what every one knows' (Bion, 1974).

Theories, whether in psychoanalysis or in philosophical counselling, are built up to define more clearly the framework in which people interpret. These are necessary, if interpretation is not to become a matter of inspired guesswork. Theory also helps to moderate the help-lessness of not-knowing. But it remains important that this should be subservient to the clinical work and not its master.

Freud described the tendency towards dogma in his paper *The Future of an Illusion*: 'And thus a store of ideas is created, born from man's need to make his helplessness tolerable' (Freud, 1927). It is all too easy to equate not-knowing with ignorance. This can lead counsellors to seek refuge in an illusion that they understand. But if they can bear the strain of not-knowing, they can discover that their compe-tence includes a capacity to tolerate feeling ignorant or incompetent, and a willingness to wait (and to carry on waiting) until something genuinely relevant and meaningful begins to emerge. Only in this way is it possible to avoid the risk of imposing upon the adolescent the self-deception of premature understanding, which achieves nothing except to defend the counsellor from the discomfort of knowing that he does not know.

Counselling has the potential for enabling re-birth of the individual personality. It is a tragedy that comes to be limited to a process nearer to that of 'cloning', whereby the adolescent comes to be 'formed in the image' of the counsellor and/or master and his theoretical orientation. In his book *Orthodoxy* (1908), G.K. Chesterton imagines:

> an English yachtsman who slightly miscalculated his course and discovered England under the impression that it was a new island in the South Seas . . . who landed (armed to the teeth and talking by signs) to plant the English flag on that barbaric temple which turned out to be the Pavilion at Brighton.

Hence, Casement, with reference to psychoanalysis, concludes, '[i]f an analyst trusts in the analytic process he will often find himself led [by the adolescent] where others have been led before' (1986). The importance for the adolescent is that any theoretical similarity in depth analysis to what has previously been conceptualised in relation to others should be reached through fresh discovery, not 'pre-conception', to use Bion's terminology.

One's openness to the unknown in the adolescent leaves more room for the adolescent to contribute to any subsequent knowing; and what is thus jointly discovered has a freshness which belongs to both. More than this, it may be that a significant part of the process of interpre-tation and therapeutic gain is achieved through the adolescent coming to recognise that we can learn from him. The adolescent is thus allowed a real part to play in helping to interpret and help and, to that extent, to discover what is needed in that therapeutic approach.

Adolescents benefit from our willingness to find out, even that which is already 'known' through working clinically with them. This makes us feel better than using short-cuts to understanding, based on what is borrowed from others – and which adolescents also borrow. Fresh insight emerges more convincingly when an analyst is prepared to fight to express himself or herself within an adolescent's language, rather than falling back upon old thinking.

When I let patients play a part in how their sessions evolve, I do not find myself being made helpless because of this. At times, I even have to become drawn into a 'harmonious mix-up' (Balint, 1968). We all need confidence in the process if we are to tolerate the vicissitudes of being used by the adolescents in these different ways, in analysing either too much or sometimes nothing. We need to be able to follow the adolescent, without feeling too much at sea to function analytically or philosophically.

It is well known that adolescents can become resistant to receiving, or to holding on to, good experience of either intellectual or sensitive quality in the analysis. This reaction is sometimes regarded as a 'negative therapeutic reaction' (Freud, 1923). Or it is interpreted in terms of envy, on the grounds that the analyst is assumed to have something that the adolescent lacks – the adolescent being thought of as preferring to attack this rather than to accept the benefit of it:

> Evelyn suddenly began weeping bitterly during a session without any reason that I could identify. We were reading a passage – surely not hilarious, but at least not very tragical – from Voltaire (the French Enlightenment philosopher). Eventually, he was able to speak again, he said: 'It is your voice. You sound kind'. I still could not understand why this had so upset him, but a few minutes later he was able to add: 'My most common childhood memory is of my parents being harsh with me, even cruel. I cannot ever remember them being kind.'

I believe that there is a further way of understanding this kind of reaction. Casement (1990) called a similar experience, 'the pain of contrast'. A negative response to experience that might appear to be 'good' seems to be an unconscious attempt by the adolescent to preserve childhood memories from comparison, particularly when there is a risk of exposing the risk of early deprivation or the true nature of damaging experiences in childhood. Thus, when good experience is encountered, and is recognised as good, the shock to any defensively held view of childhood (as better than it was) can be very acute. It was with Evelyn that I first recognised this type of reaction to good experience, and I have encountered many other examples of it since.

Bion (1975) encouraged analysts to hold together their knowing and not-knowing in what he called 'binocular vision' . The analyst can learn how to follow with one eye those aspects of a patient about which we know we do not know, while keeping the other eye on whatever it is felt we do know. There is indeed a creative tension between knowing and not knowing. We could say philosophically exactly the same about elements analysable and elements not analysable.

When an analyst learns to follow the patient's cues and listens to the resulting dialogue between two viewpoints of that 'binocular vision' of knowing and not-knowing, he or she will frequently find himself or herself led towards the understanding which is needed. In psychoanalysis and any form of counselling, our task is to find that other voice both in the person and in ourselves.

## NOTES

1    In Bionian terms, the 'point of view', 'angle' or 'perspective' from which one tries first to understand and then to communicate a particular experience.

2    According to Bion, the term 'psychoanalytic object' is not related to the word 'object' as used in psychoanalytic literature.

3    The theory of 'alpha function' postulates the existence of a function of the personality that operates on sense impressions and on perceived emotional experiences, transforming them into alpha elements. These, unlike the perceived impressions, can be used in new processes of transformation, for storing, etc. Alpha elements are, then, those sense impressions and emotional experiences transformed into visual, auditory, olfactory or other images in the mental domain. They are used in the formation of dream thoughts, unconscious thinking during wakefulness, dreams and memories. Bion called 'beta elements' those sense impressions and emotional experiences that are not transformed. These elements are not appropriate for thinking, dreaming, remembering, or exercising intellectual functions usually related to the psychic apparatus. These elements are generally evacuated through projective identification.

4    When, as a complement to 3 above, I use the term 'thought', I refer once more to Bion's proposition that thoughts exist and give rise to an apparatus for manipulating them called thinking. The activity we know as thinking was in its origin a procedure for unburdening the psyche of an excessive and overwhelming amount of stimuli. According to Bion, thoughts are considered to be genetically and epistemologically prior to the capacity to think. In the earlier stages of the development thoughts are not more

than sense impressions and the very primitive emotional experiences 'protothoughts' related to the concrete experience of a 'thing-in-itself' (following Kant's concept of what is unknowable in the object). When using the term 'thought', Bion refers to thoughts, preconceptions, conceptions, thoughts proper and concepts. He wonders whether or not to include the beta-elements as primitive forms of thought.

5  Wittgenstein (1921 # 7 ), usually translated as: 'whereof one cannot speak, thereof one should be silent'.


## REFERENCES

Balint, M. (1968), *The Basic Fault: Therapeutic Aspects of Regression*, London: Tavistock Publications.
Bion, W.F. (1962), 'A theory of thinking', *International Journal of Psycho-Analysis*, 43.
Bion, W.F. (1974), *Brazilian Lectures 1*, Rio de Janeiro: Imago Editora.
Bion, W.F. (1975), *Brazilian Lectures 2*, Rio de Janeiro: Imago Editora.
Casement, P. (1986), *On Learning From the Patient*, London: Tavistock.
Casement, P. (1990), *On Further Learning From the Patient*, London: Tavistock.
Cassirer, E. (1953), *Philosophy of Symbolic Forms*, Cambridge, MA: Harvard University Press.
Chesterton, G.K. (1908), *Orthodoxy*, London: Fontana Books.
Freud, S. (1923), *The Ego and the Id*, Standard Edition I, London: Hogarth.
Freud, S. (1927), *The Future of an Illusion*, Standard Edition 21, London: Hogarth.
Freud, S. (1937), *Analysis Terminable and Interminable*, Standard Edition 23, London: Hogarth.
Hadot, P. (1987), *Exercices spirituels et philosophie antique*, Paris: Etudes Augustiniennes.
Jones, E. (1916), 'The theory of symbolism', *British Journal of Psychology*, 9, 181–229.
Jones, E. (1948), *Papers on Psycho-Analysis*, 5th ed. London: Baillière, Tindall and Cox.
Langer, S. (1982), *Mind: An Essay on Human Feeling*, vol. 3, Baltimore, MD: Johns Hopkins University Press.
Méry, J. (1978), *Pédagogie curative scolaire et psychanalyse*, Paris: E.S.F.
Pascal, B. (1962), *Pensées*, Paris: Presses de l'Imprimerie Nationale (1670).
Piaget, J. (1950), *The Psychology of Intelligence*, London: Routledge and Kegan Paul.
Piaget, J. (1953), *The Origins of Intelligence in the Child*, London: Routledge and Kegan Paul.
Wieder, C. (1984), 'Des "analysées du texte"', *Psychanalyse à l'Université*, 19, 73, 145–168.
Winnicott, D.W. (1971), *Playing and Reality*, London: Tavistock Publications.
Wittgenstein, L. (1921) *Tractus Logicus Philosophicus*.

# 16 Philosophy as psychotherapy

*Chris Mace*

> Philosophy, throughout its history, has consisted of two parts inhar-
> moniously blended: on the one hand a theory as to the nature of the
> world, on the other an ethical or political doctrine as to the best way
> of living. The failure to separate these two with sufficient clarity has
> been a source of much confused thinking.
>
> (Russell, 1961, p.788)

At the outset of this book, the relationship between psychotherapy and
philosophy was considered as one between two independent bodies of
practice, albeit subdivided ones. Several essays have shown how some
philosophers have always viewed philosophy itself as a practical discipline, concerned with how life should be lived. This raises a question:
are distinctions between the two ultimately artificial? The view that
psychotherapy is no more nor less than practical philosophy gains
impetus from proposals that philosophers should offer their services
directly to the public, through consultations organised according to the
professional habits of contemporary psychotherapists (Lahav and
Tillmans, 1995). It is time now to review prospects for future collabo-
rations becoming even closer than those in the past.

## PHILOSOPHISING PSYCHOTHERAPY –
## A DANGEROUS PRACTICE?

Chapter 15, with its overt attention to the origins of thought and to
psychoanalysis, helps us to understand a confusion between psychotherapy and philosophy. Other writers have reinforced Wieder's themes
of the importance of avoiding theory, prejudice, or presupposition in
therapeutic work. Such intentions are common to Socratic, sceptical,
hermeneutic and positivist traditions. However, as she indicates, there

is a strand in analytic thinking which eschews pursuit of specific ends, therapeutic or otherwise. According to it, the understanding that comes from analytic insight is an end in itself – an ethic laid bare in Szasz's (1957) discussion of the 'final aims' of psychoanalysis. Analysis has not necessarily failed if a patient finds they either cannot adjust or cannot live – provided a certain recognition has taken place. Of course such a view sits uneasily with the original aims of psychoanalysis. It was conceived as a medical treatment, with definite goals. Psychoanalysis was also a product of modern culture, as it pursued objective, shared truths. Individual treatments were therefore valued for the evidence they afforded of universal processes, a motive that has sometimes competed with the drive to heal.

A major shift in recent culture has been the presumption that psycho-analytic ideas could and should be studied independently of their therapeutic intent. Philosophers have had no small part to play in this. It is only one example of assumptions prevalent in a post-Cartesian world by which theoretical understandings of ourselves have been disso-ciated from ethics and philosophies of living. The danger is that the literary image eventually supplants the therapeutic instrument. Once reduced to a set of ideas to lie alongside others in the course of dispas-sionate examination, it becomes thinkable that, with the passage of time, they should be consigned to a historical museum. As psycho-analysis has grown in stature as an object of academic and cultural fascination, it has become estranged from clinical circles in medicine and psychology where, without proper trial, it is often presumed to be anachronistic and ineffective. This fate has been familiar to many polit-ical and religious movements. It could see other psychotherapeutic initiatives founder should they stray too far from their original base.

There are more specific dangers too in philosophising psychotherapy. In the only major monograph to address it, Edwin Erwin (1997) applies the tools of modern analytical philosophy to the official statements of contemporary psychotherapy. He offers a critique of a body of practice that appears unable to substantiate the claims he attributes to it in terms of efficacy and process. However, he offers an account that might be seen as both external to the real business of psychotherapy (lacking clinical vignettes, reference to practitioners, and understanding of the inside of its problematic) but, in a less obvious sense, that remains external to philosophy too. When applied in this way, philosophy is reduced to a set of tools whose purpose is only to frame and solve tech-nical problems. This overlooks the fact that the most significant contributions of philosophy have followed from the identification of questions that are on the one hand resistant to a final answer, but on the other almost universally felt. Perhaps the freedom of either psycho-therapy or philosophy to pose difficult questions, clinically or specula-tively, can be both restricted or enlarged by the other. This will be an interesting touchstone for future work in the area.

## PHILOSOPHICAL THERAPY

There are many senses in which philosophy might be directly ther-apeutic. Exposure to philosophy may, in itself, be personally therapeutic for writer or reader, irrespective of its content. In his *Consolations of Philosophy*, Boethius personifies Philosophy as a healer who attends him privately and restores him to health. Fourteen hundred years later, Anthony Storr's provocative study of the power of the mind to uplift itself in solitude finds philosophers strongly represented (Storr, 1989). The experience does not have to be private. Needleman relates how, when a philosophical discussion is initiated among non-philosophical but intelligent adults by a charismatic teacher, a sequence of events regularly follows, involving openness, disclosure, support, catharsis and remoralisation in ways that many therapists would readily recognise as beneficial (Needleman, 1983).

Some philosophies have also seen themselves as intrinsically thera-peutic. Their claims deserve to be considered. One of the most famous was made by Wittgenstein. In attempting to redefine the role of philos-ophy in the course of his investigations, Wittgenstein suggested its essential function was a therapeutic one. Rather than attempting to erect general truths of its own, philosophy should expose the method-ological errors on which others' metaphysical edifices had been built. The philosopher's essential task was to question rather than answer. This attitude has something in common with that of a psychothera-pist, who allows the sophisticated argumentation of an intellectually skilled patient to wash over him while he listens instead for clues of emotional habitation. Nevertheless, Wittgenstein's ear was tuned to a different wavelength, and, as Heaton has reminded us, was especially critical of the hypostatisation of mental entities on which psycholog-ical theories depended. While Wittgenstein's method highlights an ancient tension between philosophy and psychology, his conception of therapy, demanding close attention to the way in which words are used, and offering grammatical correctives, might appear to be no less tech-nical and instrumental than its analytic contemporaries. However, his philosophy can also be understood to reach at the heart of practical matters at the same time, through his insistence on the connection between forms of words and forms of life, as Brennan illustrated in chapter 5 of this book.

While this conception of philosophy may appear to defy Russell's dichotomy, Wittgenstein is less than direct in addressing the great practical questions. His own life may have been lived with a single-mindedness that invites comparisons with that of Socrates, but his questions and arguments appear to be relatively remote from those preoccupying people around him. This is evidence that even Wittgenstein could not entirely escape modernist assumptions that distance thinking from the rest of human life. A central, unresolved ambiguity to his work remains. Is Wittgenstien implying that philosophy is nothing beyond a series of intriguing but essentially trivial linguistic confusions that can safely be ignored? Or is he pointing to confusions that run so deep that only a radical change in human life can bring about a resolution?

This limitation contrasts with the extent to which philosophy succeeded in being therapeutic in the ordinary sense in the ancient world. The discussion of the equivalence of personal change and philosophical progress in Socrates' teaching that introduced this book must remain speculative. However, there is little doubt how the major figures that succeeded him saw their philosophies' potential to enhance the lives of their students. Plato elaborated a therapeutic process of 'conversion' whereby the 'eye of the soul' had to apprehend a higher reality of ideal forms, and the nature of the idea of the Good, so that a change of character ensued. This brought not only the contentment of *eudaimonia* but wisdom itself (Cushman, 1958).

If Plato indicated this path with only the sketchiest of route maps, Aristotle was concerned that ethical writing should be sufficiently explicit to meet the demands of many different individual circumstances. He paid close attention to the different ways in which emotion both assisted and clouded perception. However, he believed progress for the individual depended substantially in participating in a shared code of ethical conduct. It was left to the Hellenistic philosophers to develop, with differences of emphasis, their practical philosophies. These were intended to be practised by followers within communities, the term philosopher applying at the time as much to those who practised, as to those who preached, a given philosophy. Hellenistic writings can seem unduly obscure and were usually intended to reinforce practice among those already familiar with their precepts rather than introduce them to an unprepared reader. (There is an interesting parallel here with the vast bulk of psychoanalytic literature. The latter assumes so many understandings inseparable from the analytic process that, if a paper makes sense at all to a non-clinician, it is probably not making the sense that was intended.) The attention to individual concerns is coupled to attainment of specific states which, like the *ataraxia* discussed in chapter 4, have a clear psychological as well as ethical content. As in Aristotle, there is very detailed attention to the vicissitudes of the emotions, and their perceptual value. There is relatively greater interest in the attainment of individual health rather than social good as analogies are regularly drawn between philosophical and medical arts. A full account of how the major Hellenistic schools set out to realise therapeutic aims can be found in Nussbaum (1994). It is frustrating in retrospect how little seems known about the actual personal consequences of involvement in these movements in their pure form, rather than what they promised. Whatever these were, there is little doubt that many of these schools' methods were effectively usurped by the seminaries and monasteries of the Christian church.

Existential philosophy invites comparison with the Hellenists not only because it restores practical ethical concerns to centre stage, but in its attention to concrete particulars before general principles. However, as Pierre Hadot (1995) reminds us, the position of later philosophies that seem to offer a direct vehicle for personal understanding and improvement has never been comparable because they have not been part of a similar institutional context. Kierkegaard's isolated self-examination can be taken as an invitation to follow a similar path, in private. As the existentialist movement develops, it begins to share structures as well as themes with psychotherapy. C.G. Jung chaired a year-long seminar series on Nietzsche's *Zarathustra* for analysts in his circle as a contribution to their professional development. Heidegger personally blessed the attempt to found a therapy, 'daseinanalysis' on his philosophy by Medard Boss and colleagues (Richardson, 1993). This initiative, which depended upon practising psychoanalysts immersing themselves in Heidegger's philosophy, did not last, suggesting something vital was still missing. Is there reason to suppose that the recent movement of 'philosophical counselling', usually a vehicle for the philosophically trained to assume the role of practitioner, will fare better?

## PHILOSOPHICAL COUNSELLING

Philosophical counselling is defined by a practical reality, the offer of 'consultations' directly to the public. It is often described in terms of the distinct needs it meets that contrast with those met by established forms of psychotherapy – philosophical counselling attending to the freely chosen principles by which life is lived. These might also be differentiated according to different arenas of meaning, as in Mijuskovic's (1995) distinction between meanings which are subjective and relative (the domain of psychotherapy) and those which are individually 'absolute' (the province of philosophical counselling). A distinction has also been made according to perceived differences in volition (the neurotic patient is dominated by their symptoms/past/need for relief; only the philosophical patient can freely choose to attend and place their presuppositions under the microscope). However, it is interesting that oppositions that place philosophical counselling in the exclusive business of 'worldview interpretation' (Lahav, 1995) tend to rely on mechanistic models of psychotherapy. More accurately, when they berate psychoanalytic psychotherapists for construing patients' narratives in terms of determinative events in the past, they are in danger of mistaking theory for practice in psychotherapy.

People working as philosophical counsellors have brought significant innovations to their practice. This varies from allowing specific philosophical schools to influence the way the counsellor reflects on issues, to introducing philosophical texts into the dialogue, to teaching and/or using specific philosophical tools in order to dissect and remedy constraints on the client's situation. If the latter does not bring resolution, it at least demonstrates that a dilemma is insoluble in a profound way that can in itself be healing. Readers of this book will have seen all these ways of introducing philosophical experience into psychotherapy illustrated here, prompting some doubt as to how far philosophical counselling could be distinguished by its methods alone.

A radical answer is promoted by Achenbach (1995), who is critical of attempts merely to cross-fertilise psychotherapy and philosophy. Referring to 'philosophical practice' rather than counselling, he has emphasised how the practical philosopher can enter into a personal dialectic but must not be seduced into accepting either the psychologist's problematic or their notions of mind. However, like some others, he appears to believe it is possible to have a practice free of identifying values or ideas.

There are a number of problems with such a view. It appears to be unrealisable pragmatically (once one has to deal with issues of training new practitioners, and integrating practice within the existing frameworks of clinical and legal practice). It also faces difficulties in principle. No distinct body of human practice, even Zen Buddhism, manages to avoid reference to guiding aims and values. There risks being a disparity not only with the various schools of psychotherapy, whose differentiation often depends upon differences in underlying values beyond those of method, but also the entire tradition of practical philosophy. We have just seen how ancient practical philosophy is informed by ideals of *eudaimonia* or *ataraxia*. At present, philosophical counselling that affects to abjure these in favour of a methodical instrumentalism risks having no direction at all.

A further unresolved question concerns the social rituals of philosophical counselling. At present these seem based upon a compromise between therapeutic counselling and academic interchange. It is striking how in the past transformative philosophies have created their own milieux, whether in the shape of communities organised around shared teaching (as for the Hellenists) or public exposure of very personal dilemmas (in the case of existentialism). The same has been true of innovatory psychotherapeutic movements, in the founding of analytic institutes as much as the adoption of encounter groups. In the case of philosophical counselling, there is little evidence as yet of the ideals of the movement being worked through in social practice.

Above all, what remains unclear, between the good intentions, promissory notes and specific techniques of philosophical counselling, is whether it will be based on an informed vision of what change depends upon, in the kind of circumstances it claims to ameliorate. Without this, it is difficult to generalise about what it could bring to the situation of individuals that neither an educative exposure to philosophy, nor a psychotherapy sensitive to affective, interpersonal and cultural barriers would afford.

## THERAPEUTIC PHILOSOPHY AND PHILOSOPHICAL THERAPY IN JASPERS

In looking to the possibilities for philosophy as psychotherapy, it is salutary to consider the work of someone uniquely qualified to do so. One candidate might be Jacques Lacan, were there not problems in evaluating (along with his professional peers) how far his thinking was philosophical and how far events in his consulting room were therapeutic. Roger Scruton (1994, p.ix) has suggested that philosophers will only know what they are doing if they 'express the problems of the head in the language of the heart'. Somebody who often did this brilliantly was Karl Jaspers. Jaspers held chairs in philosophy and psychiatry, and brought his own blend of existentialism to bear on clinical questions. His psychiatric masterpiece, *General Psychopathology* (Jaspers, 1963), concludes with him considering 'the human being as a whole'.

In it, he presents his views on psychotherapy. He takes its practice to be essential, although he finds much to criticise in the major schools of the early years of this century.

Jaspers says the aims of psychotherapy cannot be readily stated because of its kinship with philosophy. Successful practitoners in either field offer more than ideas, because in their comportment they also offer their being. He cites Nietzsche and Kierkegaard with greater approval than Freud precisely because they reveal far more of their own existential struggles to their readers than Freud does of his personal difficulties. Jaspers emphasises how, personal analyses notwithstanding, the psychotherapist needs to undertake a process of self-illumination that draws on a wide fund of experience and training. Because the ultimate demands in therapy will always be to understand others, and their philosophies, as found, so there is a stringent need for self-understanding on the part of the psychotherapist. He believes this might be sometimes arrived at without a training analysis, but it never comes without a struggle.

Jaspers offers a reiteration of philosophy's traditional distrust of psychologism. However, in line with his unique professional position, the grounds of this concern are essentially practical. The psychotherapist who allows himself to be seduced by mistaking psychological abstractions for reality is not only committing a philosophical error – by itself this is almost excusable as, according to Jaspers, one remains in the company of philosophers like Heidegger who produce an articulated set of hypostatisations about being that must curb further original exploration – but because it sidetracks enquiry into a cul-de-sac that is limited, self-feeding and, being relativisitic, anti-human. In Jaspers' chosen language, the dimension of being is lost through an exclusively psychological approach. However, in grasping for a point of reference that transcends particular theories and aims, he can appear to share the aspirations that prompted Wilfrid Bion to talk of vertices dividing entire universes of experience (Bion, 1990). This is not unlike Jaspers' own highly abstracted references to boundaries and limit situations in his existence philosophy (e.g. Jaspers, 1971). Bion's implication was that an analyst needed to have some capacity to traverse these vertices him- or herself in order to be capable of helping patients towards psychic freedom. Bion too was sceptical about the extent to which established methods of training and supervision could prepare someone to develop such a capacity. As Wieder hints in the last chapter, immersion in philosophy offers one experience of crossing a vertex and returning enriched. Perhaps Jaspers provides a particularly satisfying example of how philosophy and psychotherapy can mutually promote growth, meeting the test suggested earlier in this chapter. Whether this can or should lead to their fusion remains to be seen. For the present, mindful of the dangers, it seems as blind to omit philosophy from the training of psychotherapists, as to condemn philosophers to ignorance of psychotherapy.

## SOME CONCLUSIONS

Three tentative conclusions seem in order. The first is that attempts to realise philosophy as practice, in the shape of philosophical counselling, are barely in their infancy. Its prognosis is uncertain. The experience of other practical disciplines is that its survival and growth will require more distinct values and vision than are currently evident.

A second is that the interface between philosophy and psychotherapy illustrates wider crises in philosophy. Its relation to practice here is one facet of its search for a role (and for one for its exponents) in the postmodern world. Discussion of psychotherapy needs to enter philosophy's agendas in different forms than at present. In particular, these need to acknowledge the experience of two millenia of practical philosophy and over a century of (formal) psychotherapy in directly facing contemporary equivalents of the needs these had addressed.

A third is that philosophy presents opportunities to psychotherapy as it is currently constituted. At a time when it risks further ideological fission, bureaucratisation, and seduction into a probably anachronistic flight towards positivism, psychotherapy needs to recollect its roots if it is to meet wider needs in the future. Its practitioners not only need to be aware of relevant results from philosophy, but to experience its methods and spirit. A vital part of the latter is the capacity to suspend judgement and to analyse at will, while valuing diversity throughout. This is unlikely to be achieved unless philosophy takes its place on the curriculum in the future training of psychotherapists.

## REFERENCES

Achenbach, G.B. (1995) Philosophy, philosophical practice, and psychotherapy. In R. Lahav and M. da V. Tillmanns (eds) *Essays in Philosophical Counselling.* Lanham, MD: University Press of America 61–74.

Bion, W.F. (1990) *Brazilian Lectures.* London: Karnac.

Cushman, R.E. (1958) *Therapeia: Plato's Conception of Philosophy.* Chapel Hill: University of North Carolina Press.

278    *Chris Mace*

Erwin, E. (1997) *Philosophy and Psychotherapy*. London: Sage
Hadot, P. (1995) *Philosophy as a Way of Life* (tr. M. Chase). London: Routledge.
Jaspers, K. (1963) *General Psychopathology* (tr. J. Hoenig and M. Hamilton). Manchester: Manchester University Press.
Jaspers, K. (1971) *Philosophy of Existence* (tr. R.F. Grabau). Oxford: Blackwell.
Lahav, R. (1995) A conceptual framework for philosophical counselling: world-view interpretation. In Lahav, R. and Tillmans, M. da V. (eds) *Essays in Philosophical Counselling*. Lanham, MD: University Press of America 3–24.
Lahav, R. and Tillmanns, M. da V. (eds) (1995) *Essays in Philosophical Counselling*. Lanham, MD: University Press of America.
Mijuskovic, B. (1995) Some reflections on philosophical counselling and psychotherapy. In R. Lahav and M. da V. Tillmanns (eds) *Essays in Philosophical Counselling*. Lanham, MD: University Press of America 85–100.
Needleman, J. (1983) *The Heart of Philosophy*. London: Routledge and Kegan Paul.
Nussbaum, M. (1994) *The Therapy of Desire: Theory and Practice in Hellenistic Ethics*. Princeton, NJ: Princeton University Press.
Richardson,W.J. (1993) Heidegger among the doctors. In J. Sallis (ed.), *Reading Heidegger*. Bloomington: Indiana University Press 49–63.
Russell, B. (1961) *History of Western Philosophy*. London: George Allen and Unwin.
Scruton, R. (1994) *Modern Philosophy*. London: Sinclair Stevenson.
Storr, A. (1989) *The School of Genius*. London: André Deutsch.
Szasz, T. (1957) On the theory of psychoanlytic treatment. *International Journal of Psycho-Analysis*, 25: 44–56.

# Index